Computer, Self, and Society

Michael Wessells
Randolph-Macon College

D0076244

Prentice Hall
Englewood Cliffs, N.J. 07632

Library of Congress Cataloging-in-Publication Data

Wessells, Michael G., [date].
    Computer, self, and society/Michael G. Wessells.
       p.   cm.
    Bibliography: p.
    Includes index.
    ISBN 0-13-171273-X
    1. Computers.   2. Computers and civilization.   I. Title.
QA76.W472 1990   89-35698
303.48'34—dc20   CIP

Editorial/production supervision and
   interior design: Fred Dahl and Rose Kernan
Cover design: Wanda Lubelska Designs
Manufacturing buyer: Carol Bystrom

©1990 by Prentice-Hall, Inc.
A Division of Simon & Schuster
Englewood Cliffs, New Jersey 07632

All rights reserved. No part of this book may be
reproduced, in any form or by any means,
without permission in writing from the publisher.

Printed in the United States of America

10 9 8 7 6 5 4 3 2 1

ISBN 0-13-171273-X

Prentice-Hall International (UK) limited, *London*
Prentice-Hall of Australia Pty. Limited, *Sydney*
Prentice-Hall Canada Inc., *Toronto*
Prentice-Hall Hispanoamericana, S.A., *Mexico*
Prentice-Hall of India Private Limited, *New Delhi*
Prentice-Hall of Japan, Inc., *Tokyo*
Simon & Schuster Asia Pte. Ltd., *Singapore*
Editora Prentice-Hall do Brasil, Ltda., *Rio de Janeiro*

To My Family

Contents

4. THE GLOBAL ECONOMY, 73

5. NATIONAL SECURITY, 98

6. CRIME AND SECURITY, 125

Preface

The power of computers as information tools is well appreciated by now. In fact, computers have become such important instruments for managing information and solving problems in enterprises ranging from business to medicine that it is difficult to imagine living without them.

What is less apparent is that computers are instruments of social change. The introduction of computers into an office, for example, can change the quality of worklife for the office staff and it can give managers greater control over the workers. Computers have also become one of the primary sources of economic success in the international arena. Technological superpowers such as the U.S. and Japan are locked in a struggle for computer supremacy, and they both recognize that the loser may become a second-rate economic power.

Along with these social changes have come a host of difficult social and ethical issues. For example, should governments be allowed to keep extensive computer files on private citizens or would this place too much power in the hands of the government? Are the huge amounts of money being spent on computers in the schools justified by the gains in the quality of education? Should life-and-death decisions be turned over to computers? How does reliance on computers in the military affect our security? Who benefits from the use of computers?

Analyzing these issues is no mere academic exercise. Although the computer revolution began decades ago, many key policy decisions about the use of computers have yet to be made. Furthermore, technology moves at a much faster pace than policy decisions, and each wave of new computer technology can raise new issues or render the old policies obsolete. It is up to us to decide how computers ought to be used, and the decisions we make determine the kind of society we shall become. If we make wise choices and use computers in appropriate, humane ways, we can improve the quality of life. If, on the other hand, we take the attitude that anything goes, we open ourselves to a panorama of potential misuses that threaten our freedom, our values and our way of life. We have ourselves to blame if this powerful technology is used inappropriately.

Living amidst the frenzied pace of the computer revolution, most people struggle just to keep up with hardware and software. Few people have the time to step back and to ask how we are changing, to ponder social and ethical issues such as those raised above, and to get a sense of our direction. As a result, many people find life increasingly unintelligible, and they are ill equipped to prevent the misuse of our increasingly powerful computer technology.

The first step toward correcting this problem is public education, which has long held that an educated citizenry is our strongest safeguard against tyranny, whether by people or technology. This book is written in the spirit of advancing public education. It aims to provide a broad survey of the individual and cultural impacts of computers and to stimulate reflection upon the social and ethical issues provoked by current and projected uses of computers. By looking behind the computer revolution and analyzing the values that underlie various uses of computers, it attempts to help prepare readers to make their own informed decisions about which uses of computers are appropriate or ill advised.

Because the issues addressed in this book transcend the boundaries of a single discipline, I have drawn extensively upon ideas and observations from areas such as sociology, psychology, economics, cognitive science, history, and political science. In order to make the analysis accessible to students, I have included material from a large number of case studies and contemporary applications. Recognizing that a book such as this must necessarily raise many more questions than it can answer, I have provided an extensive bibliography for those who wish to pursue their inquiry further.

In order to make it easier for instructors to tailor this book to their courses, I have written the chapters in such a manner that they may be read in any order. At the same time, the book is organized around several themes and topic areas. The first chapter provides a broad social context for the inquiry by placing computers in a cultural and historical perspective and by analyzing the myths and values that often guide the use of computers. Chapters 2, 3, and 4 examine issues of business and economics, whereas Chapters 5, 6, and 7 address issues of individual and collective security. Chapters 8 and 9 inquire into artificial intelligence and its social implications. The final chapter deals with education since it is through education that we shape our future.

I want to express my gratitude to Susan McKay, Keith Miller, and Tom Porter for their many helpful comments on the manuscript. Of course, any errors that remain are my own responsibility. I also want to thank the Kellogg National Fellowship Program for encouraging me along the interdisciplinary path and supporting much of my initial work on this project

Michael Wessells
Ashland, Virginia

1

Computers, Technology, and Culture

Throughout history, technological change has fueled the engines of social change. Over ten thousand years ago, the development of early agricultural technology ended the nomadic way of life for many people, allowing them to settle in a particular place and to enjoy a relatively stable food supply. In the fifteenth century, the use of the printing press led to the widespread availability of books, making it possible to educate the masses and to transmit ideas over vast stretches of time and space. Over one-hundred and fifty years ago, the development of the steam engine spurred the Industrial Revolution, which ended the agricultural way of life and ushered in an era of living in cities and working in factories. In this century, the automobile has encouraged urban sprawl, stimulated the growth of vast corporations, and promoted the rise of a global economy.

Today we live in an era of unusually rapid technological change—the era of the computer. In the 1940s, computers were exotic items tended by a handful of technological wizards. Over the past forty years, however, the computer has made a meteoric ascent into the lives of millions. By 1988, over 18 million Americans owned a personal computer, and working in front of a computer had become a standard part of the job in business, industry, medicine, government, science, and education. In half a century, computers have become woven into the fabric of Western civilization.

Like previous technological innovations, computers have enabled and provoked significant social changes, automating work, increasing the interdependence between the U.S. and Japan, generating tremendous amounts of information, and making technology ever more central a strand in the fabric of human life. The scope of these changes is so broad that it is difficult for us to see them clearly, particularly in a time of such rapid social evolution. Struggling just to avoid falling behind, people seldom look beyond the horizons of their personal experience to comprehend the magnitude of the transformation around us.

Yet we must analyze how we are changing in order to consciously guide our society in the directions we want it to move and to avoid drifting imperceptibly into a situation in which computers detract from our quality of life and our security. The widespread use of computers has already generated a host of difficult social problems. In business, for example, many workers feel socially isolated because they spend more time with computers than with people, and in industry, the use of computers has put many people out of their jobs. In the military, malfunctions in the computers used to detect whether we are under nuclear attack have frequently generated false warnings that the Soviet Union had launched their missiles, raising the specter of an accidental nuclear war.

In addition, the widespread use of computers has raised difficult issues that have profound implications for our freedom and morality. Since the 1950s, the government has used computers increasingly to store and retrieve vast amounts of information about citizens. Although this has increased the ability to collect and to process information efficiently, many authorities on civil liberties ask whether we are drifting toward a Big Brother state in which the government uses computers to monitor and control the citizenry. Similarly, in the 1980s, artificial intelligence systems enjoy relatively widespread use, raising questions about what kinds of decisions ought to be turned over to machines. For example, there are computer programs that can diagnose infections and make suggestions regarding medical treatment. Should computers be allowed to make life and death decisions in the medical arena? And if we allow computers to make such decisions, will we become morally lazy and overdependent on machines?

There are no simple answers to these questions, and this tempts some people to avoid struggling with them. But succumbing to this temptation is dangerous since democracy succeeds best when the citizens are both informed and involved. Further, although it is impossible to stop the computer revolution, it is possible to channel it in some directions rather than others. In business, for example, there is not much choice about whether to use computers at all since not using computers would put one's company at a hopeless disadvantage. But there are real choices about how to use computers—to replace people or to increase their productivity, to get control over the workers or to increase their autonomy, and so on. Government, too, can make highly significant choices about how it will and will not use computers. Public officials can, for example, decide not to collect large files of information about individual citizens, and Congressional and military leaders can choose not to turn over to machines decisions such as whether to launch nuclear missiles.

The choices we make, both individually and collectively, about how to use computers will have a powerful impact on our government, our values, and our way of life. For this reason, it is important for every citizen to be aware of how computers are changing society and to be prepared to make informed decisions about how computers ought to be used. This book aims to cultivate this awareness and to prepare readers to make their own informed decisions on issues such as the ones raised earlier.

To achieve these aims, we need to examine the effects of computers upon diverse enterprises such as business, labor-management relations, education, government, decision-making, and national defense. These areas and the issues that arise within them are so broad as to exceed the boundaries of any particular discipline. Accordingly, this book develops an interdisciplinary perspective that is informed by ideas from disciplines such as economics, psychology, sociology, and philosophy.

In analyzing the influence of computers, it is important to recognize that the computer is the leading edge of a host of technological developments, some of which have called attention to the same kinds of issues that computers are raising today. In many respects, the computer revolution is an extension of the Industrial Revolution, which began two hundred years ago. To gain historical perspective on the computer revolution, we need to examine the Industrial Revolution and its social effects. But we need to reach back even farther in time to acquire a broad historical perspective on the linkage between computers and human culture. Throughout the course of human evolution, technology and culture have developed hand in hand, and this trend continues today as computers and culture evolve and shape each other. It is appropriate to begin our inquiry by situating computers within the framework of human evolution.

Intelligence, Technology, and Evolution

In the animal kingdom, many species have brains that are organized in a relatively simple manner and that make up a tiny fraction of their body weight (Jerison, 1982). These animals survive and pass on their genes by using strength, speed, or disguise, together with a modicum of intelligence. Changes in their behavior result mainly from the slow process of organic evolution via natural selection over many successive generations. For example, an environment containing a small number of swift prey will confer selective advantage on cheetahs who run swiftly. Over many generations, this selective pressure may change the local cheetah population in such a way that most of the cheetahs who are born are capable of running very fast.

Humans, by contrast, have more complex brains that constitute a larger proportion of their body weight. Our ancestors made their way more through prodigious intelligence than through physical prowess (Campbell, 1982), as is evident from the size of the contemporary human brain. A device of unsurpassed complexity, the human brain contains approximately ten billion neurons or nerve cells, each of which synapses or communicates with 1,000 to 5,000 other neurons. Considering each neuron as a binary unit that can either fire or remain at rest (actually, neurons can send graded signals in addition to binary ones), the brain contains over ten trillion bits of information (Sagan, 1977). This number is impressive even by the standards of the most powerful computers available today.

Our complex brain is the seat of penetrating creativity, of extensive memory capacity, and of language, an essential vehicle for complex thinking and social organization. Because of our superior brain capacity, we can change our behavior through the relatively rapid process of learning, bypassing the slow process of organic change. Equally important, we remember what we learn and transmit our ideas easily to our offspring. Though we are still bound by the pressures of natural selection, we have become cultural animals for whom the use of tools has been the key to our biological success.

Tools, Intelligence, and Adaptation

Tool use is more common in animals than was once believed. Egyptian vultures, for example, drop rocks on hard ostrich eggs, breaking the thick shell and consuming the contents. Chimpanzees occasionally scare enemies off by throwing bones or rocks at them, and they gather their favorite food, termites, by dipping sticks into termite mounds (van Lawick-Goodall, 1971). Similar uses of tools probably occurred among our distant primate ancestors who inhabited trees and forests in Africa.

As severe drought parched the African continent, the forests diminished, opening vast expanses of grassland or savanna. In adapting to life on the savanna, our ancestors began walking in an upright posture, freeing their hands for using tools. Later, they began making tools, and their brain size increased dramatically over what in evolutionary terms is a small period of time. These developments interlocked, and each drove the others onward. With free hands for carrying and using tools and an enlarged brain to be used in designing new tools and the ends to which they could be put, our ancestors began using tools more and more, thereby obtaining a substantial advantage over their competitors. In turn, the advantages of producing and using tools may have increased the selective pressure leading to upright walking and brain enlargement. Thus tool use, upright locomotion and brain enlargement were mutually enhancing developments that formed an intricate causal web (Campbell, 1982).

The early tools produced by hominids were relatively simple yet quite effective. In the Olduvai Gorge in Tanzania, Louis and Mary Leakey have discovered many stone choppers nearly two million years old. Held in the palm of one hand and used to strike another rock, a good chopper can knock off a flake useful for cutting meat and gristle. Gradually, a primitive technology for making tools developed. Over many years, our ancestors refined this technology and invented more sophisticated tools such as spears, clubs, and axes. Of course, they passed on their skills and the tools that they made to their offspring. Tools thereby became part of a culture that reflected the cumulative wisdom and experience of previous generations.

Owing largely to their use of tools, humans have adapted effectively to a remarkable variety of environments. The fossil record shows, for example, that our ancestors lived for a time alongside many large mammals. Because meat provides an excellent source of calories, hunting the large mammals would have provided much of the food required for survival. Using spears with sharp stone points, the relatively weak hominids killed the powerful mammals for food. Similarly, in adapting to colder climates, our ancestors used sharp scrapers to clean animal hides, which they then stitched into clothing using needles made of bone. Using flint stones, they produced fire at will, gaining warmth and protection from nocturnal predators. This process of adaptation through the use of tools continues today. Rather than adapting to new environments through the slow process of organic change, we use sophisticated tools to create liveable environments on land, beneath the sea, and even in space.

The use of tools has gone hand in hand with the development of complex social organization. Using tools, people lived as hunters as well as gatherers of food. In turn, hunting favored cooperation, for group hunting succeeded more often than individual hunting, and only a group of hunters could kill the large mammals that provided abundant food. Moreover, in a group of hunters, individuals can share their techniques and can divide the labor, performing the tasks which they do best. This coordinated group activity requires effective communication by gesture, or, more likely, by spoken language, which leaves the hands free for using weapons. Living as hunters may also have contributed to the division of labor between the sexes, since women who were either pregnant or who were nursing children were better suited for activities other than hunting. As humans used tools more and more effectively in hunting, they had to devote less time to securing food, allowing more time for additional social activity such as visiting other groups. On these visits, they exchanged and learned about new tools, perpetuating the cycle consisting of tool use, hunting, and social activity.

The basic human propensities for communication, cooperation and group living, then, owe partly to the extensive use of tools. The complexities of social living required substantial brain capacity, the evolution of which had already been fostered by the use of tools. Though we often think of tools as instruments, they are much more—they are shapers of our social character and our evolutionary path. So it is with computers.

Information and Intelligence Tools

The collection and management of information has been important throughout human evolution. People have always gathered information about what is edible or poisonous, about which situations are safe and which are dangerous, and so on. In prehistoric times, people remembered and managed the information that they used on a daily basis without the aid of written records and technology. As human knowledge increased, however, it became necessary to store information outside of the brain in devices such as books.

Today there is an ever increasing need for tools that enhance our ability to store and process information. In the last hundred or so years, human knowledge, particularly scientific knowledge, has expanded enormously. We live amidst an information explosion of immense proportions, leading to concern that society will be swamped by a glut of information. Although books continue to be useful in storing information, they are of limited use in organizing and selecting from the information stockpile. What we need now is a powerful technology for managing and processing information.

This technology is now available in the form of the computer, which is unsurpassed when it comes to information management. Computers can search a vast amount of literature or data in a fraction of a second and then transmit the results instantly to the farthest parts of the planet. They can also manage huge financial accounts, processing hundreds of transactions each second and calculating the results automatically. This is not to say that computers have solved the problem of the information glut. Some would say that computers are actually increasing this glut by generating too much new information. Used appropriately, however, computers make it possible to handle large masses of information with much greater efficiency than had been possible in previous eras.

In addition to managing existing information, computers advance our intellectual and creative pursuits by enabling us to simulate or mimic the real world and to design new tools, which can then be tested via computer. Computer models of volcanic eruptions, for example, enable us to enter existing information about volcanoes and to make predictions about future eruptions. Similarly, new aircraft are now designed by entering the specifications of the desired craft into a computer. A computer model then tests the design using information about weight, stress loads, and so on, thereby identifying flaws in the design. In this manner, computers amplify our ability to create new tools, moving us faster along our evolutionary trajectory.

Computers, then, are mind tools that can expand our creativity and that enable us to do outside of our heads much that we previously had to do inside of our heads (Stonier, 1984). Whereas many tools amplify our physical power, allowing us, for example, to lift heavy objects, computers amplify our mental power, allowing us to perform immense calculations and to store, retrieve, and manipulate vast amounts of information. In short, they extend our intellectual reach.

Artificial Intelligence

The embryonic field of artificial intelligence (AI) seeks to create machines that perform tasks we typically think of as requiring intelligence. Although the successes of AI have been exaggerated consistently in the popular media, real advances have occurred, particularly in the area of expert systems, which embody in a computer part of the specialized expertise of a person. Using expert systems, it is possible to have computers make decisions and solve problems, thereby extending the reach of human intelligence and saving money in the process.

Oil drilling, for example, is an expensive operation. When problems in drilling occur, it is usually necessary to shut down operations and to fly an expert to the rig site. Since the costs of doing this are in the range of $100,000 per day, large savings could be reaped by developing a computerized expert system to be kept at the rig site. Teknowledge Inc. has done just that in developing a system called DRILLING ADVISOR for a French oil company (Harmon and King, 1985).

DRILLING ADVISOR was designed to solve the problem of what to do when the oil drill sticks, that is, when its rotary and vertical motion are thwarted. First DRILLING ADVISOR asks the operator to enter information about the type of well and the nature of the material being drilled through. Then it asks what kind of drill bit was being used and at what depth the problem was encountered. This information gives the system a description of the episode in which sticking occurred. Next DRILLING ADVISOR asks what is the specific gravity of the mud, shale, sandstone, and other materials surrounding the drill. It also asks what is the type of the mud and in which directions the drill can move.

Applying this information, the system makes suggestions about the possible causes of the sticking and recommends actions for overcoming the problem. It does this by using its knowledge base of 250 rules, which were formulated with the help of human experts on oil drilling. So far, the system has performed very well, handling a number of cases that differed from those used in designing it (Harmon and King, 1985).

Largely because of the recent advances in artificial intelligence, computers have indeed become mind tools that extend and amplify our intelligence. Unlike books, automobiles, and other highly influential technologies, computers have the unique ability to make inferences and complex decisions. By uniting tools and intelligence in a new way, the computer continues us on an evolutionary trajectory that began millions of years ago on the African savannas.

Throughout evolution, tool development interacted extensively with the social order. As pointed out above, our ancestors' social organization enabled the creation of particular tools and made it a priority to build new ones. But the development of new tools changed the social order, allowing people to live and hunt in new ways. The extensive interaction between technology and the social order occurs with regard to the computer today, only it is difficult to see since we are immersed in the computer revolution. Fortunately, history provides models of the interaction between technology and society, and we now turn to that history.

Technology and Society

The evolution of human culture seems to occur at a gradual, steady pace. In fact, however, cultural evolution has been punctuated by several major upheavals or revolutions. For example, in the first Industrial Revolution, which occurred between 1780 and 1840, the pace of technological development increased dramatically. The appearance of new technologies, coupled with changes in population, transportation, and economic conditions, transformed the social landscape, restructuring the conditions of work and firming the grasp of the capitalist way of life. The events of the Industrial Revolution illustrate the profound influence of technology on society and point out the complex interplay between technology and economic and social conditions.

The Industrial Revolution

In 1750, the textile industry in England was a domestic system, a cottage industry. The weaver spent much of his time in his cottage, which often consisted of a single room that served as both living place and workshop. Working a loom similar to those which had been used for centuries, he wove threads of wool or cotton into fabrics which he sold at the markets. The loom used so much thread or yarn that five or six spinners were needed to keep a single loom in full supply. Typically, the spinning was done in homes other than the weaver's, thereby specializing the local labor. The weaver, however, was his own master, for he controlled production and determined his own work schedule, often setting aside a weekly holiday on "Saint Monday." Further, even the relatively wealthy weaver who owned multiple looms often worked alongside his employees, and he did not regard himself as belonging to a higher social class (Mantoux, 1961).

Owing partly to an increase in population, the demand for cheap woven goods increased sharply. This increased demand, coupled with extensive land enclosures which discouraged many from agriculture and from sheepherding, led men to take up weaving. In turn, this increased the demand for thread and yarn. The supply of spinners, however, fell far short of the demand. This situation created strong economic incentives for the invention of machines that increased the spinners' productivity. In 1765, James Hargreaves invented the spinning jenny, which allowed a single workman to spin several threads simultaneously. Thread production increased still further through the use of Richard Arkwright's water frame, a completely mechanical, power-driven device.

These inventions created a new imbalance, for the supply of thread and yarn now outstripped the weavers' capabilities. Edmund Cartwright's power loom, particularly when used in the factories of the 1830s and 1840s, corrected the imbalance. Operating two steam-driven looms, an adolescent boy could outproduce a skilled weaver using a hand loom by over three to one. This led large numbers of children to enter the workforce, and they often worked long hours under harsh conditions.

The power looms were so productive, however, that the demand for skilled weavers declined, leading to unemployment and low wages for weavers. On more than one occasion, the enraged weavers smashed the looms and the buildings that housed them (Mantoux, 1961). The conflict between men and machines, then, is one unfortunate byproduct of the Industrial Revolution, one that reminds us of the potential social costs of technology.

The mechanization of the textile industry made it possible to increase the quantity of production, the volume of sales and, ultimately, the amount of profit. But the new machines required power, which was difficult to distribute to homes scattered in different places. It was most efficient to establish one central power station that could drive many machines. The result was a significant reorganization of work: work moved out of the homes and into larger facilities in which many people worked using machines. Further, managers were needed to supervise many workers and to coordinate production operations. The workers no longer owned their own materials and tools, and factory owners or supervisors controlled the work. Labor had lost ownership of and control over the means of production.

Like the factories of the Middle Ages, the early factories of the Industrial Revolution were powered mostly by water, so they had to be built near swift streams and rivers. But the demand for power fostered the invention of new sources of energy, particularly James Watt's steam engine. In turn, the steam engine fostered the demand for coal and iron, and it also made it possible to construct factories in many different locations. In the 1790s, the use of steam pread rapidly, and dense urban concentrations of factories soon arose ... Lancashire and Yorkshire. The rise of the factories stimulated urbanization because they employed so many people and because the workers found it convenient to live near their workplace.

The Industrial Revolution thoroughly transformed labor and the relationship between workers and owners. In earlier times, personal life and work had been interconnected, and people did not have highly specialized work roles. During the Industrial Revolution, work became structured according to specialized roles designed to maximize the efficiency of production, and work activities became sharply separated from personal life. In other words, work had become rationalized; it had been organized according to rules established by the factory owners. In addition, labor had become a commodity to be bought and sold according to its market value, and a rationally organized system of wage labor had evolved. Workers' wages were far below the earnings of the factory owners, and many workers were forced to live in poverty and under the threat of unemployment. Being impoverished and uneducated, the rising masses of workers constituted a new and lower social class that lacked the power and influence of the factory owners and capitalists. The class system about which Karl Marx wrote had been born.

As the Industrial Revolution progressed, technical advances proliferated and became interdependent, just as the power loom became dependent upon the steam engine. At the same time, people became increasingly dependent upon machines. The result was a web of interconnecting elements, the beginnings of the industrial network that still pervades civilization. The Industrial Revolution, however, was not just a technological revolution—it was equally a social revolution. It radically altered living and working conditions, it stimulated the development of a new social class, and it bound people and machines more tightly into a common cultural web.

The dramatic social impact of the Industrial Revolution has encouraged numerous social and political theorists to advocate a view called technological determinism, which states that technology is the primary cause of the social order, of social consciousness and of social change (Ellul, 1964; Galbreath, 1969; Heidegger, 1966; White, 1949; Winner, 1977). This view finds support in the observation that the steam engine fostered the formation of factories and large urban centers, leading eventually to a division of social classes and a rationalized system of labor.

Technological determinism, however, is too extreme, implying incorrectly that people have little or no choice over whether and how to use technology. During the Industrial Revolution, factory owners did have choices, albeit constrained ones, about what to make and in what quantities. As one noted historian put it, technology opens a door, but it does not compel us to enter (White, 1966). In addition, technological determinism errs by overemphasizing technological innovation to the exclusion of other factors. In the Industrial Revolution, the desire for increased productivity and profit motivated the invention of devices such as the steam engine. To be sure, the steam engine had a powerful impact, but the steam engine itself was brought about by economic factors. Further, the British control of the seas and of an expansive colonial market also contributed to the Industrial Revolution. It is inappropriate, then, to single out technology as the prime mover of social change.

Computers in the Fabric of Culture

Society is best thought of as a vast system in which technological, economic, social, and political factors interact extensively and feed back on each other, making it difficult to identify a single cause of social change. In the U.S. automobile industry, for example, many manufacturing plants have introduced computer-driven robots to do much of the welding previously done by people. Economic factors motivated this change. And the use of computers in production has in fact reduced production costs, increased the quality of the product, and enabled many companies to survive in a highly competitive market dominated increasingly by Japan. In turn, these economic benefits drove manufacturers to buy more sophisticated computers and to use them even more extensively in building automobiles. The result has been a transformation of the manufacturing process and a substantial change in the work life of millions of people. But the computer alone did not cause these changes. As in the Industrial Revolution, it was the interplay between economic and technological factors that produced social change.

Political and technological factors interact in a similar manner, as is evident in the use of computers in the Soviet Union. For example, under the leadership of Mikhail Gorbachev, the Soviet Union seeks to increase sharply its imports and production of personal computers and to create a national computer network that will uplift the sagging Soviet economy (Dizard, 1986). Movement on Gorbachev's agenda will significantly enhance the technological capabilities of the Soviets, who lag approximately ten years behind Americans in the high-tech arena.

The proliferation of personal computers in the Soviet Union, however, will have impacts far beyond the economic and the technological (Roberts and Engle, 1986). Using personal computers, ordinary citizens and even dissident groups can produce and distribute information on a scale never possible before. This will make it very difficult for the Soviet government, which historically has exercised powerful control over the flow of information, to control the flow of information in the future.

The loss of centralized control over information may advance Gorbachev's political agenda, which includes increased openness (glasnost) and citizen participation in public debate and decision-making (democratization). But it may also promote social upheaval by allowing nationalist groups and dissident factions to distribute their ideas and to increase their political influence. Although it is too early to tell exactly what the effects of personal computers in the Soviet Union will be, this case and many others point out that technology never acts alone. Instead, technology interacts with a host of economic, political, and social factors.

This insight has deep significance for the study of computers in society. Because technology never acts alone, what appears to be a social impact of computers is in fact an impact of computers in conjunction with other factors. Strictly speaking, computers by themselves have no social impact—they have an impact only when they are used in a particular social context. As discussed above, their use is guided by numerous influences outside technology. In addition, because computers have been created and programmed by people, social changes that appear to be the product of computers are equally the handiwork of people. Thus we must go beyond technology in order to understand its social effects.

This interactionist view of technology and society suggests that technology is not the single, dominant force underlying culture. By analogy, it is an important fiber that permeates the fabric of culture, interweaving with social, political, and economic factors. Indeed, the divisions between these different factors are often unclear, and, in many cases, arbitrary (Pacey, 1983). At many points in the cultural fabric, technology interweaves with science, for scientific discoveries lead to new forms of technology. And the application of new technologies generates new problems and questions, stimulating additional scientific inquiry. The result is a cultural fabric of immense richness and complexity, with science, technology, and society tightly interconnected.

From this perspective, it is an oversimplification to say that technology is a neutral tool to be used for good or ill, according to our free choice. For one thing, social and political values are often embodied in the design of technology. The value of political control, for example, informs the design of computer systems that enable industrial managers to control production centrally and to monitor the activities of the workers (Shaiken, 1984). In addition, technology is an important part of the causal network that also involves economic, social, and political factors. For example, the presence of a handgun does not compel one person to shoot another. But the presence of a handgun in the context of a fight or a political coup may well increase the likelihood of a shooting. Similarly, general purpose computers can be used for everything from writing great literature to fighting a war. In the context of a large military organization, there is little doubt that computers will be put to military uses. Because technology exists in and is used in a social context, it is appropriate to view technology as an element of society that, like any other, is laden with social values.

In addition, economic, political, and social factors shape the development and the use of technology—choice alone does not guide technology. This is not to say that our choices are insignificant in regard to technology but to recognize that they are constrained by the social context, which is suffused with beliefs and values. In order to make informed choices, we need to examine the beliefs and values that surround the use of computers.

Computers, Myths, and Values

In every culture, there is a matrix of beliefs and values shared by large numbers of people. Most Americans, for example, believe in free enterprise, and they cherish freedom as a value, viewing it as a fundamental right. These beliefs and values shape the technology of our culture, and particular uses of the technology increase the strength of particular values.

Computers, for example, embody the Western belief in the usefulness of science and logic as well as the values of speed and efficiency. Indeed, these beliefs and values, coupled with a highly developed infrastructure for science and engineering, made the U.S. and England fertile centers for the development of computers. In contrast, there have been few opportunities for the invention of computers in relatively primitive cultures that attached little value to speed and efficiency and that were based upon religion and mysticism rather than science and logic.

The dominant beliefs and values of a society also shape the use of computers, which in turn can strengthen the influence of those beliefs and values. If, for example, a strict, totalitarian society used computers extensively, it would undoubtedly use them to assert the values attached to central control and authority. And the use of computers in the pursuit those values could certainly increase the ability of the government to control the citizenry. It is chilling to imagine, for example, how much more effective Hitler could have been if he had had computers at his disposal. Like other forms of technology, the computer is not a passive tool but an instrument for implementing or strengthening particular values and beliefs.

In entering American culture, the computer has penetrated into a social system permeated by the belief that technology will make life better and that it is therefore a good idea to develop more technology. This belief is evident in the writings of computer optimists, who have trumpeted that computers will usher in a golden age of human-machine partnership in which computers will perform tasks that are dull, dirty and dangerous, and will liberate people for intellectual and leisure pursuits (Jastrow, 1981; Provenzo, 1986). This belief is also embodied in popular film characters such as R2D2 and C3PO, the entertaining droids from *Star Wars*.

This belief, which sometimes shades into a blind faith in technology, acts as a lens that distorts our perception of computers, leading to false beliefs or myths about them. These myths are often difficult to spot because they usually are partly true—they tend to be oversimplifications rather than outright falsities. In addition, computer myths are so deeply embedded in the culture of some companies and industries that they are taken for granted and pass unnoticed. Left unidentified, these myths are pernicious because they can silently shape expectations and guide decision making down inappropriate paths. The best way to immunize ourselves against these myths is to identify and analyze them explicitly. The following section addresses three of the most prevalent myths.

Three Computer Myths

Myth 1: The computer is correct. In many circles, people attach excessive credibility to computer models and to data analyses conducted by computers. Particularly among people who know little about computers, there is a tendency to view the computer as mysterious and powerful and to regard computer output as unassailable. Whether making a presentation in business, in education, or in government, the use of a computer can dazzle the audience with snappy graphics and overwhelm them with mountains of data, leaving the impression that no stone has been left unturned. And if the audience enters the presentation expecting the computer to produce correct results, they are biased toward believing what they have seen. Expecting to see the truth, they respond to flawed analyses as if they were words of wisdom handed down from above. As one wag put it, this is a problem of "Garbage in, gospel out."

In reality, computers operate according to the principle of "Garbage in, garbage out." If computers are fed inaccurate or incomplete data, the results they produce will be flawed, no matter how believable and impressive they may appear. For example, on November 9, 1979, a test tape designed to simulate a Soviet nuclear attack was inadvertently fed into the computer system that the U.S. uses to detect actual missile attacks. During the following alert, which lasted six minutes, the U.S. responded as if it were under a real attack, and it launched ten fighter aircraft from bases in the Northern U.S. and Canada (Borning, 1987). Fortunately, the mistake was caught and World War III was prevented. But this case provides a sobering reminder of what could happen if the output of computers were accepted uncritically or believed too readily.

Even people who understand computers very well may fall into a credibility trap, but for a different reason. Computer experts often have tremendous faith in technology and in their own ability to create highly accurate computer systems. In addition, they have a thorough knowledge of the model on which a computer program is based. Having designed a model, embodied it in a computer program and checked the program repeatedly to make sure that it works, they too may tend to believe too strongly what their computers tell them.

In 1983, for example, the lower Colorado River flooded, killing six people and producing millions of dollars in damage. This disaster, which should have been prevented by the elaborate flood control system in place on the river, stemmed from serious mistakes in federal computer projections of the melt-off from heavy snows (Borning, 1987). Not expecting an unusually heavy water flow from the mountains, the state kept too much water dammed up prior to the spring thaws. In this tragic case, computers made incorrect projections because they were guided by an incorrect model of the water flow.

On the surface, this problem of basing computer programs upon incorrect models appears to have a ready solution—test the model and the program more thoroughly before actually using them to make decisions. In fact, however, comprehensive testing is much more complex than it appears to be at first glance. Because humans cannot foresee the future perfectly, they cannot foresee all of the factors that might affect the operation of their computer system and that ought to be tested. Understandably, they fail to run tests of truly unexpectable events.

On October 5, 1960, for example, the U.S. computer system used to detect enemy missiles indicated that the Soviets had launched a massive missile attack against us. It turned out that the early warning radar system in Greenland had picked up a signal from the rising moon, not from a missile attack. The designers of the system had never thought about the moon when designing and testing the program. Although this problem was corrected subsequently, the point remains that computer systems can never be tested perfectly since we cannot foresee all of the events and situations that they will encounter in the future. It is unrealistic to expect computers to be perfectly correct since they were designed and programmed by imperfect beings. For these reasons, we should be humble about our computer systems, and we should examine the output of computers and claims about the accuracy of particular systems with a critical eye.

Myth 2: Using computers always improves efficiency. In many pursuits ranging from writing to conducting scientific research, the use of computers has often improved efficiency. But there is nothing inevitable about these efficiency gains. In fact, it is quite possible to suffer decreased efficiency through the use of computers.

In 1985, for example, the Internal Revenue Service (IRS) became swamped in a quagmire of unprocessed returns and unanswered inquiries from taxpayers. The IRS also made many incorrect or delayed refunds totalling hundreds of millions of dollars and sent out many unjustified threats to seize property. These problems, which cost the taxpayers millions of dollars, resulted from the receipt of a record 100 million tax returns that year, coupled with the implementation of a new computer system. As it turned out, the computer system lacked the capacity to handle so many returns. Not only was it plagued by a variety of hardware and software problems, but inefficient procedures for entering data onto the system created a tremendous bottleneck. One U.S. Senator described the IRS as a "computerized chamber of horrors" (Sawyer, 1985). As this example shows, adding computers can create as many problems as it solves.

Using computers efficiently requires careful attention not only to computers but also to their users and to the requirements of the job. The computer system itself—the hardware and the software—must have the capabilities needed to handle the tasks it is intended to do. In addition, the people who use the system must receive adequate training on the new system so that they can trust it and use it effectively. And the procedures carried out by the computer and by the users must be efficient. Otherwise, the system will run afoul of a corollary of Murphy's Law: Anything that can be done wrong can be done wrong faster by computer.

Myth 3: *Every computer-related problem has a technical solution.* This is the myth of the technical fix. Like the two myths discussed above, this statement contains an element of truth since many problems do have technical solutions. Commercial airlines, for example, have often worried about how to train their pilots to handle emergencies. Using computers and van-size simulation chambers, airlines have begun to address this training problem (Elmer-deWitt, 1988). The trainees sit in front of a flight control panel and see realistic computer-generated images of such scenes as flying over Manhattan or approaching a runway on a foggy night. In this computer-generated world, they encounter emergencies such as failed landing gear or an engine bursting into flames. The experience is made even more realistic by accelerating and tilting the simulation chamber so as to mimic the feelings of speed and body orientation that pilots have in flying real aircraft. Because of this training, pilots can make mistakes and learn from them without harming anyone, becoming better prepared to respond effectively to real emergencies.

Not all problems, however, have technical solutions. The problem of automating an office, for example, consists of a mixture of technical problems and people problems. The technical problems such as how much and what kinds of hardware capacities are needed have technical solutions. But the problems concerning people do not. If the office workers fear computers and are satisfied with a manual mode of operation, they may resist learning about or using the computer system. Improvements in the computer system or in computer-assisted training will not solve this problem, which is fundamentally human rather than technical.

Similarly, the problem of communicating effectively is not entirely technical. Telecommunications satellites, coupled with computers, allow people from different countries to talk with and see each other, creating a global village. Although bridging large gaps of time and space fosters communication, it does not guarantee effective communication. Even when talking face-to-face, it can be very difficult to get one's point across effectively and to really understand what someone else is trying to say. Effective communication requires more than technology—it requires open-mindedness, sensitivity, and empathy.

Living in a high-tech society that places enormous faith in technology, we find it all too easy to believe that there is a technological fix for every problem. But there is not. Problems that appear to be strictly technical often turn out to include significant human elements as well. In working to remedy a social problem, it is as important to think about the human dimensions as it is to think about the technological dimensions of the problem. Furthermore, new technology can be either used appropriately or misused. In order to use computers appropriately, we need to think carefully about our values.

Computers and Values

Traditional American values have undergone a number of wrenching changes in this century. Technology has not been the sole cause of these changes, but it has exerted a powerful influence. The mass production of the automobile, for example, fostered a decline in the value attached to living in a stable community and increased the value attached to mobility. In the 1960s and 1970s, advances in birth control technology spurred the sexual revolution, which radically altered sexual values and behavior. Advances in abortion technology have enabled sharp increases in the numbers of pregnant women choosing not to deliver, raising profound questions about the right to life.

The use of computers, too, presents significant challenges to our values. If, for example, computers were used mainly to consolidate the power of central government and of large corporations, then we would become a very different society, one that attaches less value to individual freedom. The trouble is that shifts in values may occur so gradually as to pass unnoticed, allowing society to drift away from its moorings. In order to avoid aimless drifts in our value systems, we need to be conscious of the values that are implicit in our choices and of the value conflicts that may result.

Economic Values

Animated by the prospect of huge profits, thousands of entrepreneurs, engineers, and corporations have followed the gold rush into the computer market. From 1980 to 1985, the computer market went from offering only a few personal computers, mostly for mechanically inclined hobbyists, to offering over one hundred brands of microcomputers and thousands of related products, many of which could be used even by avowed computerphobes. In addition, the computer boom spawned new meccas of computing such as Silicon Valley in California and Route 128 in Massachusetts, near Boston. Seemingly overnight, firms such as Apple Computers and Lotus Corporation burst onto the scene, enjoying tremendous profits and becoming household names.

Besides being profitable business items themselves, computers are often used to boost productivity. Through the use of computers, AT&T operators now handle 600 to 700 customers daily, whereas they processed only 150 calls per day in the early 1970s (Koepp, 1986). This makes for huge savings and larger profits in the telephone industry. In fact, the Bell system saved twenty-four million dollars in one year by using computers to cut one second from the average directory assistance call (Howard, 1985).

Managers looking to maximize their profits often introduce new technology in order to reduce labor costs, which rank high among all of the costs of production. The average cost per hour of work for a robot that does welding on an automobile assembly line is less than half of the hourly wage of a skilled human welder (Shaiken, 1984), and the robot often makes better welds. These benefits tempt many managers to introduce robots instead of hiring additional human laborers and to replace human laborers with robots. Thus economic values may conflict with social values such as full employment.

This is not to say that economic values always conflict with social values in the development and use of computers. For example, the expansion of the computer industry creates many new jobs. Furthermore, workers who have been displaced by robots can be retrained and moved into a different type of work. The pursuit of economic values, then, may have socially useful consequences. In fact, the pursuit of economic values often goes hand in hand with the pursuit of social goals such as the elimination of poverty.

Political Values

Although many Americans are not aware of it, the computer has become one of the most powerful political instruments of our time. In a political campaign conducted in the midwest ten years ago, the challenger knew that he had to boost his name recognition in order to challenge the incumbent. Using voter registration lists and the telephone directory, he created a list of the voters' addresses and telephone numbers. Next, volunteers asked the voters several questions by phone and recorded their answers on the list. Using this list and computers, the challenger generated a personal mailgram for each voter. If voters had mentioned environmental issues, they received mailgrams that began with "Knowing of your interest in protecting our environment..." and that then outlined the candidate's position on environmental issues. Because of this technique, the challenger went from having no name recognition to winning the primary (McDonald, 1988).

Many other politicians have rushed to computerize their campaigns, and personal computers have become staples of even the smallest campaigns. Firms such as Below, Tobe & Associates now sell candidates selected files, which cover 71 million registered voters across 42 states and which provide information about ethnic group, household type, gender, and so on. Using these lists and computers, many campaign managers now send what appear to be individually tailored letters to every potential voter in their districts. Of course, this type of letter can be highly misleading, since the candidate is in a position to tell a particular voter only what he or she wants to hear. Nevertheless, computers have become cemented into the American political system.

Computers also increase political power by adding to the prestige of particular people or nations. Technology is often perceived as an indicator of creativity, intelligence, and social organization. To have the most powerful supercomputer, for example, speaks loudly for a nation's scientific, engineering, and industrial capabilities, giving the nation additional influence in the international arena. Within an organization, individuals often gain prestige by acquiring the most powerful computer and by using it to do things that fellow workers cannot do. Thus the computer is more than a powerful tool—it is a symbol of power.

Political values are particularly important when considering issues such as who decides whether to use a particular technology and who will benefit from it. All too often, it is the wealthy and the powerful who make the decision to buy an expensive new computer system for a hospital, for example, rather than to expand health care services for the poor. Typically, relatively wealthy doctors and hospital administrators make this type of decision even though it has profound implications for the disadvantaged.

The decision to acquire a new computer system may appear to be a technical decision that is either value-free or guided only by the desire for improved efficiency. In fact, however, it is also a political decision that advances the values of one group over those of other groups. Furthermore, the decision to buy a medical group a new computer increases the power of the doctors by boosting their prestige and by giving them powerful new resources with which to wield influence. In evaluating the use of computers, it is essential to probe beneath the stated justifications and to identify underlying political values.

Aesthetic Values

Computers having high-resolution capabilities have created new horizons in the realm of graphics. In 1947, for example, Bedouin shepherds near Jerusalem discovered the Dead Sea Scrolls, ancient documents over 2,000 years old that contain originals of celebrated religious works. Although this was considered to be the greatest manuscript discovery in history, the enthusiasm of biblical scholars was dampened by their inability to read more than a few individual letters from the badly decomposed parchment. Using computers and high-resolution graphics, however, the scholars created digitized images of the scrolls from infrared photographs. Then they enhanced the images by making the darker points darker and the lighter points even lighter. As a result, they are now able to read original scriptures that might soon have been lost forever (Elmer-DeWitt, 1988). Scientists now use similar techniques routinely for enhancing images transmitted by satellites and space probes, creating dazzling pictures of the earth and of other worlds.

Computers have also become a means of creating new forms of art. At an art conference in San Francisco in 1985, an artist exhibited a new form of art that consists of 256 square feet of computer paper. The sheets were covered with print created by programming an Apple computer to read and to print out the contents of each of its 65,536 memory addresses in the form of zeroes and ones, creating a variety of distinct and visually engaging patterns (Hohn, 1988). The power of the computer as an artistic medium became evident to millions of people following the introduction of Apple Corporation's Macintosh computer, which includes a Macpaint program for painting sophisticated images.

In music as well as in the visual arts, computers have become an increasingly important medium. Computers make it possible to generate a tremendous array of sounds and to organize and synthesize them into aesthetically appealing pieces. Composers use computers to blend electronic sounds with those produced by traditional instruments, creating symphonies whose sounds are bounded only by the imagination (Boulez and Gerzso, 1988). In recording studios, computers have enabled the production of digital recordings of such high fidelity that they have reached the upper limits of the human hearing capacity.

As these examples illustrate, the computer is more than a powerful tool for obtaining external goals such as building faster cars or earning larger profits. It is also a powerful medium for promoting aesthetic sensitivity. Used in the service of aesthetic values, the computer is not the silicon Frankenstein that it has on occasion been made out to be (Reinecke, 1984; Shallis, 1984). Rather, it is a medium that can nourish human creativity and sensibility.

In the era of computers, the aesthetic and technical realms are increasingly interconnected. New technology has a beauty of its own (Florman, 1974), and computer gurus such as Steven Jobs, the co-founder of Apple computer and the developer of the NEXT computer, recognize the importance of making computers with which people can develop an aesthetic bond. In addition, engineers who design technology often speak of the beauty of working on problems that are technically sweet, ones that push the limits of human technical virtuosity (Kidder, 1981).

The tremendous amount of effort now devoted to increasing the memory capacity of computers is born partly out of the practical desire to do bigger jobs and to do them faster. But it also reflects the aesthetic impulse to achieve technical virtuosity, to do what had once seemed to be technically impossible. And it is impressive to see just how far we have come. For example, the most powerful supercomputer in existence in the early 1970s had a memory capacity of 500,000 15-digit numbers. Over

the following fifteen years, the capacity of the most powerful supercomputer expanded 512 times. The Cray-2 supercomputer of the mid-1980s had
a memory capacity of 256 million 15-digit numbers (Erisman and Neves,
1987). This enormous increase in technical capacity had aesthetic as well
as practical appeal to both the designers and the users of supercomputers.

This value of the technical aesthetic can mislead us into developing new
technology for its own sake, without careful attention to the social consequences. For example, the author once asked one of the most prominent
computer scientists in the world if he would, given the opportunity, complete
the construction of a superintelligent computer, even if neither he nor anyone
else could tell in advance whether the computer would serve or kill people.
He answered that his aesthetic and scientific impulses would require him to
complete the machine, without moral agonizing. Not all computer engineers
feel as this one did, but many feel the lure of technical sweetness. In order to
protect human survival, much less our humanity, technical sweetness cannot
be treated as the most important value.

The value of the technical aesthetic, coupled with the myth of the
technical fix, gives technology a powerful one-two punch in American society.
Believing in the power of technology, both policy makers and the public look
to computers to solve societal problems ranging from crime to nuclear war.
They can often find a ready core of computer engineers who, guided by the
value of the technical aesthetic, are eager to work on any technically sweet
project, even if the project stands little chance of doing what it had been
intended to do. As a result, technical solutions are often sought for problems
that cannot be solved through technology alone. In working to solve social
problems such as unemployment or homelessness, we must look beyond
technology and consider humanitarian values.

Humanitarian Values

On a national computer bulletin board used widely to send and receive
messages, one of the most popular users is a woman who can neither speak
nor walk. For her, the computer is an instrument of liberation, one that allows
her to meet and to talk with people from all parts of the country. Larry M., a
victim of cerebral palsy, uses the computer to work from his rural home in
Virginia and to circumvent the physical difficulties he experiences in walking
and driving. In an urban ghetto in New York, Mark H. uses computers to teach
problem solving skills after school to disadvantaged youths who would otherwise be on streets permeated by drugs and crime. Knowing that boys tend to
use computers more than girls do, Mark makes a conscious effort to encourage
girls to work with the computers.

These cases illustrate that computers can be used in the service of
basic human values such as togetherness, compassion and social equity.

It is the pursuit of these values that sets humans apart from machines. If we allow these values to erode, we lose a piece of our humanity, and the quality of life declines. If, on the other hand, we actively cultivate these values, our quality of life increases, and we achieve the highest human potential of caring for others as we care for ourselves.

Awareness of humanitarian values offers an antidote to the unthinking pursuit of technology for its own sake. Although engineers and technicians may be tempted to build more powerful bombs, increasingly potent nerve gases, and sophisticated new weapons of mass destruction, humanitarian values persuade us to resist these temptations. Whereas the technical aesthetic encourages us to push ahead and to solve whatever technological challenges we face, humanitarian values caution us to reflect upon the social consequences. Not every technology improves human well-being. Practically every technology, from nuclear technology to computers, may be used to achieve humanitarian goals or to create powerful new vehicles of war and destruction. By reflecting on humanitarian values, we prepare ourselves to resist the tendency to use computers in every situation and to use computers in a socially appropriate manner.

Thinking about humanitarian values is particularly important in this era of computers. For one thing, many of the most important policy decisions on how to use computers have not been made yet, and if we make careful and appropriate choices, we can protect our humanity and use computers to improve the conditions of living and working. Furthermore, computers have become so central in science and engineering that they drive the pace of technology development. Without constraining the uses of computers, there is little hope of guiding technological development down socially productive avenues.

Conclusion

Technology has played a key role in human evolution and has contributed to such monumental social changes as the agricultural revolution of 10,000 years ago and the Industrial Revolution that is still underway. The march of technology may seem inexorable, as if civilization were driven by a technological imperative. But there is no technological imperative per se—technology is embedded in a richly interactive social system in which individuals, organizations, institutions, belief systems, and values influence and are influenced by technology. Although the social system constrains the realm of choices, it is nevertheless true that people have real choices to make about whether and how to use a particular technology.

In no other age has the capacity for the misuse of technology been so great. Ours is the first era in which people have had the capacity to annihilate the planet through nuclear war or to alter life itself through biogenetic engineering. Whether we like it or not, each of us now shoulders part of the responsibility for choosing to use technology wisely and in the service of human values. In order to exercise this responsibility, we need to be well informed about the social consequences and issues associated with our most powerful technologies, which surely include computers. In the chapters that follow, we examine the social implications of computers in a wide variety of areas, beginning with the world of work.

2

Work Transformed

Ten years ago, West End Printing was a small, family owned publishing company in Virginia that specialized in preparing handsome marketing brochures for local businesses. Producing a brochure required a skilled typesetter, a creative pasteup artist, and an expanding array of expensive printing machines. Typesetting alone cost West End's customers over $20 per page, and the costs for unusual graphics ran much higher. Today, however, West End does all of the printing using an Apple Macintosh desktop publishing system, which cost only $10,000, far below the costs of the previous equipment. Henry Phillips, the owner, no longer spends long hours on the laborious tasks of typesetting and pasteup, tasks that are now done entirely by computer. Using the Macintosh, he can rapidly create dazzling graphics, select attractive type for the text, and print out remarkably clean and precise copies on his laser printer. In six months, West End has recovered its modest investment in the desktop system, and it has doubled its production without expanding the staff. The customers praise the system for having reduced the costs from over $20 to under $5 per page. Moreover, the workers enjoy using the system since the computer does most of the drudge work, leaving them free to exercise their creative talents.

In the past two hundred years, automation has had a powerful influence on work, modifying the organization of work, changing what workers do, altering the power and the satisfaction of workers, and so on. As illustrated by the use of desktop publishing systems (Rogers, 1986), computers extend this impact on work both quantitatively and qualitatively. The use of computers allows a quantum leap in productivity, a leap as great as that of the Industrial Revolution. Because they perform work that requires extensive skill and intelligence on the part of humans, computers are changing the kind of work that people do and strengthening the bond between people and machines.

It is important to analyze these changes since work is such an essential part of life. Although work is often thought of as a means of building a career and earning the money needed to buy things, it is in fact much more. Through work, individuals define their identity and take on a set of socially accepted responsibilities and roles, for example, those of doctors, lawyers, businessmen, and so on. For many people, work adds purpose and structure to life, and it meets important psychological needs for social interaction, self-esteem, and self-improvement. Work also enables people to reach beyond the narrow corridors of the self and to contribute to the improvement of society.

At the same time, many workers are subjected to inappropriate uses of computers that decrease the quality of working life by making them passive monitors, by increasing stress and health problems, and by fostering social isolation. In addition, workers often do not receive the training they need in order to work effectively with computers. In the absence of proper training, they feel bewildered by the new technology and incapable of doing the quality of work that they want to do. To make wise decisions about using computers in the workplace, we need to be aware of both the potential advantages and perils involved in using computers.

Productivity

Although the use of computers by itself does not guarantee increased efficiency, the computer is nevertheless an important productivity tool. For example, an airline clerk, having immediate access to current information about flights on different airlines, about the numbers of seats available, and about fares, can make many more reservations each hour than could be made without computers. American Airlines relies so heavily on its computers to govern its reservation and flight control systems that it recently spent thirty-four million dollars to shelter its computers in a steel-reinforced, concrete bunker that can withstand hurricanes, floods, and earthquakes (Burgess, 1988).

In analyzing productivity, it is tempting to think only about quantity, for example, about the number of items produced in a factory. In fact, both quality and quantity must be taken into account. Workers on an assembly line, for example, could double the number of units they complete each hour, and this might look like a doubling of productivity. But increases in the number of units produced could be accompanied by decreases in the quality of the work. This decreased quality could lead to reduced sales and costly lawsuits, thereby decreasing the overall productivity of the company. Used properly, computers allow significant increases in both the quality and the quantity of production.

The Electronic Office

In 1958, Mary M., who filed claims for an insurance company, worked in an office in which a typewriter sat on every desk and the walls were covered by massive banks of file cabinets. She was in constant motion, shuttling between offices and moving claims documents back and forth between her desk and the file cabinets. In 1988, Mary works in an electronic office in which computers have replaced typewriters and in which the computer is the main tool that she uses to do her work. Sitting at her terminal, she types documents via word processor, files them on hard disks, and transmits information to other workers and offices via electronic mail. Using computers, she has nearly tripled the number of claims she processes each day, much to her manager's delight.

This case is far from exceptional. Indeed, it is unusual now to find businesses that do not make extensive use of computers. Already typewriters appear to be relics of a bygone age. In the 1990s, as many as forty or fifty percent of all workers in the U.S. will probably be using some sort of electronic terminal daily (Giuliano, 1985).

The rush to computerize offices is easy to understand in light of the substantial gains in efficiency and quality that can result. The word processor, for example, makes it possible to move around large blocks of text with a few keystrokes, without extensive retyping or cutting and pasting. In addition, many writers testify that the word processor can improve the quality of the finished document by facilitating revision, one of the keys to effective writing. The use of word processors also produces substantial savings, reducing the secretarial costs of preparing a letter from seven dollars to less than two dollars (Giuliano, 1985). Word processing, however, only scratches the surface of the productivity gains that can be reaped by using computers.

Electronic Mail and Conferencing

In the increasingly competitive business world, both workers and managers need rapid access to the information that other workers have. Although the telephone is a highly useful tool, it is limited by the need for both parties to be available simultaneously. It can be extremely difficult for two very busy workers to contact each other by phone, and workers complain frequently about the frustration of playing telephone tag. In addition, frequent telephone interruptions interrupt workers' concentration and make it difficult to complete the work that the office is supposed to do.

Many businesses have reduced these problems through the use of electronic mail, which involves sending and receiving typed messages by way of computers that are networked. Using electronic mail, the sender types in a message and indicates the intended receiver, and the computer then transmits the message to the receiver's terminal or stores it until the receiver signs on and requests to see the mail. The advantage is that the sender transmits the message without delay, and the receiver reads the message and responds at his or her convenience, as the following transaction indicates.

LINDA: [sending message to Frank at 10:14, 9/27/88] Frank, I can't locate the sales figures from August, 1988, for our pliers, Model No. 4318. Please send me the figures.

FRANK: [responding to Linda's request at 11:02, 9/27/88] No problem, Linda. The volume for #4318 was 13,029 items with a retail value of $28,174.

In this interaction, there was no work interruption and no telephone tag. In addition, the electronic request gave Frank time to look up the sales information that he needed in order to respond to Linda's request. At its best, electronic mail makes it possible to solve difficult problems through a single exchange rather than through a string of telephone calls.

Computers also increase communication efficiency by allowing the instantaneous transmission of large amounts of information over long distances. In the past, sending a document from New York to Los Angeles required waiting approximately one week for mail delivery. Although express mail services reduced the delivery time significantly, they were too expensive for many businesses to use regularly. Now, however, FAX (facsimile) machines and ordinary telephone lines coordinated by computers shoot pictures and text across the continent at the speed of light. As a result, stock analysts in New York can send a ten-page report of a company's stock performance to headquarters in Los Angeles in minutes, saving large amounts of time and money.

Operating any large business requires holding periodic conferences at which people exchange information, make decisions, and plan future activities. But live conferences are very costly, and they typically require many workers to use valuable time in traveling. Many businesses have circumvented these problems through the use of computer conferencing, which allows the participants to hold a conference from their workplaces so long as they have access to a terminal or computer connected, perhaps by telephone line, to a central computer. The conference begins when one participant types in a statement, making a proposal and asking others to respond. The other participants type in their responses to this item, and everything that is typed in by the various participants appears on everyone's screen, as in the following dialogue.

RONALD T.: [beginning conference between corporate vice-presidents of Acme Computer at 2:45, 6/17/88] Mikhail Gorbachev and other Soviet leaders want to import a large but unstated number of U.S. microcomputers. We have been invited to send a team to Moscow to discuss the matter. Should we move ahead on this? If we send a team, who should be included?

JAMES R.: [responding at 9:05, 6/18/88] Ron, I think we should look into this, but first we need to know what the U.S. government thinks about selling U.S. computers to the Soviets.

FRED B.: [responding at 3:19, 6/18/88] As corporate attorney, I'll look into that, Jim. My understanding is that the government plans to loosen its restrictions on transferring micros to the Soviets so long as older models with 8-bit processors are all that are involved. I'll post another message on this within the next two days.

HELEN F.: [responding at 11:24, 6/19/88] Ron, I think we should go ahead on this so long as we make it clear we aren't making a deal in coming to Moscow— all we're doing is opening a discussion about the possibilities and problems. As for the team makeup, Ted Bannister would be an excellent choice. He's fluent in Russian and knows a lot about our international business operations....

One of the chief advantages of computer conferencing is that it allows a group to carry on a conversation even though the participants talk at different times. In the dialog above, the initial message was posted on June 17, and the first reply occurred the following day. This gives participants time to think the item over carefully before responding and to communicate at their convenience, avoiding disruptions in their work flow. In addition, computer conferencing allows the participation of many people, whereas telephone conferencing is best suited to a smaller number.

The main drawback of computer conferencing is the lack of face-to-face interaction, which makes it less personal and more difficult to identify the other person's feelings. For example, it can be very difficult to detect sarcasm and humor via computer since there are no smiles or body language to signal that a remark is intended to be humorous. Face-to-face communication is possible, however, in some systems of communication by computer. For example, computers play a key role in telecommunications networks which have both visual and audio capabilities and which can be used to hold teleconferences among groups on different continents.

Using computers, companies can create vast networks that connect thousands of workers and managers, improving the flow of information within the organization. For example, Digital Equipment Corporation

(DEC), one of the largest producers of computers, links together 75,000 employees by means of the Easynet network, which includes 27,000 computers located in 26 nations (Helm, 1988). Functioning as the central nervous system of DEC, Easynet allows teams of engineers in different countries to exchange software, memos, and circuit diagrams at high speeds. It also allows DEC to coordinate work on a product in various departments such as marketing, sales, and manufacturing, even though these departments may be located in different countries. As this example illustrates, the use of computers in communications fosters the development of multinational corporations and of a global business community.

Electronic Funds Transfer (EFT)

For many years, paper money, silver, and gold were the primary means of buying and paying for goods. But the use of money and gold carried a high risk of theft, and it was impractical for making the very large transactions required by many corporations. The use of checks, which account for over ninety percent of all transactions, alleviated some of these problems.

Unfortunately, the checking system created another serious problem—a paper explosion. From 1940 to 1970, the number of checks written increased ten times over. Over 40 billion checks were written in 1980, and the number of checks written each year continues to increase at a rate of approximately six percent. This tremendous volume, far too large to be processed manually, has forced banks to automate their processing of checks, using devices such as optical scanners. A typical scanner can read the identifying information at the bottom of checks at the rate of over 10,000 characters per second, processing more checks in a minute than a person can process in a full day. This type of automation eased the burden on the checking system substantially.

The checking system, however, still faces numerous obstacles. Even with the aid of optical scanners, the ever increasing volume of paperwork is staggering, increasing the costs of banking operations. In addition, payment by check remains a relatively slow method. A check sent by mail, for example, could be in transit for a week or more, and still another week might be required for the supplier to clear the check and to fill the order. In making a purchase from a supplier overseas, this system could require a wait of several months. Besides being frustrating, such long waits can impede the flow of one's business.

These problems have spurred the development of electronic funds transfer (EFT), the transfer of money by computer. U.S. banks make huge financial transactions via EFT every day. A large commercial bank, for example, transfers $30 billion daily, and banks around the world transfer over $600 billion each day (Parker, 1983). Individuals also use EFT extensively in forms such as the debit card, which is used in the same manner as a credit card, only it results in immediate payment from the customer's bank account. Typically, the seller puts the customer's card into an automatic card reader connected to the bank's computer via telephone line. The computer checks whether the customer's account contains sufficient funds for the purchase. If it does, the computer immediately transfers the amount of the purchase from the purchaser's account to the merchant's account. An electronic transfer of funds also occurs when using a credit card, but the transaction is between a credit account such as a VISA or MasterCard account and that of the merchant. Whether paying by credit card or debit card, the electronic transfer produces substantial savings of time and paper.

The use of the electronic transfer of funds is increasing rapidly through the use of Point of Sale (POS) terminals. These devices resemble cash registers in appearance, but they are actually computer terminals. They can automatically record sales, update inventory, and, when a charge card is used, debit the customer's account. In a rapidly increasing number of stores, these terminals are used in conjunction with a Universal Products Code (UPC) in the following way. The checkout clerk passes each item to be purchased over a small holographic scanning window. Wrapping a laser beam around the product, the scanner reads the product code, transmitting the data to a computer which then indicates the price and records the sale, updating both the inventory list and the merchant's financial accounts. All this occurs very rapidly, reducing the waiting time of the customers. This system boosts productivity by allowing the clerks to process customer purchases more rapidly and by eliminating the need for taking inventory and for updating the financial records by hand.

A third form of EFT is preauthorized banking. This includes activities such as the direct deposit of salaries into employee bank accounts and the direct payment by the bank of mortgage and car payments. Extensions of preauthorized banking, coupled with the uses of EFT described above, allow for truly electronic banking, leading some prominent bankers to envision a checkless and even a cashless society. This approach, however, faces serious problems concerning crime and the invasion of privacy, which will be discussed in Chapters Six and Seven, respectively.

The most popular form of EFT device is probably the Automated Teller Machine (ATM), which is a sophisticated computer terminal now located in many supermarkets and shopping centers, particularly outside banks. The user activates the ATM by inserting a plastic card containing an account number and by entering a secret personal code. The user can then make deposits and withdrawals, transfer money from a savings account to a checking account, and so on. The computer updates the user's account automatically, without human labor or paperwork. This system improves banking service by allowing customers to make transactions at virtually any time. It also increases the productivity of the banks, allowing them to process large numbers of transactions automatically.

Because of these gains in productivity and cost effectiveness, banks and businesses are offering an expanding array of integrated banking and shopping services that customers can use with the aid of a personal computer. In 1989, IBM will team up with Sovran Financial Corporation and Sears, Roebuck and Company to offer a home banking and shopping service called PRODIGY (Witt, 1988). Simple enough to be used by children, PRODIGY will allow families to sit in the comfort of their homes and pay bills, apply for loans, play the stock market, or buy items such as cars and stereo systems. The developers plan to make this service available in most metropolitan areas by the mid-1990s. Millions of consumers are already using Compuserve, a computer service that provides access to thousands of data bases and banking and financial services and that allows customers to purchase goods, apply for loans, and make airline reservations. These and other computer services will continue to expand rapidly, strengthening even further the connection between computers and business.

Expert Systems

In industry, too, computers have become indispensable productivity tools. Media coverage has focused largely upon the success of computerized robots performing relatively routine jobs such as welding on an automobile assembly line. But computers also contribute to the performance of nonroutine tasks that require intelligence. For example, in the 1970s, Digital Equipment Corporation (DEC), one of the largest U.S. computer manufacturers, relied on human experts to examine orders for computer systems, to prepare diagrams for the assembly of the systems, and to ensure that each system had all the necessary parts and no extras. This configuration process was crucial since DEC offered a large and constantly changing array of components, and incorrect combinations of components produced systems that did not work properly. In order to avoid configuration errors, DEC technicians designed each system initially. Then ninety percent of the systems were put together and checked at a final assembly facility in Westminster, Massachusetts. If a computer system ran properly, it was disassembled and shipped to the customer.

The trouble with this process was that the final assembly and testing was costly and time consuming, and it often delayed the customer's receipt of the system. Moreover, DEC foresaw that its components were changing so rapidly that it was difficult to keep workers trained to configure new systems properly. This led DEC to build an expert system called XCON (for eXpert CONfigurer), which is now used routinely to configure its popular VAX-11/780 computer systems (Kraft, 1984). Having received a customer's order that specifies the capabilities the system should have, XCON selects from an array of over 400 possible components an appropriate system configuration for that customer.

The use of XCON allowed DEC to eliminate the final assembly and testing procedure and to ship components directly to the customer site for assembly. By eliminating the final assembly step, XCON produced a savings of $25 million, and it also enabled DEC to fill customers' orders in a more timely manner. XCON testifies to the power of the computer as a mind tool, which is evident in applications such as computer-aided design.

Computer-Aided Design (CAD)

Computer-aided design, CAD, involves the use of a computer-graphics terminal to design, draft, and analyze a prospective product. CAD is used widely in designing printed circuit boards, automobiles, and aircraft, to name but a few applications. In designing an airplane wing through manual drafting, for example, engineers typically spend many hours drawing. Then they evaluate the new design by constructing a model and subjecting it to a series of stress analyses, simulated flight in a wind tunnel, and so on. This process is very slow and time consuming.

The development of CAD has changed this procedure radically. Now engineers sketch the design using a special light pen and a cathode-ray tube. The computer polishes this drawing, smoothing the lines and making many small adjustments. Having completed the design, the engineers can compare it to many others stored inside the computer. They can also rotate it in order to view it from different angles, zoom in on particular sections for a closer examination, and so on. Further, the wing design can be evaluated by computer, which, through simulated flight, performs many tests concerning factors such as weight, carrying capacity, wind drag, and stress performance. This reduces the need to build and to test physical models by weeding out grossly impractical designs early on. Although there continues to be a strong need to build real models and to test them in wind tunnels, CAD has helped to eliminate the needless testing of models destined for failure.

CAD produces stunning gains in the productivity of engineers and architects. A manager at Boeing, for example, reports that CAD doubles the productivity of his engineers. CAD users have also reported that they have been able to maintain high standards of quality. Because it facilitates creative design and the construction of new tools, CAD is a prime example of computers extending and amplifying human intelligence.

Robotics

A robot is a mechanical manipulator that may be programmed to perform a number of different tasks. Contrary to the popular impression of robots as humanoid devices such as R2D2 and C3PO from the film *Star Wars*, most robots now in use consist of arms that can bend and twist in addition to grasping, holding and turning a product. Most are unsophisticated and have very limited or no sensory capacity, though the new generation of robots is expected to be able to recognize an impressive variety of objects by both sight and touch.

The number of robots in use in the U.S. is currently rather small by comparison to Japan, although the number in the U.S. is expected to increase rapidly in the early 1990s. The reason behind the expected increase has to do with some dramatic increases in industrial productivity. For example, at one General Electric locomotive plant, it once took 68 machine operators 16 days to produce a locomotive frame. But with the use of several robots, it now takes only eight unskilled workers one day to complete the same job. Similarly, at the warehouses of a major drug chain, robots are now used as packers, and they handle nine times as many loads each hour as the human workers they replaced (Foulkes and Hirsch, 1985).

Robots offer numerous advantages in addition to increased productivity, not the least of which is lower labor costs. In the automobile industry in the mid-1980s, for example, a human welder earned approximately $23 per hour, including benefits, whereas a robot welder cost only $6 per hour and often did work of higher quality (Foulkes and Hirsch, 1985). As a result, robots are now used widely in tasks such as welding joints on and painting automobile frames. Further, many managers favor the use of robots because they can work around the clock without fatigue or complaint, and they do not stage strikes and work slowdowns. Workers, who typically fear being replaced by robots, are often relieved to have robots perform dull, dirty, or dangerous jobs.

Computer Numerical Control

Traditionally, highly skilled machinists having years of experience were responsible for the design, production, and use of machine tools, the drills, saws, and other tools which are used throughout industry to produce different products. Computers, however, are increasingly being used to perform these tasks through a set of processes referred to as computer numerical control (CNC). In computer numerical control, a computer program controls machines such as lathes, mills, and drill presses, guiding the speed at which the machines operate, the depth to which they cut, and so on. In essence, this method transfers control over complex machines from skilled workers to computers.

CNC boosts productivity by increasing both the speed and the ability to produce small batches of items. Using conventional methods, the first step in production is the construction of expensive jigs and fixtures that hold each part in position for machining. This labor-intensive method was very expensive, and it required large amounts of time for setting up machines, handling materials, and moving from one machine to the next. In this system, only mass production is cost effective, for the startup costs are too high to make the production of small batches profitable, and this limits the flexibility of production. CNC, however, requires only that a part be clamped to a single table. Then a computer guides a cutter through all of the motions required to produce the desired part. When a particular number of one type of item has been produced, one needs to take only a few seconds to change the computer program in order to begin producing an entirely different part. Consequently, a greater variety of parts can be produced in small or large batches and without long delays.

This ability to produce small batches of products is significant because in industries such as the aerospace industry and the ship-building industry, the market favors the current trend toward the production of a relatively small number of items (Wright and Bourne, 1988). The ability to produce small batches of items increases the manufacturer's flexibility of production signif-icantly. For example, the Yamazaki Machinery Corporation, a Japanese machine tool manufacturer, uses a sophisticated CNC system that can produce 74 different products in 1,200 variations (Shaiken, 1984). This enormous flexibility allows manufacturers to change their production rapidly in response to market demands. It also allows them to produce customized products on short notice, much to the delight of the customers.

Computer-Integrated Manufacturing (CIM)

In manufacturing, the wave of the future is to link together CAD, CAM, and CNC systems into truly integrated systems that allow completely automated production (Adler, 1988). A glimpse of this future is provided by Fanuc Limited, a Japanese company that uses robots to build drive motors for other robots. At the factory, unmanned vehicles under the control of a central computer carry materials from a warehouse to the production area. Forty-nine robots on four assembly lines use the materials to build robot motors, which are then carried automatically back to the warehouse (Salerno, 1986).

In 1987 at the Advanced Manufacturing Systems Exposition in Chicago, GTE unveiled a powerful CIM prototype that manufactures printed circuit boards, which contain many chips and drive computers, start to finish (Feder, 1987). The process begins when someone places an order for a board that can do particular things. Next, computers design the board to meet the specifica-tions and pass the design data automatically to computer controlled machinery that schedules production, prepares a plastic board, places the appropriate chips on it, and tests the board to make sure it works properly. The system does all of this without human intervention.

These heady accomplishments, however, should not distract us from the enormous complexities and unexpected costs involved in putting integrated systems into place. The U.S. government, for example, unveiled in 1981 the National Airspace System (NAS) Plan for using computers to help overworked air traffic controllers guide planes safely and to alleviate travelers' frustrations over chronic flight delays (McWilliams, 1987). The NAS Plan called for the introduction of a $10 billion system that integrated computers, software, radar, and communications equipment. Initially, proponents of the plan anticipated that it would produce savings of $26 billion for the government and $37 billion for the airlines. By 1988, however, it appeared that the actual savings would be minimal and that the cost of the system would exceed $16 billion. Because of unexpected technical difficulties, substantial benefits from using the system are still eight to ten years away. Planning miscalculations and underestimations of the complexity of the project have been blamed for the delay.

This type of example, which is all too common, reminds us that the route toward increased productivity is an arduous, uphill path that is strewn with risks and uncertainties. If planning is simplistic or misguided, the result is not higher productivity but an undesirable form of CAD—computer-assisted disaster.

Automation, Craft, and Skill

Historically, work was something that people did with their hands under the guidance of a rich array of sensory information. For example, long before the Industrial Revolution, skilled clothing makers made hand-stitched items by means of their manual and visual skills. Knowing that a finished item of clothing reflected their creativity and skill, the workers had a strong sense of pride in craftsmanship. Their work was a seamless web of manual and sensory experience—to work was to see, to touch, and to make. Because it was their own, their work was an extension of themselves, an expression of their qualities of mind and creativity.

The rising tide of automation has rapidly changed the nature of work. During the Industrial Revolution, working with machines largely replaced the older system of manual labor. Yet craftsmanship flourished as a new breed of skilled machinists arose. Although they made their products by machines rather than their own hands, they were the ones who guided and controlled the machines. And they still relied extensively on their own sensory experience in guiding the machines, checking belts and pulleys, adjusting cutting blades, and looking carefully at their work to ensure that they were making their product correctly.

The advent of computers is taking this modification of work one step further, making work something that is done increasingly with the aid of a machine or even by a machine. For millions of people, to work is to use the computer. In business, industry, and many other areas, the use of computers is radically changing the skills that are needed on the job. Whereas the skill levels required in some jobs are declining, the skill levels required in other jobs are increasing. Further, the use of computers is changing the kinds of skills that are needed. The electronic environment in which many people work is relatively abstract, and it places a higher premium on intellectual skills than on manual skills. In short, computers are transforming work itself.

The Deskilling of Jobs

As a mind tool, the computer offers an avenue for expanding and enhancing the intellect. But it also enables employers to turn over complex jobs to computers, leaving the human workers to watch over the machine. When this occurs, there is a deskilling of jobs, a reduction in the skills required of the human workers.

In industry, the use of computer numerical control has in many cases produced a downgrading of skilled jobs. Traditionally, the operators of machine tools such as lathes have been highly skilled workers who learned their craft by serving a long period as apprentices and by working many hours with their machines. For skilled machinists, the machines became an extension of their own bodies and sensory experience. Standing over a workstation and guiding tools such as drills and various metal cutters, they smelled and listened carefully for the sound of a drill operating at too high a speed or for the need for additional lubricant. Although they relied on machines to produce things, it was their skill that ultimately shaped the product.

Of all the workers in industry, the highest levels of skill were found among the diemakers, who, with blocks of steel, drawings and their knowledge of design, made a steel form used in stamping sheet metal parts such as automobile fenders. Diemakers were planners and producers who used both their heads and hands to develop their products. Typically, the diemakers took great pride in their craftmanship and worked with a fierce independence calculated to maintain high standards of quality. Because they had extensive skill, experience, and creativity, and because they produced the tools upon which industry is based, diemakers enjoyed high levels of prestige and control over how they did their jobs (Shaiken, 1984).

The advent of computer numerical control has undermined this prestige. Using CNC, the computer controls the machine tools, leaving the machinist in the position of a watchman who simply observes and makes sure that the system is operating as intended. The skilled machinist does no actual cutting and, in general, does little with his hands. And he also does little with his head since the operation of the tools is determined by programmers and systems engineers. In short, his mental and manual skills have been rendered useless (Braverman, 1974).

This job deskilling has made many skilled machinists feel useless and frustrated. As one worker said, "On my old job I controlled the machine. On my present job, the machine controls me" (Shaiken, 1984, p. 130). In addition, the use of CNC has dealt a heavy blow to the skilled machinists' traditional pride in craftsmanship. Because the machine does the work, the machinist neither identifies with the product nor derives satisfaction from producing an item of high quality.

Thinking of craftmanship in the narrow sense of manual skill, pride in craftmanship may not seem very important. But there is much more at stake than the preservation or the loss of manual skill. True craftsmanship is as much mental as manual. In order to build effectively, the craftsman must have a keen mental image or conception of what a quality product is and of how to produce it. Craftsmanship involves a unity of the labor of the mind and the hand; it blends artistry, mastery, and manipulation. For the craftsman, the product is an extension of self, the expression of creativity, skill, and pride in mastery. To rob the craftsmen of their craft is to strip away a part of their creativity, satisfaction, and humanity, making them feel like parts of a machine. It also reduces their concern with the quality of the product and the success of the company, and this can extract a heavy economic toll.

The problem of the deskilling of jobs reaches far beyond the machine shop. In the printing industry, for example, the traditional skilled jobs in typesetting, proofreading, and layout are being replaced by relatively unskilled jobs in which workers type at a video display terminal while computers do most of the skilled work (Evans, 1980). In the watchrepair business, the skilled job of fixing a mechanical watch having hundreds of parts has given way to the relatively unskilled job of replacing one of the five basic components of an electronic watch. And in banking, the job of making a loan, which previously required an understanding of ledgers and the loan process, has been reduced to filling out forms (Zuboff, 1988). With additional advances in the field of artificial intelligence, white collar, professional jobs in law, medicine, and engineering may be deskilled in similar fashion.

Abstraction

The use of computers has also made work more abstract. As more and more people have begun working in front of a computer, the work environment has become increasingly set apart from the manual and sensory experience that once pervaded the world of work.

At Piney Wood, a pulp plant of a large paper company, one of the most important and treacherous jobs is to bleach brown, digested pulp into the gleaming white used to make paper. In order to bleach the pulp, thousands of gallons of brown pulp are piped each minute into large vats where it is washed and treated with chemicals such as chlorine.

In the 1940s, human operators guided the bleaching process, watching temperature gauges, controlling valves and checking vat levels. In nearly every stage of their work, the operators walked the floor of the plant, relying on their senses to evaluate and to correct the bleaching process. They touched the pulp to check whether it was sticky or slippery, they sniffed the vats to tell whether the proper amount of chemicals had been added, and they visually inspected the color of the pulp. Their world was one of motion and of rich sensory experience, and the operators were understandably proud of their hard earned skills in interpreting what they saw, smelled, and felt.

In the early 1980s, everything changed at Piney Wood, owing largely to the introduction of a central computer system (Zuboff, 1988). The operators no longer monitored and controlled the bleaching process by walking the plant floor but by studying information on the screen of a central computer that provided data on all aspects of the bleaching process. Whereas the operators had previously walked the floors of the plant and collected sensory information, they now sat in swivel chairs in an air-conditioned area, watching screens glowing with numbers, letters, and diagrams and typing in commands to modify the bleaching process. Their work world had become the world of the computer.

Cut off from the rich array of sensory information, the operators worked in a highly abstract environment. They could neither see nor smell the pulp as it was being bleached, and they relied on the computer, which provided symbolic information on various facets of the bleaching process. They could not tell by sight or smell whether too much bleach had been added to a vat. Their only means of discerning this error was by reading codes and symbols from the computer screen. Whatever knowledge the operators had about the production process at a particular moment came from the computer, not from their own senses. Their knowledge of the current production process had been wrenched apart from their sensory experience.

Because their work had become more abstract, many operators felt cut off from the bleaching process, and they saw their jobs as having become more thought-oriented. The operators said they felt as if they were operating blind and without having a good "gut feel" of what was actually going on in the plant. Although they saw the information that they needed on the screen, they often found it difficult to link this information to their image or concept of what was actually happening on the plant floor. In order to make this linkage, the operators had to do much more thinking than acting. Before the computers had been installed, operators actually saw and smelled problems such as too rich a mix of chemicals, and they knew exactly what to do because of their previous experience in handling these problems. In fact, most operators felt they had been trained to do rather than to think. But after the computer had been installed, the operators had to think carefully about how to interpret what they were seeing on the computer screen and about what steps to take to correct the problem.

Even when the operators understood how to interpret the information on the computer screen, they were not always willing to believe it since they trusted their own senses more than the computer. Having changed the process by typing in a command on the computer, the operators often felt a gnawing doubt about whether the system had actually done what they had requested. Their work felt not only more abstract but also more ambiguous.

This problem of the workers distrusting the computer has cropped up in many other areas. Before computers, clerks for insurance companies manually retrieved claims documents, recorded payments of premiums, and calculated credits and debits to customers' accounts. But the use of computers has eliminated much of the manual work and paperwork, since clerks now call up files on the computer and record payments on the screen. Because the computer automatically adjusts the accounts, the clerks no longer do calculations by hand. Despite the efficiency of this procedure, many clerks say they have trouble believing that the computer is actually doing what it is supposed to do (Zuboff, 1988). Their trust that the appropriate changes had been made in an account was rooted in their ability to hold the paper account in their hands and to manually change it and file it away. Using the computer, the processing of an account had become not only more abstract and remote but also more difficult to trust.

Aside from making sure that the computer actually does what it is intended to do, the best antidotes to this problem of distrusting a computer system are to involve the workers in the selection and the implementation of the system and to provide effective training in using it. No matter how well a system works, the workers will not trust it unless they have learned to use it effectively and have seen that it actually does what they have told it to do. Training is also the key to preparing people such as the operators at Piney Wood to make the transition from acting to thinking in a computerized work environment. The widespread use of computers has created the need for new skills, particularly skills of acquiring and interpreting information.

From Manual to Intellectual Skills

Although the use of computers has deskilled many jobs, deskilling is only part of a larger picture. For example, the rising demand for computers and related services has created many new jobs requiring high levels of skill in areas such as electrical engineering, systems design, and software production. It would be a serious oversimplification to say that computers are deskilling jobs and making people less important in the workplace.

The use of computers is also increasing the skill levels in existing jobs. Before computers, workers needed finely tuned manual and sensory skills. But in the age of computers, workers need the intellectual skills to use computers effectively and to interpret and make decisions about the complex information that computers make available. In the traditional process of cookie making, for example, the ovensman's job was to monitor the weight and size of the cookies after baking. If the cookies were too large or too heavy, the ovensmen adjusted the amount of batter used and the temperature of the oven, and they notified the wrapping department if adjustments were needed in the packaging of the cookies. This manual process was relatively inefficient since the ovensmen had time to sample only a few cookies out of a large batch, and they obtained the weight and size information they needed only after a large numbers of cookies had been baked.

In order to remedy this inefficiency, cookie manufacturers have introduced computerized weighing systems that weigh each cookie rather than a sample and provide information about cookie size and weight much earlier in the baking process. Having this earlier feedback, the ovensmen can make the appropriate changes in the oven or tell the roller operator to adjust the thickness of the cookies before large batches have been produced incorrectly. In addition to reducing waste and improving quality control, this system has changed the ovensmens' jobs by increasing their control over the baking process and freeing up time for them to learn about and monitor the entire production process. If, for example, the cookies were too light, the ovensmen would have to issue orders rapidly for changes in a particular aspect of the production process. Through the use of the computerized weighing system, the ovensmen spent less time doing manual work and more time doing the intellectual work of making decisions and overseeing the production process. As a result, they perceived their jobs to be more interesting, and they saw their work as more responsible since both the quantity and the quality of production had improved (Buchanan and Boddy, 1983).

In the paper industry, too, the use of computers has increased the levels of intellectual skills required of plant operators. At Piney Wood, for example, the operators said that they had to use their minds more to link what they saw on the computer screens with the flow and the thickness of the pulp, even though they could not see these directly. As Piney Wood's training director put it, "To be successful in this new environment you need a mental picture of what the systems refer to" (Zuboff, 1988, p. 86).

In addition, the computer systems at plants such as Piney Wood provided a rich array of information about the production process, giving the operators a much more global picture of what as occurring in the plant than had ever been available before. Having this global picture and centralized control, the operators tried out the effects of new combinations of changes in variables such as the temperature and the amount of bleaching chemicals. Thus the operators did not simply do what they had done before using computers. They approached their jobs differently, using their intellectual skills to conceptualize what was occurring in the entire production process and to decide what changes to make. As a result, many of the operators became more satisfied with their jobs (Zuboff, 1988).

Overall, the use of computers has had mixed effects on work, deskilling some jobs and skilling others (Attewell and Rule, 1984). These mixed effects, which may be expected to continue, caution us against making blanket generalizations about whether the skilling or deskilling of jobs will be the dominant change. Whether a particular job will be deskilled is a matter of managerial choice, a choice that reflects the values discussed in Chapter One. The choices that managers make will have a powerful impact on the quality of work life.

Quality of Work Life

Productivity and profitability are the benchmarks that managers and corporate executives use to gauge their success. Emphasis on productivity and profit, however, should not distract attention from the important social and psychological functions of work. Stated bluntly, high levels of productivity are detrimental if they are accompanied by a decline in the quality of work, which of course influences the overall quality of life. If, for example, practices that increased productivity also impaired workers' health or made them feel bored, useless, and alienated, then it would be difficult to advocate these practices.

While quality of work is difficult to define with precision, a high quality work environment has several typical characteristics (Walton, 1980). These include health and safety, positive social interaction, opportunity for advancement, challenge, pride in a job well done, low stress, and fair compensation, among others. Computers, like other machines, may increase or decrease the quality of work, depending upon the economic and social objectives that guide their use and upon the manner in which they are introduced. It is appropriate to focus on the potential misuses of computers, not because they are more common than appropriate uses, but because it is only through an awareness of misuses that we can minimize or avoid them.

Alienation and Depersonalization

People feel alienated when they feel estranged and personally distant or dissociated from a particular social context. Feelings of alienation go hand in hand with depersonalization, the relative lack of ordinary contact with and care for others. In work settings, people become alienated and depersonalized when they feel manipulated by management and when their work has become demeaning and socially impoverished.

The introduction of computers can induce alienation by stripping workers of their job control and autonomy. Working on a system that gave clerical workers little decision-making responsibility, one worker complained "I have no decision-making on that computer. It's been programmed to do this, and this, and this, and we are programmed to do the same thing. I don't want to be programmed. It does things automatically, and if you feel it's wrong, you really have no choice but to let it go that way on this formatted screen" (Zuboff, 1988, p. 138). Working in automated offices and plants, workers often feel excessively dependent on the computer. When the power goes off or the computer shuts down, workers feel helpless and frustrated in their inability to do their work. At Piney Wood, this frustration was evident in a control room, which had a large axe mounted on the wall above a sign that read "IN CASE OF COMPUTER FAILURE, USE FIRE AXE" (Zuboff, 1988, p. 269).

Alienation can also occur as a result of changes in the organization of work that leave people socially isolated. Before computers had been introduced, many secretaries worked in open offices with other workers nearby, allowing them to ask their fellow workers questions and to talk while they worked. In introducing computers, however, many companies have isolated workers by partitioning the office into separate cubicles and by training workers to turn to the computer rather than to other workers for answers to questions. Socially isolated and tied to the computer, many workers feel more like machines than human beings.

The extensive use of electronic communications media may also induce feelings of depersonalization. In some offices that use electronic mail extensively, there are fewer face-to-face conversations. Yet many people feel that face-to-face interactions are emotionally and communicatively richer than are interactions by electronic mail, and it is not difficult to see why. In face-to-face interactions, there is a rich exchange of both verbal and nonverbal information—smiles, frowns, changes in posture, downward glances, and so on. In order to appreciate the communicative importance of this nonverbal information, consider whether you would trust the promise of someone who, as he spoke, looked down at the floor constantly and shuffled his feet nervously. Most people enjoy the company of others and the sharing of laughter, handshakes, and eye-to-eye contact, but electronic mail provides for none of these. Similarly, in a computer conference, differences in the status of the participants may be less apparent than in a face-to-face conference. This may make some participants more impulsive, and it may alter the decision-making process (Kiesler, Siegel and McGuire, 1984).

Communication by electronic mail also provides very little immediate feedback from one's audience, and this can reduce the speaker's concern over the listener's feelings. One result is flaming, the uninhibited expression of oneself more strongly by computer than by other means of communication (Kiesler et al., 1984). In flaming, messages range from the tactlessly blunt to the downright hostile. While flaming is not a necessary outcome of the use of electronic mail, electronic media do foster bluntness by virtue of the lack of immediate feedback and accountability. In addition, telling jokes and using sarcasm can be very difficult via electronic mail since the receiver cannot see the sender's smiles and body language. For this reason, experienced users of electronic mail usually identify smiles by a sideways grin symbol ":-" or by writing the word "smile" in parentheses (Turner, 1988).

Big Brother is Watching

People who love freedom and the open road have long been attracted to the job of truck driving. Sam, a driver who had forty years of experience in driving for the Safeway Company, once loved his job because he felt free and on his own. That changed, however, when the company installed a small computer called Tripmaster on the dashboard of his truck. Tripmaster continuously monitors his truck's speed, when shifts occur, excessive idling, and even the length of Sam's coffee breaks or lunches. Now he complains that "They push you around, spy on you. There's no trust, no respect anymore" (Marx and Sherizen, 1986, p. 67), and he plans to end his career as a driver.

Worker surveillance is also occurring in many other occupations. Pacific Southwest Airlines, for example, uses a central computer to monitor exactly how long its workers spend on each incoming call and how much time passes between calls. Workers who spend more than an average of 109 seconds handling incoming calls receive negative points. They also receive negative points for taking more than twelve minutes on a bathroom visit outside of the one hour that is allotted each day for lunch and coffee breaks. If the employees receive more than 37 points in a year, they are fired (Koepp, 1986). Secretaries, too, are experiencing the effects of computer monitoring, as an increasing number of employers keep an exact record of how many keystrokes an employee has produced in a day or a week. By comparing the output of one employee with that of others, managers can decide who should be rewarded and who should be warned or fired.

The use of computers to monitor workers has boosted worker productivity in numerous cases. But computer surveillance also has high psychological and social costs for the nearly six million workers who are monitored each year (Office of Technology Assessment, 1987). Surveillance decreases the morale of workers, who usually feel that the practice is oppressive and degrading and that it embodies excessive concern with the quantity rather than the quality of production (Irving, Higgins and Safayeni, 1986). In addition, computerized monitoring has in some cases produced such high levels of resentment among the workers that their productivity actually declined (Walton and Vittori, 1983). Many customers worry that the increases in efficiency are coming at the expense of quality of service and friendly human contact.

By keeping workers constantly under the gun to produce, computer surveillance also produces excessive levels of stress. A flight reservationist for United Airlines, for example, claimed she had suffered a nervous breakdown after her supervisor threatened to fire her for spending thirteen minutes over her allotted break time (Miller et al., 1988). Describing what it is like to have very high production standards and to be monitored continuously, one reservationist said "You're a nervous wreck. The stress is incredible" (Koepp,

1986). These high levels of stress contribute to high rates of absenteeism and to decreases in the health of the workers.

Health

The use of computers has contributed to the health of workers by freeing them from dangerous tasks such as welding. But computers have also introduced a number of health risks. In 1981, for example, a Japanese worker was killed while trying to make an adjustment on the industrial robot he was responsible for operating. He made the mistake of entering the off-limits area around the robot while it was operating. While trying to repair it, he apparently brushed up against a control button that made an arm move, pinning him against the machine and crushing him (Norman, 1983). This type of incident is relatively rare, however. Health problems are far more common for clerical workers who spend most of their day at a video display terminal (VDT).

Alice, for example, uses a computer all day to process insurance claims. By the middle of day, she has difficulty focusing her eyes, and she suffers muscular pains in her shoulders, forehead, and neck. Tense and irritable at the end of the day, she goes home wanting only to be left alone in order to recover (Brod, 1984). The problems Alice experiences are typical. Indeed, major studies conducted by the National Institute for Occupational Safety and Health and by Mt. Sinai Hospital indicated that VDT operators have higher levels of eye disorders than any other group of office workers. And in 1985, a legal writer who alleged that severe eyestrain forced her to leave her job in San Francisco won a worker's compensation claim of $15,000 (Cowart and Amirrezvani, 1986).

Vision problems, however, are only the tip of the medical iceberg. For example, recent research suggests pregnant women who use VDTs more than twenty hours a week have almost twice as many miscarriages as working women who do not use VDTs (Seligman, Abramson, and Hager, 1988). In addition, a 1985 study conducted by the North Carolina Occupational Safety and Health Project reported that VDT users suffered higher rates of angina (chest pain) than comparable workers who did not use VDTs (Cowart et al., 1986). There have also been nagging concerns over the low-level radiation emitted by VDTs (DeMatteo, 1985), although the Office of Technology Assessment (1985a, 1985b) concluded that the evidence available does not warrant the establishment of VDT regulations.

The use of computers can also produce high levels of stress, which over long periods of time can reduce resistance to disease and increase the incidence of stomach ulcers, high blood pressure, and heart attacks. Workers who use computers often experience increased task demands and mental strain (Turner, 1984; Zuboff, 1988). This strain owes in part to a faster pace of work, as architects who use computer assisted design make up to nineteen times as many decisions each hour as they would have made using a pencil (Cooley, 1980). The mental strain also stems from being tied down to one spot and watching the VDT, leading to eyestrain and muscle fatigue. Combined with the stress of being monitored, the mental strain can reach unbearable proportions.

The stress of VDT workers is amplified by the nature of their work situation. Most VDT operators have clerical jobs, which typically afford workers very little autonomy and power to make decisions. At the same time, the job demands are high. And when job demands are high and autonomy is low, the result is a high strain job (Karasek, 1979). Further, having little control over the events in one's job can be highly stressful. When people are exposed to uncontrollable events or even perceive that events are beyond their control, they enter a psychological state of helplessness (Seligman, 1974). This state increases the incidence of stomach ulcers, reduces motivation and the desire to achieve, and induces depression.

Stress can be produced by any one of the factors discussed above—high task demands, eyestrain, muscle fatigue, monitoring, and low autonomy. However, in the work of VDT operators, particularly clerks, these factors combine into a dangerous brew that threatens workers' health.

Health hazards are also a serious concern in the high-tech work of making computers, particularly the silicon chips which allow computers to do things such as store information. Chip manufacturing is a chemical intensive process that utilizes a variety of hazardous chemicals such as solvents, acids, and gases. A large chip manufacturing plant could store over three thousand chemicals and gases for use in the production process. The people who work with this kind of chemical arsenal face high risks. In 1980, the California Department of Industrial Relations reported that the occupational illness rates in the electronics (semiconductor) industry ran three times higher than rates in other areas of manufacturing. Over forty percent of all occupational illnesses in the semiconductor industry stemmed from toxic poisoning (Eisenscher, 1985). The burden of these illnesses falls primarily on the craft workers, most of whom are women (Fuentes and Ehrenreich, 1983).

The health hazards posed by the electronics industry extend to the communities surrounding the manufacturing plants. In the fabled Silicon Valley of Santa Clara County in California, where there are over 1,400 high tech firms, storage tanks from a manufacturer leaked 58,000 gallons of trichloroethane into the groundwater. Tricholorethane is toxic to internal organs and is a suspected carcinogen, and the toxic pollution from it is believed to have increased the miscarriage rates in nearby San Jose (Geiser, 1985). Similar cases of groundwater contamination have been reported in other high-tech areas in Massachusetts and Virginia. The tragic irony is that the same workers in the semiconductor industry who shoulder the risks of handling toxic chemicals at work are also exposed to them at home through drinking water.

Electronic Cottage or Electronic Sweatshop?

Sharon J. rises each morning at 6:30 and goes to work, not by driving but by walking downstairs to her computer. Sitting in front of the monitor during the next nine hours, she processes approximately 500 Blue Shield medical claims, for which she earns $80. During the day, she rarely leaves the basement except to dress her son for nursery school and to make herself a sandwich, which she eats in front of the computer (*New York Times*, May 20, 1984). Like thousands of other workers, Sharon is a telecommuter, someone who works from home with the aid of a computer and often with the aid of communications devices such as modems and fax machines.

Telecommuting has been hailed as the wave of the future since it allows people to choose their own work hours and to work at home, avoiding the frustrations of driving and office politics. It also opens many avenues of work to the physically disabled and to parents who have need to care for their children at home. Telecommuting arrangements can also cut employers' expenses on office space and furniture. Telecommuting is so attractive that the World Futures Society has predicted that by the year 2000, one half of the workers in U.S. service industries such as insurance and banking will be working at home (Cetron, Rocha and Luckins, 1988).

Although telecommuting seems to be an attractive arrangement for many professional workers who enjoy having flexible schedules and the time to complete challenging work projects, the story is not so happy for nonprofessionals. Clerical workers, for example, believe that working at home decreases their chances of promotion, and many of them experienced deteriorating relationships with their employers (Zureik, 1985). Although working at home in the presence of one's family sounds inviting, many people working at home encounter significant family strains that can lead to divorce and alcoholism (Salomon and Salomon, 1984). In addition, the constant presence of the computer in the home invites workaholic behavior at the expense of family interactions (Olson and Primps, 1984).

In the wrong hands, telecommuting arrangements are reminiscent of worst aspects of working in sweatshops. In the nineteenth century, European immigrants often worked at home for twelve to sixteen hours a day in the garment industry for a salary of pennies (Fuentes and Ehrenreich, 1983). Working at home today, clerical workers, most of whom are women, receive few benefits and very low pay, typically on a piecework schedule. In the early 1980s, for example, female workers on the Caribbean island of Barbados earned a paltry wage of $1.50 per hour to process data for American companies (Nussbaum, 1983). Because of computer surveillance, employers have the ability to monitor worker output exactly and to obtain very high rates of work. Thus the opportunity exists for making the home a highly oppressive work environment. Prospective telecommuters would do well to keep these possible abuses in mind in making their choices.

Conclusion

Computers are transforming the manner in which people work, increasing our dependence upon machines and changing the kinds of skills that are required to work effectively. Although computers have boosted productivity significantly, they have also been used in ways that detract from the quality of life at work. In addition to making work more abstract, they have often led to a deskilling of jobs, health problems, worker surveillance, and feelings of social alienation and isolation.

There is nothing inevitable, however, about these ill effects of computers. It is quite possible to use computers in ways that minimize or avoid the problems raised above and that contribute to a high quality of worklife. For example, structuring work in ways that foster quality social interaction reduces worker alienation. Similarly, computer monitoring can be used to assess how much work has been done and to adjust the work system in ways that increase work efficiency without spying on workers or increasing the time pressures on them. In numerous cities that use computers to process traffic tickets and to perform other jobs, clerks reported that computing had decreased the time pressures on them and raised their sense of accomplishment (King and Kraemer, 1985; Kraemer, Dutton and Northup, 1981). Further, potential health problems such as visual impairments can be reduced through the use of proper lighting and high resolution monitors and by assigning workers diverse tasks, some of which take them away from the computer screen.

For these reasons, it is inappropriate to point to the computer as the spoiler of worklife. Ultimately, it is people who decide how computers will be used in the workplace, so people must accept the responsibility for misuses of computers. In particular, it is managers who decide whether computers will be used and to what ends. In making these decisions, they are often forced to consider tradeoffs between productivity on the one hand and quality of worklife on the other. As discussed in the following chapter, their decisions have significant implications not only for the workers but for the social fabric of their organizations and the communities in which they are rooted.

3

Management and Labor

Jack P., vice-president of a large grocery products group, found it a nightmare to keep track of his division, which sells 500 products under 15 separate brands to 33,000 grocery stores. Each day at 3:00 P.M., the president and six vice-presidents received stacks of paper showing the sales results of the previous day. Different departments often reported different figures for the same activities, making it difficult to interpret the information. In addition, plowing through the reports ate up valuable time, and by the time he had done so, the information was no longer current. Now, however, Jack and the top management team uses a system of personal computers to obtain the information he needs by 8:30 A.M., enabling him to respond rapidly to problems and market changes. And because the entire group uses the same data base, now there are no more disputes about whose numbers are correct. Jack summarized the transformational effects of the computer when he said "we conduct our work lives differently" (Gelfond, 1988, p. 84).

Jack is one of a rapidly growing breed of new managers who recognize that new information tools are needed to carry out the four primary management functions of planning, organizing, leadership, and control. Gone are the days when managers organized and controlled companies through the use of manually collected information. Large insurance companies, for example, manage millions of customer policies, respond annually to tens of thousands of claims, and have thousands of employees. Managing by hand the payroll, not to mention millions of customer accounts, would require inordinate amounts of time and labor and would be highly cost-inefficient, perhaps unworkable. Because the business environment changes rapidly and is highly competitive, managers need rapid access to information about the activities of their company and those of their competitors. In order to lead effectively, they need a holistic picture that pieces together elements such as current internal operations, market conditions, government regulations, and available supplies.

Designed properly, computer systems can meet these rapidly evolving needs for information. Computers put vast amounts of information at managers' fingertips, allowing for timely and effective planning. They have also opened new avenues of communication and organization, allowing managers to restructure the corporate environment. Further, integrated systems can give a chief executive officer a global look at current company activity and the positioning of the company relative to its competitors. It is no wonder, then, that managers are relying increasingly on information systems and that most corporations now have a manager or a vice-president of information systems to guide the company in acquiring and using computers.

The decision to use computers, however, is not simply a decision about technology. It is also a decision about the social relations and the organization of the company. For example, in every company, there is a delicate balance of power maintained by stated and tacit agreements between management and labor. The use of computers can tip the balance and upset the relations between management and labor. As discussed in Chapter Two, management can use computers to increase their control over the workers. In automated plants, management can use computers as strikebreakers, replacing dissatisfied workers with machines and eroding the power of labor unions. On the other hand, management can choose to install computer systems that give workers much more information about the company and much more power to make decisions. This choice not only decentralizes the company's information but also erodes the traditional lines of authority and distinctions between managers and workers.

Decisions to use computers also have implications that extend beyond the company. For example, managers have often introduced computers in order to streamline their workforce. In fact, some companies have made conscious decisions to use computers to replace human workers. Whether temporary or permanent, unemployment causes extensive personal unhappiness, and it also exacts a high social toll in lost productivity, welfare payments, and social unrest.

In order to be responsible leaders, managers need to know more than how to use state-of-the-art technology for meeting their needs for information.

They also need to be sensitive to the social implications of their decisions about using computers. For these reasons, this chapter examines computers both as information tools and as instruments of social change.

Information Management and Decision Making

Richard S. is president of a large retail outlet for consumer electronics goods such as stereos, radios, and microwave ovens. Concerned about lagging profits over the past month, he asks the sales department to provide detailed information about the sales volume, and he checks some business reports to find out about the sales volume of competitors during the same period. He also asks the purchasing department for a report on the costs and availability of various items, and he instructs the marketing department to conduct research on ways to improve marketing. He experiences a warm rush of adrenaline when he learns that his main competitor is tied up in a major lawsuit and when the marketing department reports independently that the upcoming month will be an excellent time to hold a large sale. Smelling a victory, he checks the current inventory and calculates the probable costs of buying the items for the sale. Then he sets the date for the sale, notifies personnel in various departments, and coordinates the activities of the purchasing, marketing, and sales divisions in preparation for it.

For Richard and many other top executives, obtaining and using information effectively is a vital part of leading a company. Operating in information-intensive environments, managers worldwide are integrating computers into their managerial activities and using them to make key decisions.

Essential Information Tools

In the 1970s, the electronic spreadsheet was a luxury enjoyed by a relatively small number of companies. By the early 1980s, however, the electronic spreadsheet had become a standard tool in most companies. A spreadsheet is an accounting record that itemizes the assets, the expenditures, and the income of an organization, allowing managers to determine the "bottom line" or the total financial resources available. Figure 3.1 shows part of an electronic spreadsheet of the sort that is commercially available for microcomputers. The spreadsheet consists of a thousand rows and several hundred columns, creating thousands of cells, each of which can store information. Cells can also store formulas, allowing computations to be performed automatically. For example, cell E2 stores the formula +B2*D2, which instructs the computer to multiply the entry in cell B2 by that in cell D2 and to store the product in cell E2. Similarly, cell E8 contains a formula which instructs the computer to add all of the entries in columns E2 through E7, yielding the total sales.

Electronic spreadsheets have numerous advantages over paper and pencil spreadsheets. By performing computations automatically, they produce sub-

E2: + B2 * D2   READY

	A	B	C	D	E
1	Item	No. Units	Code	Price	Sales
2	Power Saw	36	0013	36.95	1330.20
3	Drill	25	0141	27.95	
4	Screwdriver	148	0291	4.50	
5	Hammer	97	0295	12.95	
6	Handsaw	18	0019	21.95	
7	Level	26	1248	18.95	
8				Total Sales:	

Figure 3.1. Sample spread-sheet.

stantial savings in labor. In addition, they provide accurate and immediate information about the current transactions and financial resources of a company. When financial records were kept manually, the various sales offices had to send their sales information to a central office, where accountants would calculate the total sales of the company. This procedure was laborious and slow, and it created substantial delays between the actual sales and the appearance of the results on the books, making it difficult for managers to make decisions about sales and purchasing. Computers now allow different sales offices to transmit sales information immediately via electronic mail, and the spreadsheet program records the information and calculates the results immediately. Further, point of sale terminals can be used to automatically record the sales and to transmit the information to the computer running the spreadsheet, allowing the entire recording, transmission, and calculation process to be performed electronically. This procedure provides a wealth of information about sales as they occur, and it manages the company books automatically.

Another essential information tool is the data base management system (DBMS). Figure 3.2 shows part of a hypothetical data base that stores information regarding the customers of a business. Each row contains information for a particular customer, listing items such as customer number, address, discount eligibility, and credit status. This system sorts customer records according to various criteria. If, for example, managers wanted to send out an announcement to each customer who qualified for an educational discount, they would use a high-level query language to instruct the system to print a list of names and addresses for those who are eligible. This automatic sorting and printing saves enormous amounts of time and labor, particularly when there are thousands of customers to be considered. Similarly, the DBMS is very useful in answering unexpected questions, such as how many customers come from a particular state that is about to undergo a change in tax laws. By making a few keystrokes, a manager can access a rich array of information in a very short period of time.

Name	Customer No.	Address	City	State	Discount Eligibility	Credit Status
Andersen, Darin	45029-623	119 Maple St.	Portland	Oregon	Y	1
Eagley, Anne	84052-927	226 Mullen Dr.	San Antonio	Texas	N	1
Grubbs, Donald	99574-023	14 Richmond Ave.	Alexandria	Virginia	N	2
Harper, Steven,	74613-804	159 Henry St.	Orlando	Florida	Y	1
Mason, Hillary	20176-112	93 Dover Circle	Durham	N. Carolina	N	1
Perry, George	73812-993	834 High St.	Boston	Massachusetts	Y	1
Thompson, David	10085-119	742 Beacon Hill	Boston	Massachusetts	N	2
Wells, Howard	47259-186	13 Salem Ave.	Cleveland	Ohio	Y	1

Figure 3.2. Part of a hypothetical data base.

Management Information Systems

A business may be thought of as an organization of subsystems or departments—marketing, sales, manufacturing, payroll, executive office, and so on. In the early days of computing in business, many firms computerized the operations of each department independently. This decentralized approach had the advantage of increasing the productivity and the information management capabilities of each department, thereby facilitating the work of the mid-level managers who ran each one. Although a computer shutdown stopped operations in one department, it does not shut down the entire company as can occur when a central computer is used.

On the other hand, the decentralized approach was inefficient because of the duplication of data. Typically, for example, the annual salary of an employee was listed in the computer records of both the personnel department and the payroll department. While some redundancy in information storage may be desirable, unnecessary redundancies such as this one can be very expensive, particularly if the company has thousands of employees. Another problem was that different departments used different computers. If the computers were incompatible, it was difficult to transfer the information from one department's computer to another. But the most severe problem was that the decentralized approach did not give top executives a holistic view of the company. All too often, managers found their desks piled high with long reports from various departments. What they need most, however, is not isolated information about individual departments but an integrated picture of the entire company.

For these reasons, many firms have developed a centralized management information system (MIS), a coordinated network of computer subsystems within a company that integrates information from different departments or corporate operations. Rather than having separate data bases for each department, a management information system provides a single, central data base that is accessible to all departments. Used properly, this approach can minimize costly storage redundancies and give executives comprehensive information about the company. By accessing the central data base through a terminal in their offices, managers acquire current information about sales, payroll expenses, personnel absences, manufacturing productivity, and shipping expenses.

This comprehensive information increases managers' ability to coordinate the work of different departments and to slash production costs. For example, the costs of maintaining a large inventory of parts for assembly lines are very high. But management information systems enable managers to cut inventory costs through a process called just-in-time delivery. Instead of storing large numbers of parts, parts are delivered to the assembly plant just before they are to be used. By tying delivery trucks into the MIS, managers know at all times where their incoming shipments are and how much they can produce in a particular period of time. In 1984, Centronics Data Computer Corporation installed a just-in-time system for its production of printers. Within a year, Centronics reported a fourfold increase in its daily printer production (Reiss and Dolan, 1989).

Management information systems also allow managers to coordinate the activities of their companies with the needs of customers (Miron, Cecil, Bradicich, and Hall, 1988). For example, Westinghouse Electric Supply Company has furnished its customers with terminals connected to its central computer system (Porter and Millar, 1985). This gives the Westinghouse managers a clear and timely picture of what they need to produce. And it gives the customers the satisfaction of being able to place orders directly and to receive immediate feedback about the production and delivery schedule. As these examples suggest, the MIS changes the way in which companies operate.

Management information systems allow managers to not only coordinate the internal activities of their companies but also to tailor what their firms do according to changes in the external environment. If, for example, the demand for a particular drug goes up or if a new federal regulation regarding that drug is passed, the managers of pharmaceutical firms need to know immediately in order to adjust their activities accordingly. Similarly, an international banking firm that does business in Argentina needs to know immediately if there is a sudden change in the rates of inflation in Argentina or if the Argentine government is about to impose new restrictions on loans. By making this type of information available to managers, management information systems increase the ability of companies to compete effectively in a rapidly changing environment. They also transform the business environment by increasing the interdependence of suppliers and builders, of retailers and customers, and of governments and businesses.

Decision Support Systems

Managers would love to have a crystal ball in order to foresee the future and prepare for it. Although the computer is no crystal ball, it can still help managers to prepare for the future. In particular, managers can use powerful resources called decision support systems (DSS) to ask the "what-if" questions that assist in making decisions.

At a small college, for example, top management wants to increase the amount of money the college can spend on new projects during the next academic year by a million dollars. But the managers are uncertain about whether to commit themselves to the one million dollar goal since they are unsure about where the additional money will come from and about whether it will cover new expenses. Using the college information system, coupled with decision support systems, the managers ask "What if we increase tuition by eight hundred dollars the following year?" Having entered the new tuition figure into the information system, they immediately receive an estimate showing that this tuition hike will give the college just under one million dollars. The Treasurer, however, expresses concern that one million dollars will not cover the expected increases in insurance premiums for the following year. Accordingly, he asks "What if our premiums increase by thirty percent?" He enters the new insurance figure into the computer, and the decision support system indicates that the thirty percent increase in insurance premiums could by itself require nearly one million dollars. Shaken by this unexpected result, the team rapidly issues a set of new what-if questions aimed at finding ways to enable the college to handle even its worst case scenarios.

The great advantage of this type of system is that it enables management to anticipate possible negative consequences without actually suffering them. By forecasting the effects of variables such as increased competition from neighboring colleges, cutbacks in student aid, and decreases in the numbers of high school graduates in the area, the system promotes effective strategic planning, enabling the college to position itself effectively relative to its competitors.

But decision support systems are not foolproof. A DSS incorporates a model, and the system is only as good as the model that guides its predictions. For example, in answering a question about the effects of a tuition hike on funds available for new projects, the DSS assumes that a particular percentage of tuition fees will be uncommitted, that is, available for new projects. If this assumption is incorrect, then the prediction made by the DSS will also be incorrect.

Further, a DSS can err by not taking into account all of the variables that a decision will bring into play. For example, a tuition increase of eight hundred dollars could bring in more money if the same number of students enroll in the following year, but the increase could drive away applicants, thereby producing a net decrease in funds. Large corporations and the international business environment are so intricate that it is difficult to include all of the important factors in a decision support system. Although computer models do contribute to the decision making process, they cannot eradicate the uncertainty that inevitably surrounds many of the decisions that people must make.

System Analysis, Design, and Implementation

Despite the many potential advantages of management information systems in business and industry, the use of these systems does not guarantee success. Management information systems are very expensive, and the costs of implementing a system might outweigh the benefits. Further, these systems are highly intricate, and they do not always work as intended.

Systems analysis is a vital step in designing a work system that does what it is intended to do. The Eastern Financial Group, for example, was a large financial group that used a computer network of 15,000 terminals spread across six states. The Group's managers received a multitude of complaints that programs did not work and that terminals did not get fixed on time. Desperately in need of help, the managers turned to Bill G., an IBM systems analyst, with a general cry for help: "Our network is out of control" (Reiss and Dolan, 1989, p. 446).

Through an extensive set of interviews with people such as the Group's managers and the engineers who ran the network, Bill learned that the network had grown so rapidly that the network engineers had little time for planning and spent most of their time responding to crises. They also learned that call switching was one of the main problems that the network users encountered daily. Although the Group had established twenty-five "help" stations to respond to customer questions, customers who called station one were often told "Sorry, you'll have to call station four to handle that." All too often, station four referred the caller to yet another station, ending in the consumer getting frustrated and no one taking responsibility to make sure that a particular problem was eventually fixed.

On the basis of his analyses, Bill recommended that the Eastern Financial Group establish a first call responsibility system in which the first "help" station contacted was responsible for following up a customer's call to make sure the problem had been fixed. In order to reduce the heavy workload on the system personnel, Bill also recommended that the Group add artificial intelligence capability to the network. In this arrangement, simple problems could be handled by the computer, with the computer "talking" through synthesized voice and the customers responding via telephone touchpads.

As this example illustrates, the systems analyst is a key figure in designing a system that works properly. Working closely with management, the analyst gathers information regarding the policies and goals of the company and the sources of its problems and dissatisfaction. Having identified the problems, the analyst then works together with management to design a new system or set of procedures.

An effective design alone, however, does not guarantee that the system will work as intended. Because designs that look good on paper often fail to work properly when actually put into place, managers have learned that it is necessary to test the new system rigorously before actually installing it (Howard and Hammer, 1988). Human concerns must be taken into account at every stage of the process of system analysis, design, and implementation. If, for example, the installation of a new computer system isolates workers and degrades their work to the status of pushing buttons, worker morale could plummet, decreasing productivity.

No matter how well designed and carefully tested a system is, it can also fail if the workers who actually use the system do not receive proper training (Tornatzky, 1985). Lacking effective training and unable to perform jobs they previously knew how to do, workers become frustrated and angry at management. In this atmosphere, the new system becomes symbolic of the conflict between managers and workers, fueling resistance to the computer. If managers fail to give adequate attention to the needs and desires of the people who will use the system, they may allow their companies to suffer from unintended shifts in power and organization.

Control, Power, and Organization

Most companies have a well-defined organization and established lines of command and control. The most widely used form of organization is hierarchical, and it consists of numerous layers of management. At the top is the president, who supervises a small group of top managers, mainly vice-presidents. The top managers supervise a larger team of middle management. Each mid-level manager is in charge of a particular plant or department and supervises a relatively large number of workers. In a hierarchical organization, the lines of authority are very clear—the workers answer to the mid-level managers, and the mid-level managers answer to the vice-presidents, who in turn report directly to the president. Typically, the people at each level have clearly defined roles that prescribe everything from dress to proper demeanor and work responsibilities.

Companies, however, are more than formal structures or organizations within which people work. Companies also have their own culture, their own rituals, values, attitudes, and ways of doing things. Some companies pride themselves on innovation and welcome the creative ideas of workers, while other companies are highly resistant to change. Whereas some companies encourage friendly relations between managers and workers and invite the participation of workers in making decisions, others have adversarial relations between managers and workers and keep a large social distance between the two groups. In some companies, workers enjoy learning to use new technology and welcome the introduction of computers, while in others, workers have very negative attitudes toward technology. Although these cultural features do not appear on organizational charts, they are often as important as the formal structure in determining what a company does.

The introduction of a computer system may have far-reaching implications for the structure and the culture of an organization. By implementing an integrated information system, for example, a company may give its workers access to much more information than they ever had before. Having additional information, the workers may feel they are in a position to make decisions that had traditionally been made by managers. In addition to blurring the distinction between the roles of managers and workers, this situation can lead to shifts in the power and control exercised by the workers. These shifts can be productive if they are anticipated and managed. But if they are allowed to occur without conscious direction, the result can be severe conflict between labor and management. When managers make decisions about adopting a new computer system, they are making decisions that are social as well as technical and that may reshape their organization.

Scientific Management

Theories of management shape the way in which managers structure their organizations and the work process, and they also influence the use of technology. In the U.S., management theory and practice bears the indelible imprint of the work of Frederick Taylor (1911, 1947), the father of scientific management. Taylor's goal was to develop a scientific system of work and management that maximized workers' efficiency, thereby increasing productivity and profits.

Eager to move beyond workers' intuitions about how to work most efficiently, he performed many studies of time and motion, analyzing tasks such as drilling down to the minute details of the optimum drilling speed and the most efficient workbench layout. By measuring the fastest way to do a job, he identified an optimum procedure, a recipe of steps that the efficient worker must follow. In Taylor's view, workers are themselves part of a rationalized system of work, an efficient machine for getting the job done.

Taylor also analyzed the obstacles that management must overcome in order to maximize worker efficiency and productivity. The chief obstacle was soldiering, which occurred in two forms. The first was natural soldiering, the nearly universal tendency of workers to take it easy. He viewed this form of soldiering as much less troublesome than the second, which he called systematic soldiering. In systematic soldiering, workers not only work slowly but also deceive their employers about how fast the work can be done. In order to do this, the workers watch each other to ensure that no one gives away the secret by working at the maximum rate. From this perspective, the workers' knowledge is a source of political power used to promote the interests of the workers, typically at the expense of the managers and the company.

Because Taylor believed that workers and managers have opposing interests, his theory of management emphasized the importance of managerial control. Taylor stated that managers, not workers, should gather the traditional knowledge of workers and then reduce this knowledge to rules and formulas. This strips workers of their monopoly on knowledge and erodes their ability to engage in effective soldiering. Taylor also recommended that managers use this knowledge to establish optimal work procedures that specify the exact steps that each worker must perform according to demanding standards of time. In addition, Taylor recommended that "...all possible brain work should be removed from the shop and centered in the planning or laying-out department..." (Taylor, 1903, p. 98) For Taylor, the task of the worker is not to think but to follow strict prescriptions formulated by management. The task of the manager, on the other hand, is to act as the final authority and to maintain tight control over the workers.

Taylor's theory, though no longer accepted widely among theorists of management, helped to establish views and practices that have strong effects today (Braverman, 1974; Shaiken, 1984; Zuboff, 1988). By emphasizing the need for a corps of managers to watch over the workers, Taylor's theory set the stage for the expansion of middle management. His theory has also encouraged the idea that work is a rational process that can be broken down into a series of steps which can then be performed at optimal rates. Captivated by this idea, American managers such as Henry Ford based their assembly-line methods upon the extensive subdivision of labor guided by elaborate time-and-motion studies. Taylor's influence is also visible in modern corporations, which are divided into separate departments, each of which performs a specialized set of functions. Working in Taylor's tradition, many managers do the important planning and decision making, and they expect workers to do what they have been told. This approach to management has helped to put relations between managers and workers on an adversarial footing and to make efficiency and control the benchmarks by which managers are judged.

Computers and Hierarchical Control

In relatively traditional companies in which there is an established hierarchy, managers often choose to use computers not to innovate but to automate work currently done by people. Their goals in automating are to not only increase the efficiency of operation but also to increase their control over the work process and the human workers. Used in the service of these goals, the computer is a tool that reinforces the existing hierarchy and lines of authority.

At the Acme Metal Plating Company, for example, the managers were dissatisfied with the manual system of plating, which involved dunking metal plates into a series of solutions in order to coat them with a plate of chrome, zinc, and so on (Wilkinson, 1985). Three workers used levers to immerse the metal plates in the different vats of solutions for particular amounts of time. Management, however, complained that the workers were unreliable and sometimes left metal in the vats longer than necessary, wasting time and valuable plating materials. Management also believed that the workers worked too slowly and took excessively long breaks.

In order to remedy these problems, the Acme managers introduced a computerized system that automatically controlled the movements of the jigs and barrels. This system required only two workers, whose job consisted mainly of loading and unloading the components to be plated. Under the old system, the workers had extensive control over the job, and they made decisions such as whether a particular item needed to remain immersed in a vat a few seconds longer than usual in order to ensure proper plating. But in the new system, the computer guided the entire plating operation. Since the managers governed the computer, this system increased the managers' control over the work process. To ensure that they had complete control, the managers placed the control panel for the new system in a back room that was off limits for the workers.

The desire for control is also one of the primary motivations behind the introduction of computer numerical control. As the engineering manager of one major industrial plant put it, "We're going to NC [numerical control] because it puts the process in our hands" (Shaiken, 1984, p. 51). CNC is a logical extension of Taylorian theory, for it uses optimally efficient production procedures and gives management a high degree of control. It does this in part by separating planning and execution, just as Taylor recommended. In the use of CNC, a planning department decides what to do, and a team of programmers then writes the programs which direct the computers to accomplish the specified tasks. When a particular job needs to be done, the planning department loads the appropriate program into the computer, which then performs the task. The worker, even if he or she is a skilled machinist, acts as little more than a monitor. By taking this approach, management transfers the knowledge required for effective production from workers to machines that are kept under strict managerial control.

Managers use computers to cement their control not only by taking control over the work process but also by controlling information. Traditionally, only management has had access to key information regarding profits, salaries, overhead, and the cost efficiency of various production processes. By limiting access to this kind of information, managers put themselves in the position to make decisions and simultaneously limited the ability of the workers to make decisions or to challenge those of the managers. In implementing computers, many companies have built managerial control into the system by providing the full scope of information only to a handful of managers who hold secret passwords. Even if a rich array of information is available to the workers, managers often retain control by not training the workers to use the system effectively (Zuboff, 1988).

Although computers have revolutionary potential, they are often used in the service of traditional values such as managerial control and the maintenance of the existing social order. Far from being a neutral tool, a computer system such as a CNC system is suffused with values, particularly those of management. Embedded in an authoritarian social environment, the computer becomes a tool for strengthening the traditional divisions of labor and patterns of domination and subordination.

The Struggle for Control

Of course, the hierarchical system sows the seeds for power struggles because it establishes adversarial relations between managers and workers. These struggles are increasingly played out in the medium of the computer. Tony M., for example, was a skilled machinist who was angry over the decision of his plant's managers to introduce a numerical control system, which had degraded his job to watching over the machine. He decided to slow production by means "unavoidable delays." Ostensibly, these delays are for technical checks on the cutter and for precise manual measurement of the dimensions of a part. But in fact, Tony and other machinists adjust the frequency and length of these delays to reflect the degree of tension between managers and workers. By means of these slowdowns, the workers regain a measure of the control they had lost, and they use the computer in a struggle for power with the managers (Shaiken, 1984).

It is not always the workers, however, who see computers as a threat to their power and who struggle to reclaim control, as is illustrated by the case of the Tiger Creek paper mill (Zuboff, 1988). The Tiger Creek managers worried about the lack of quality data about the operation of their paper machine and the costs of each run. At the end of each work shift, they performed laborious analyses of hundreds of variables and of what had happened in sixty-five different control loops of the paper machine, estimating the production costs of that shift. Next they prepared a report for the machine operators, indicating how the machine should be set up for the following day. Although this system preserved the division of labor in which managers made the decisions and the workers (the operators) followed orders, it was troublesome because there were no cost data on each run. What they needed in order to reduce costs was to put detailed information about the operation costs into the hands of the operators on a minute-by-minute basis.

The Tiger Creek managers decided to install a computer based Expense Tracking System (ETS), which provided the operators with on-line information about the costs of the current run. Using this information, the operators adjusted the process in a manner that minimized the costs while maintaining the high quality of the paper. To the managers' delight, the ETS saved $456,000 in the first year alone. The operators, too, enjoyed using the ETS since it enabled them to do a better job, gave them more responsibility for making decisions, and provided an intellectually challenging environment in which they experimented with many different combinations of variables to develop the most cost-efficient process. In addition, the ETS provided hard data concerning the optimal process, allowing them to justify their decisions to management.

Before long, however, this happy situation turned sour as the workers and managers became locked in a turf struggle for control over the system. The managers felt threatened by the ETS since they no longer had control over either the information regarding the production process or the process itself. Their fear was amplified by the knowledge that upper management wanted the ETS project to succeed and would hold them accountable if it did not. Worried over their loss of control and fearful that they would become obsolete, the managers moved to regain power and control. They did this by making changes in the system and not explaining them to the operators, who consequently felt that they were operating in the dark. In addition, the managers began to formalize new procedures and to demand that the operators follow them. To ensure that the operators obeyed their orders, the managers began using the ETS to monitor the operators' activities. These changes not only discouraged operators from experimenting with the system but also enabled the managers to take the credit for any savings that occurred.

Naturally, the workers felt that the managers had stolen their thunder and undermined their ability and to make decisions that maximized the cost savings. Feeling demoralized, the operators began calling the system the "electronic tattletale," and they lost interest in trying to maximize its effectiveness. As a result, the costs savings from the use of the ETS leveled off, and the ETS never achieved its full potential for savings (Zuboff, 1988).

The Tiger Creek case, which is not exceptional, illustrates how fragile the boundary is that separates managers and workers. The introduction of computers can create ambiguity over job responsibilities, amplify tensions that already exist between workers and managers, and upset the existing social order. At Tiger Creek, the failure of the ETS to reach its full potential stemmed from the managers' fear of losing their power and even their jobs. Seeking to avoid just this kind of problem, many organizations are rethinking the role of management and decentralizing the control over information.

Toward Decentralization

At the Cedar Bluff paper plant, top management introduced a sophisticated computer system that controlled all aspects of the plant's production on a moment-by-moment basis. At the same time, they installed an integrated data base that provided detailed information throughout the plant about the current production process, costs, market data, and personnel records. This was a much more egalitarian arrangement than that of Tiger Creek since both the workers and the managers had equal access to the information about the entire plant (Zuboff, 1988).

The decision to make these data available throughout the plant was part of a broader commitment to a team-based organizational structure. In a traditional, hierarchical organization, the managers control information, which flows upward from separate departments. But at Cedar Bluff, the top management made a conscious decision to break down this hierarchical arrangement in favor of a more decentralized organization in which information flowed laterally, across departments, as well as vertically. In the new scheme of things, the managers did not have the right to control information and to dictate limits on what the controllers could and could not do. The managers' role was to bring people together to discuss problems and to facilitate the collection of the information needed to solve the problems. In this decentralized environment, their role emphasized coordination and problem solving rather than control.

Managers at Cedar Bluff who had previously worked at plants such as Piney Wood praised the new system of distributing information widely, saying that it enabled them to see and to do new things that could not have been done otherwise. At Tiger Creek, the operators had wanted to experiment with combinations of variables but had been held back by middle management. But this was less of a problem at Cedar Bluff, where managers realized that productivity and profits would be maximized only if the plant used to the fullest possible extent all of the information at its disposal.

The operators at Cedar Bluff praised the new system because it provided the information they needed in order to do their jobs better. It also documented their ideas about how to run the machines in the most efficient manner, providing concrete evidence to the managers that one particular setup was more efficient than another. In essence, the integrated information provided an objective standard against which both the workers and the managers could measure their activities. If a worker and a manager disagreed about the most effective operating procedure, the data provided by the system could be used to resolve the dispute. This situation changed the very ground of authority. Whereas authority had previously derived from position in the corporate hierarchy, it now derived from the ability to use and to interpret information. Under the new system, the workers enjoyed the functional authority of making decisions and using information to back them up.

As the leaders of Cedar Bluff realized, it makes little sense for management to withhold information and to maintain rigid hierarchical control in a business environment that is information intensive. In order to maximize success in such an environment, companies may need to reorganize themselves in ways that maximize their ability to produce and use information effectively. Making the transition from centralized to decentralized use of information, however, is very difficult. Because the transition involves shifts of power, conscious steps must be taken to transfer power without excessive conflict. In particular, upper management must help educate lower management in order to show them the value of their new role and to prepare them to assume it without fear.

The case of Cedar Bluff indicates that computers have not made middle management expendable. Thirty years ago, predictions were made that new information technologies would eliminate or sharply reduce the middle levels of management by improving the vertical flow of information and the centralized control over decisions (Leavitt and Whisler, 1958). Although some case studies supported this prediction of the decline of middle management, many others have not (Attewell and Rule, 1984). As illustrated by Cedar Bluff, computers can lead to decentralization, which changes the functions and duties of middle managers. But this change in organization does not render managers obsolete. On the other hand, computers do pose real threats to the employment of managers and workers alike, and it is to issues of unemployment that we now turn.

Unemployment, Retraining, and the Unions

Unemployment is one of the most serious problems confronting contemporary society, as 1988 found some 6.8 million Americans without jobs (Rothschild, 1988). Joblessness is a problem even in expansion industries such as high-tech. In an eighteen-month period beginning in January, 1985, over 7,000 of the approximately 200,000 high-tech workers in Massachusetts alone were permanently laid off (Early and Wilson, 1986).

Unemployment induces deep personal unhappiness by reducing individuals' self-esteem, status, independence, and access to expected goods and services. It also exacts a high social toll by contributing to alienation, depression, health problems, and reduced social mobility (Warr, Jackson, and Banks, 1988). High levels of unemployment fuel crime and antisocial behavior, and they require that society spend large sums of money to support or to retrain those without jobs.

Fear that technology will inevitably swell the ranks of the unemployed was common long before the invention of computers. During the Industrial Revolution in 1811, for example, textile workers calling themselves Luddites rioted and destroyed the textile machinery which they saw as a threat to their survival. Ironically, however, the use of new technology often creates many jobs. In England from 1851 to 1901, the steam engine was used widely in the rapidly growing railway industry, and the number of employees in the industry increased from 29,000 to 320,000. Similarly, levels of employment tripled in the chemical and metal manufacture industries that emerged during the Industrial Revolution (Jenkin, 1985).

In the age of computers, fears of unemployment run strong, particularly since intelligent machines could replace people in a wide variety of jobs. Traditionally, fearful workers often looked to labor unions to protect their job security. But the advent of computers has put unions in a precarious position, as striking workers may find that they have been replaced by machines. Although this situation adds urgency to workers' fears, it is worth remembering that computers cannot be singled out as the primary cause of joblessness. Overall levels of employment depend upon myriad nontechnological factors such as government fiscal and monetary policies, the size and composition of the labor force, the rate of inflation, and so on. Further, technology can be used in many different ways, some of which create jobs and some of which eliminate jobs. For these reasons, it is inappropriate to view the computer as either villain or savior.

Structural and Frictional Unemployment

Computers are often introduced in order to reduce the costs of production by decreasing the number of workers. For example, the use of computers enabled the Bell system to lay off 60,000 workers between 1972 and 1977, a period in which the number of Bell System telephone calls increased by eighteen percent (Dizard, 1982). Further, in the banking industry, some companies require that one human worker be reassigned or laid off each time an automatic teller is put into place (Garsson, 1984).

This trend is international, encompassing many of the highly industrialized societies. In the United Kingdom, for example, thirteen percent of the people who are capable of working are unemployed (Galkin, 1985). From 1972 to 1976 in Japan, the seven major television manufacturers reduced their work force from 48,000 to 25,000, and they simultaneously increased production from 8.4 million to 10.5 million sets (Bessant, 1984). Similarly, in the United Kingdom, the introduction of word processors has cut the office staffs of numerous companies by as much as fifty percent (Downing, 1980), and over two jobs have been lost for each robot introduced (Draper, 1985). In the breakfast cereal industry, the introduction of computerized weighing systems that reduce the amount of waste has in many cases cut the number of workers by thirty percent or more (Leach and Shutt, 1985).

Not all of this unemployment, however, is permanent, for a distinction must be made between structural and frictional unemployment. In many contemporary economic systems, a percentage of the population is unemployed and likely to remain so because of a lack of skills, education, or adaptability. This percentage is classified as structural unemployment since it is a relatively stable feature of the economy. In the United States, the structurally unemployed includes approximately five percent of the work force. All who rank among the structurally unemployed carry a heavy burden with little hope of improvement.

The ranks of the structurally unemployed include disproportionately large numbers of blacks and members of other minority groups. In 1978, for example, the rate of unemployment for nonwhite youths between ages sixteen and nineteen was twice that of white youths and six times the overall rate of unemployment (Faunce, 1981). This state of affairs generates a serious equity gap and also contributes to alienation and social unrest among minority groups.

In contrast, frictional unemployment includes individuals who are out of work temporarily. Among the frictionally unemployed are people who want some time off from work, perhaps to raise a family, or who wish to change jobs in order to improve their situation. Also included are workers who have been displaced by technology but who have the motivation and the skills required to obtain other jobs.

Because frictional unemployment is temporary, it is less damaging than structural unemployment. Indeed, many economists view frictional employment as a necessary feature of a dynamic economy having a fluid labor market. Following the laws of supply and demand that govern a free market economy, some types of labor stay in high demand and even increase. Others suffer decreased demand, which leads to temporary displacement. This frictional unemployment, while unpleasant for the displaced workers, is viewed as a small price to pay for the maintenance of a healthy economy that maximizes productivity and profitability.

Most of the unemployment brought about by the widespread use of computers seems to be frictional rather than structural (Jenkin, 1983; Robinson, 1977). The highest rates of job displacement have occurred in areas of manufacturing in the industrial midwest, where robots have been substituted for human workers such as welders and painters (Tournatzky, 1985). Most of these displacements count as frictional unemployment since many of the workers who are displaced by computers will eventually move into other jobs. For example, many skilled welders, who worked for General Motors but who were replaced by robots, have been retrained by GM to do other jobs. Similarly, clerks who are replaced by computers in one office often find jobs in other offices.

Nevertheless, frictional unemployment stemming from the use of computers poses serious problems. In many cases, several weeks or even months pass before a new job can be found, and this places severe stress upon both the unemployed individuals and the society which supports them. Moreover, there is no guarantee that the new job will be satisfying. Some frictional unemployment reflects the movement of individuals look-ing for a better, higher paying job. But this rosy interpretation does not apply in cases in which computers have displaced a worker who lives near the poverty level and who, in a desperate attempt to support a family of four, must take any job that becomes available.

In addition, frictional unemployment can be damaging at times when the workforce is shrinking. There is not much cause for worry in years such as 1988, which had the lowest rate of joblessness in nearly a decade (Byrne, 1988). But in a tighter job market, workers find it much more difficult to obtain a new position. How serious a problem frictional unemployment is depends upon which industry workers are in. In indus-tries such as insurance and finance, which are enjoying an employment boom, frictional unemployment is not too serious a problem. But in industries such as mining that are suffering major cutbacks in the number of workers, job displacement can mean long-term unemployment.

Another problem is that minority and disadvantaged groups are often forced to carry a disproportionate share of the burden of frictional unem-ployment. For example, in the United Kingdom, over ninety-five percent of the secretaries and typists are women (Werneke, 1985). The introduction of word processors into many offices has reduced office staffs by thirty to fifty percent, and most of the displaced workers have been women (Downing, 1980). Similarly, in the 1970s, California tomato growers employed 40,000 migrant workers to harvest their crop. In the 1980s, by using a robot called the Tomato Harvester, the growers cut the workforce to 8,000 and now harvest a crop three times as large (Draper, 1985).

With regard to structural unemployment, the effects of the widespread use of computers are mixed. Unskilled workers, such as the black teenagers that constitute much of the structurally unemployed, may not find other jobs easily after having been displaced by computers. On the other hand, the use of computers creates many new jobs, a point that will be elaborated upon below. In addition, it may be possible to integrate groups such as unemployed black youths into the work force through ambitious training and employment programs.

Rapid technological change frustrates attempts to make exact predictions regarding the impact of computers on structural unemployment. Some observers predict that research on artificial intelligence will spawn intelligent systems that will replace unprecedented numbers of both unskilled laborers and skilled managers and professionals, including physicians and lawyers. If this prediction seems fanciful, consider how many workers would be displaced by the development of a program that could prepare tax forms for most people automatically and affordably. While very few programs of noteworthy intelligence are currently available, one cannot rule out rapid developments in the future. These could lead to dramatic increases in structural as well as frictional unemployment. However, many optimists argue that these job losses will be offset by the preservation of many existing jobs and by the creation of many new ones.

Job Preservation and Job Creation

In numerous cases, computers contribute to relatively high levels of employment by stimulating productivity and keeping large companies and even entire industries competitive. The U.S. automobile industry, for example, has suffered from low productivity, high labor costs, and a number of other problems, all of which have given foreign manufacturers a significant advantage. The survival of U.S. companies, indeed of the entire U.S. automobile industry, may require the adoption of state-of-the-art technology. The increased use of robots, each of which displaces from 1.7 to 6.0 workers, is expected to displace 100,000 workers by the early 1990s (Hunt, 1983). But even greater numbers of jobs may be lost if computers are not used. Kenneth Baker, former Minister of Information Technology in the United Kingdom, provided a succinct summary of the situation: "the choice for U.K. firms today is stark—automate or liqui-date!" (Bessant, 1984, p. 170).

The extensive use of computers also creates many new jobs. The computer industry itself is an expanding part of the economy, employing many hardware and software engineers, manufacturers, consultants, sales-people, and repair personnel (Bessant, 1984; Jenkin, 1983; Robinson, 1977). Because these industries have a relatively small base, however, they may provide fewer new jobs than the extensive media attention might lead one to expect. Larger numbers of new jobs may open up as companies adopt computers, increasing the demand for system managers, program-mers, technicians, repairmen, analysts, and so on.

Computers may also increase the levels of employment indirectly by creating jobs in traditional areas of business and industry. By reducing production costs and improving product quality, computers allow many man-ufacturers to increase both production and sales, thereby increasing profits. Increasing profits in turn stimulate increased investment and expenditures on research and development, creating new jobs in the industry. In order to take advantage of these new jobs, however, workers will need additional training.

The Problem of Retraining

Thirty years ago, it was the norm for people to receive training in a particular field such as chemical engineering or business and to then stick with one career in that field. By the 1980s, however, this pattern had become the exception, as most workers could expect to make two or three major changes of career during their lives. To make these changes, they need to be retrained.

The rapid changes in computers and other forms of technology have added to the need for retraining. By 1995, approximately twenty percent of workers will need to have four years of college education (Fields, 1986). At the headquarters of the Digital Equipment Corporation in Boston, managers point out that knowledge in the computer industry is changing so quickly that engineers need to be completely retrained approximately every five years. As companies introduce new computer systems, they need to provide effective training to the workers in order to reap the benefits. And when a company decides to reassign workers whose jobs were taken over by robots, the workers must be retrained in order to integrate the workers into their new setting.

It is the failure of the schools, however, that has created much of the current needs for retraining. To their chagrin, companies nationwide are discovering that their workers cannot read manuals or understand order forms. At IBM, for example, so many of the workers lacked basic math-ematical concepts that the company has begun teaching elementary algebra to many of its employees. But mathematical illiteracy is only the tip of the iceberg, for twenty percent or more of the current U.S. population is functionally illiterate (Kozol, 1985). Approximately twenty-five percent of teenagers drop out of high school, and, of those who graduate, only one of four meets standards expected of eighth graders (Gorman, 1988). The rates of illiteracy are highest among minority groups such as blacks, Hispanics and Asians, which is a significant problem since minority peoples will comprise one-third of the U.S. population by the year 2000.

These problems are compounded by the fact that highly successful international competitors such as Japan have a well trained workforce and are in a position to surge ahead of the U.S. economically. At precisely the moment when the needs are greatest for literate, well-trained workers who are equipped to build and to use high technology effectively, America is saddled with an ill-trained labor force.

A significant issue is who will pay the costs of retraining. Eric K., for example, was a welder in a plant in Detroit, the center of the American automobile industry. When he was laid off because the company he worked for decided to turn the welding over to robots, he was left to live off of welfare, which was as degrading as it was difficult to do. He spent large amounts of time looking for new jobs but found that the available jobs paid too little to support his family of four. Although he dreamed of returning to school and studying to become a computer engineer, he had no money to support his reeducation. He also dreamed of starting his own welding business, but he lacked the assets needed to obtain a loan. He felt betrayed by the system that he had previously enjoyed being part of, and, fearing the inevitable rent increase on his low income housing, he wondered how his family would cope with the looming prospect of homelessness.

Cases such as this one indicate that many individuals cannot possibly pay to retrain themselves. Understanding this, some states have launched retraining programs aimed at maintaining an employable labor force and a competitive state economy. The state government of California, for example, is spending 55 million dollars a year for a retraining program aimed at preparing 15,000 experienced workers for employment in high-tech industries. The companies that participate in the program select the workers they wish to retrain, and they in turn assure that there will be a job for the retrained worker.

Many companies, recognizing that it makes no sense to modernize plants and introduce new technology if the workers are unprepared, are also developing retraining programs. For example, UNISYS, a company based in California, discovered that many of its workers, who were Hispanics, lacked fluency in English. Accordingly, UNISYS developed a $150,000 training program designed to improve skills of reading, writing, and speaking English (Gorman, 1988).

This approach of having the company pay for retraining allows management to retain dedicated workers and to have an adequate supply of the skilled workers. It also avoids the unfortunate practice of displacing workers who live in the surrounding community and hiring outside technicians, many of whom may never live in the local community. This practice harms the community by increasing local levels of unemployment and by reducing the level of consumer spending, impairing the local economy. Understandably, this creates tension between the company and the community, and this can result in a political and economic backlash against the company. Both the company and the workers gain when the company retrains displaced workers. This insight is laying the groundwork for a new relationship between management and labor.

A New Role for the Unions

Traditionally, labor unions have had a strong restraining influence on management. If management announced a freeze on salaries, for example, labor unions could seek to obtain pay increases by threatening or actually staging work slowdowns and strikes. Computers, however, have changed this by giving management a powerful tool to be used as a strikebreaker.

In 1981, for example, the Professional Air Traffic Controllers Organization (PATCO) staged a walkout because management had not met their demands for higher wages and better working conditions. Twenty-five years ago, when the work of the air traffic controller was relatively unautomated, this type of strike might have crippled the flow of air traffic. But in 1981, the federal government successfully worked around the PATCO strike by using a computerized flow control procedure that maximized the use of the air traffic facilities, controlling departures and distributing traffic equally along major routes. In order to use this computerized procedure, the Federal Aviation Administration employed supervisors, nonstriking controllers and military personnel. Although the work force was only half of what it had been before the strike, the flow control procedure kept traffic moving at tolerable levels. This crippled the PATCO strike, which ended in the firing of 12,000 air traffic controllers (Shaiken, 1984). In this case, computers eroded the influence of the union.

The influence of labor unions has also suffered from the use of ineffective strategies for bargaining with management. In many cases, unions have waited until computer systems have been installed before negotiating with management over layoffs, salaries, and the use of the new systems (Moore and Levie, 1985). Furthermore, unions have often engaged in single-issue bargaining, leading them to positions that do not take into account all of the interlocking factors that influence the life of the company (Leach and Shutt, 1985). If, for example, a union successfully resisted the introduction of a computer because it would cause the deskilling of many jobs, the company could lose its ability to compete effectively, leading eventually to lower salaries and job losses.

Seeking to resolve these problems and to recover their influence, the unions are taking on a new role as participants in long-range planning with management (Katz and Sabel, 1985; Moore and Levie, 1985). By immersing themselves in the planning process, they gain the ability to negotiate over the use of computers before they have been installed and while there is still time to have an impact on how the systems will be used. This planning role also gives unions the opportunity to become informed about and to negotiate over the full range of options that companies must consider in order to remain competitive. This role enables the unions to move beyond single issue bargaining.

The problem of retraining is a central focus of the planning effort, for both labor and management. From labor's perspective, retraining is the key to keeping workers employed and to preparing them to feel effective and creative in using the computers that permeate the workplace. From management's perspective, retraining is essential for increasing productivity and competitiveness. Without effective training, workers may reject the new technology and fail to use it properly. By involving workers in planning and by providing proper retraining, managers increase the likelihood that workers will get behind the new equipment and boost productivity (Bylinsky, 1984). Both the unions and management recognize that it makes more sense to retrain loyal workers in whom the company has already invested a lot than it does to recruit a new set of workers who will eventually need retraining themselves.

Guided by this idea, many companies are creating what amounts to a second educational system that exists outside of the schools. Although the costs of this retraining effort are high, they are lower than the costs of the failure to retrain, for at stake is our ability to live with technology while maintaining a high quality of life.

Conclusion

Collecting and using information effectively is a high priority for contemporary managers, who must navigate in an increasingly competitive environment. Effective managers rely increasingly on information tools such as integrated management information systems that provide a global picture of their corporate operations and enable them to ask the what-if questions that are part of any strategic planning effort.

Decisions to introduce or to upgrade computers are decisions about social relations as well as technology, and these decisions can change the life of the company. Depending upon the choices that managers make, computers can reinforce or erode managerial authority, alter the functional corporate organization, and provoke power struggles between managers and workers. In making decisions about how to use computers, managers must struggle with the difficult issues of unemployment and retraining, which impact the life of the surrounding community and the social and economic vitality of the nation.

These decisions will not become simpler—if anything, they are destined to become more complex. In the past, most managers made decisions about local and regional sales. But now international goods flood the shelves of stores in virtually every city. Computers will become ever more important to managers as they work to cope with the vicissitudes of the global economy.

4

The Global Economy

On Wall Street in the mid-1980s, the rapid increases in stock prices stirred occasional concern that a "correction" in the market was inevitable. But no one foresaw an impending disaster. Suddenly, on Monday, October 19, 1987, the unimaginable happened. Prices tumbled downward, producing a collapse of a magnitude that surpassed even that of 1929. By the end of the day, the Dow Jones industrial average had plummeted 508 points, a staggering drop of 22.6%. In a single day, which became known as Black Monday, $500 billion had vanished, eliminating the spectacular gains of the preceding year. Computers played a role in the disaster by making automatic trades whenever prices dropped and by sending information about the crash around the globe via electronic networks (Tate, 1988). As panic spread around the world, stock prices on the following day plunged by 12.2% in London and 15% in Tokyo, creating fears of a global depression (Church, 1987).

The synchronized crashes in New York, London and Tokyo on Black Monday show that the economies of different nations have become richly interconnected into a larger, global economy in which the events in one nation ripple throughout many others. The existence of a truly global economy is also apparent in the huge volume of trading that goes on between different countries. Whereas imports and exports accounted for less than ten percent of the

U.S. Gross National Product (GNP) in 1950, trade constituted over twenty percent of its GNP by 1980. International investments have also soared. For example, the percentage of Americans employed by foreign-owned companies doubled between 1975 and 1985, leaving one of every fourteen factory workers to answer to a foreign boss (Norton and Black, 1989).

Trading and investment between the U.S. and Japan has been particularly active. In December of 1987, a record was set when imported cars, mostly Japanese, captured 34.5% of the American auto market (Poe, 1988). By the late 1980s, Japanese investors were using their credit cards to buy $500,000 California homes from catalogs (Norton and Black, 1989), and they were buying huge chunks of real estate in Hawaii. Throughout the 1980s, buying a television or a video recorder in the U.S. meant buying a foreign product made in Japan or in another Asian nation of the Pacific Basin. Because of the large volume of imports and exports, the U.S. economy is best thought of not as a self-contained entity but as a thread woven into the fabric of a global economy.

The existence of a global economy is also indicated by the rise of immense multinational corporations that reach across national boundaries in order to take advantage of cheap labor, low costs of materials, and favorable exchange rates (Shaiken, 1988). In Tennessee alone, there are 35 Japanese-owned factories that employ 10,000 American workers (Buckley, 1988). Similarly, the Honda Corporation is often thought of as a Japanese firm that makes the popular Honda compacts. In fact, it is a multinational corporation that is based increasingly in the U.S. Honda makes its engines in Japan and then ships them to plants such as the one at Marysville, Ohio, where Honda automobiles are assembled in large quantities. Indeed, the Marysville plant can turn out 360,000 cars each year. From Marysville, the completed Hondas are sent to American Honda dealers, which sell forty-three percent of the Hondas made worldwide. Or they are shipped from Portland, Oregon back to Japan, where they will be sold in cities such as Tokyo (Toy, Gross and Treece, 1988). By producing in the U.S., Honda takes advantage of the high value of yen compared to dollars, and it avoids the high costs of shipping entire automobiles from Japan to the U.S.

Computers have contributed to the rise of the global economy and to the development of multinational corporations. For one thing, computer networks are the nervous system of the global economy. They enable rapid exchanges of information and money across vast distances, allowing companies to have their headquarters in one country, manufacturing plants in three others, and sales centers sprinkled worldwide. They also give multinational corporations a means of managing the enormous volumes of information that they produce, allowing them to handle the complexities of doing business daily across several continents. In addition, computers and computer-related services are a huge source of international business and are the focus of some of the largest multinational corporations. In 1987, for example, IBM had a sales volume of over $54 billion, a figure that exceeds the gross national product of many nations. And IBM is not alone. From 1977 to 1979, the American Telephone and Telegraph Company, now one of the largest suppliers of computers, had a gross income that exceeded the gross national products of 118 individual nations (Dizard, 1982).

The development of a global economy has significantly increased the interdependence among nations. For example, garment retailers in the U.S. depend upon the productivity and the economic health of garment exporting countries such as Korea and Taiwan. Conversely, countries having a low agricultural yield depend upon the productivity and economic health of food exporters such as the U.S. Furthermore, the success of a multinational corporation requires economic and political stability in the countries in which it operates. The collapse of a multinational corporation may set off a ripple effect in which waves of economic unrest spread out to even the most stable countries. Owing in part to the existence of the global economy, regional political and military conflicts that might once have had mainly local effects may now have global repercussions. In a sense, the global economy has brought individual nations into a broader economic family, producing an unprecedented degree of economic and political interdependence among nations.

Realizing that the international economic environment has changed dramatically, the nations of the world have begun to rethink their economic destiny and are developing new strategies for putting themselves in position to benefit from the new economic order. Japan, which views the computer as the key to vaulting itself into a position of economic ascendence, has initiated an ambitious attempt to develop a new generation of computers. Unwilling to relinquish its leadership in high technology and wanting to regain its manufacturing prowess, the U.S. is developing new strategies for competing with countries such as Japan. In the background of this struggle between economic and technological titans, the relatively impoverished Third World nations, which include three fourths of the world population, are working to improve their standard of living and to protect their economic and political sovereignty. By examining these developments, we put ourselves in a position to comprehend the global reach of the computer revolution.

Information, Technology, and Economics

Nowhere is the link between computers and economics more apparent than in the sales potential of large computer companies. In 1987, the top twenty-two U.S. manufacturers had sales of over $120 billion, and the top seven of these manufacturers ranked in the top 100 of all U.S. companies (*Business Week*, April 15, 1988). Sales of supercomputers, the most powerful computers that are capable of performing hundreds of millions of operations each second, are soaring and are expected to surpass $20 billion in 1991 (Gullo and Schatz,

1988). There is also a booming market for computer networks worldwide, as over 200,000 computer networks were installed in 1987, compared to 52,000 installations in 1984 (Wilson, 1987). In addition, the appetite of big government for computers is increasing. The U.S. government alone spent $16 million on computers in 1986, nearly twice the 1982 level of spending on computers (Seghers and Lewis, 1987).

Just how lucrative the computer industry can be is indicated by the tales of legendary entrepreneurs such as Steven Jobs and Stephen Wozniak, who invented the Apple personal computer in a home garage in 1976 and who saw their company reach the Fortune 500 by 1982 (Forester, 1987). In order to understand the meteoric rise of the computer industry, it is necessary to examine factors such as the pace of technological development, cost trends and the range of computer applications.

A Paradigm for Growth

The first modern computers bore little resemblance to the sleek desktop units available today. In 1945, researchers at the University of Pennsylvania completed the first completely electronic, general purpose computer, called ENIAC, an acronym for Electronic Numerical Integrator and Computer. A mammoth machine, ENIAC weighed approximately 30 tons and consumed vast amounts of electricity. It contained 18,000 vacuum tubes which generated tremendous amounts of heat and which are said to have failed at the rate of once every fifteen seconds. ENIAC performed calculations much faster than its predecessors, peaking out at approximately 5,000 additions per second.

Whereas ENIAC's speed was measured in terms of thousands of instructions per second, the speed of current computers is measured in millions of instructions per second (MIPS). Furthermore, the speed of supercomputers is measured in billions of instructions per second. As Figure 4.1 shows, the personal computers of today are more powerful than even the mainframe computers of twenty years ago. Yet most weigh under 35 pounds, fit on a desktop, and cost under $2,000, making them highly attractive and accessible to consumers and businesspeople alike.

Behind these improvements cost and speed has been a steady trend towards the miniaturization of electronic components in each generation of computers. The first generation of computers, developed between 1951 and 1959, utilized many bulky vacuum tubes. The second generation, which lasted from 1959 to 1964, used transistors, which had been developed at Bell Laboratories in 1948. Transistors had great advantages over vacuum tubes because they were smaller, more reliable, consumed less power and generated far less heat. The third generation, which ran from 1964 to 1970, featured the integrated circuit, a tiny silicon chip that contained the equivalent of hundreds and even thousands of transistors.

In the fourth generation, the current one, many thousands of transistors are routinely placed on a small silicon chip, thus resulting in dramatic reductions

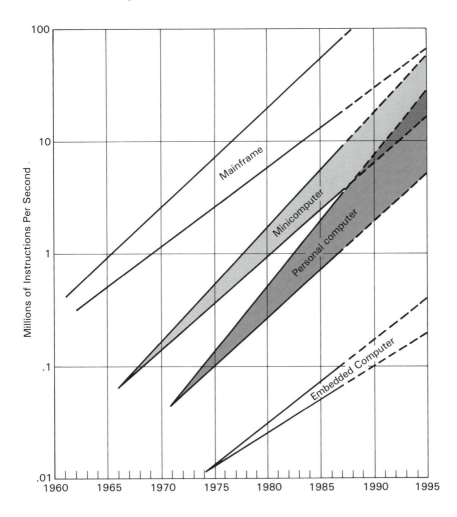

Figure 4.1. Computer speeds have risen dramatically since the 1960s. From "The Next Computer Revolution," by A. Peled, Copyright © 1987 by SCIENTIFIC AMERICAN, Inc. All rights reserved.

in size and power consumption relative to the early technology. As Figure 4.2 shows, the number of components that can fit on a single chip has increased dramatically. Many of these chips, which are no larger than a fingernail, are much more powerful than the early computers and are so small that they fit easily into products such as automobile ignition systems and microwave ovens. This miniaturization trend is expected to continue, as optimistic industry watchers predict that chips containing one billion components will be produced by the year 2000. And the next generation of chips, which will be made of gallium arsenide, will be 2.5 times faster than silicon chips (Meindl, 1987).

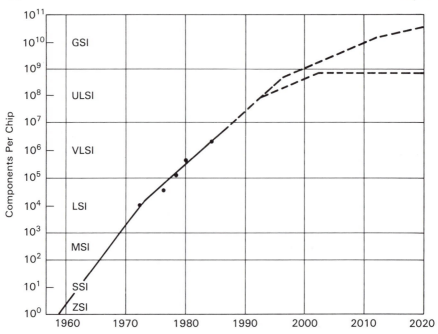

Figure 4.2. The number of components placed on a single computer chip has increased sharply since 1960, and optimists predict that a one billion component chip will be developed by the year 2000. From "Chips for Advanced Computing," by J. D. Meindl. Copyright © 1987 by SCIENTIFIC AMERICAN, Inc. All rights reserved.

Impressive cost reductions have accompanied these rapid size cuts. Over the past fifteen years, the power of computers has increased by nearly 10,000 times, yet the cost of each operation has simultaneously decreased 100,000 times. It has been said that if automobile technology had undergone the massive gains in power and reductions in cost achieved by computer technology, today a Rolls Royce would get three million miles per gallon, cost $2.75 and have enough power to drive the Queen Elizabeth II (Bernstein, 1978).

This combination of fast speed, high reliability, small size, and low cost has produced rapid increases in the marketability and the range of applications of microelectronics and computer technology. A sample of these applications is shown in Table 4.1. Nearly every area of contemporary life provides in one way or another a marketable use of computers, and new uses are being invented daily. For example, plans are afoot in the U.S. automobile industry to create "smart cars" having computerized dashboard navigation systems that communicate with centralized traffic control systems that monitor the flow of traffic (Brown, 1989). The dashboard navigation system will notify drivers of accidents or traffic jams ahead, and they will even suggest alternate routes.

A particularly important application of computers is in the telecommunications industry, which provides the networks that connect nations in the

TABLE 4.1
A small sample of the many applications of computers.

Area	Applications
Business	word processing, electronic funds transfer, accounting, data-base management, payroll, billing, credit assessment, management information systems, point-of-sale terminals
Industry	robotics, computer-aided design, computer numerical control, process control, materials handling
Military	weapons guidance, communications, intelligence, simulation, targeting and weapons control, warning and analysis of attacks, battle management, training
Communications	electronic mail, computer conferencing, videotex, telecommunications management, automated message-sending, electronic bulletin boards
Education	drill and practice, tutoring, simulation, computer-managed instruction, literature search, experimental control, data analysis
Medicine	medical record keeping, instrument control, analysis of disease and health data, computer-aided diagnosis, training

global economy. Over 500 banks in 15 countries are now interconnected by means of the SWIFT world banking network. This system allows banks to transmit payments across great distances, enabling them to make international transactions immediately (Bessant, 1984). Similarly, 105 nations belong to the INTELSAT satellite network, which can beam many different kinds of information to all parts of the globe (Dizard, 1982). Only a few hundred years ago, international communications traveled the slow channels of shipping and mail, which was routed through a small number of gateway cities. Now, however, global telecommunications networks have made it possible to transmit information immediately to people anywhere on the planet, overcoming the longstanding barriers of time and geography.

The economic influence of computers, however, extends far beyond their role as business items and communications devices. Computers also increase the importance of information as an economic resource.

Information and Economic Power

In early civilization, economic activity centered around two processes, the first of which was agriculture and the exchange of food items. The second was the extraction and use of natural resources such as timber and minerals. In these activities, the key resources were raw materials and the dominant technology was the craft of the skilled worker and artisan, acquired through individual experience.

The Industrial Revolution changed the economic base from agriculture and extraction to the mass production of goods. The key resources became financial capital and sources of power such as coal, oil, gas, and, more recently, nuclear power. Machine technology replaced the earlier craft. The production of goods no longer depended upon the craftsman's experience, and the knowledge of how to produce a particular item was embodied in a machine that could be used by anyone with enough money and power. The Industrial Revolution also forged new links between science and technology, for scientific principles were useful in designing new machines, which in turn provided the route to wealth. This increased role of science, which generates theory and codifies knowledge, began an enduring trend toward the use of theoretical knowledge in the production of goods.

In the current economy, which includes many jobs in service areas such as banking, insurance, and health care, information is a crucial resource, so much so that some analysts now view the U.S. economy as an information economy (Bell, 1973, 1980; Hawken, 1983). The importance of information is particularly apparent in the primary information sector, which includes industries such as accounting, education, media, advertising, telecommunications, computer manufacturing and computer services (Bell, 1980). This sector also includes many government employees, for workers in the Postal Service, the Census Bureau, the Treasury, and many other agencies, all deal extensively with the management of information.

What is perhaps less obvious is that information has become a key economic commodity even in a traditional heavy industry such as the automobile industry. Although automobile manufacturers still rely upon the acquisition and the manipulation of material resources, they rely increasingly on computer-aided design systems, robotics and computer numerical control systems that embody the knowledge of designers and programmers in the form of information. And, as seen in Chapter Three, managers rely on management information systems for both analysis and planning. Information, then, is a crucial commodity in the production and sale of automobiles, and the same is true in other industries such as the aircraft and paper industries.

The increasing influence of information in many economic activities marks a trend toward knowledge intensification. Information has always been important in the design and production of goods, but the current business environment places even greater demands for information acquisition and use. For one thing, current products are much more complex than ever before, and much more information must go into their design and production. This is apparent in considering now commonplace items such as jet aircraft, automobiles, televisions, submarines, and computers. Each of these is the product of extensive research and development costing many billions of dollars. And each is based upon vast amounts of information, more than can be handled by any single individual. The large corporations that produce these items are themselves very complex, and their effective management requires large amounts of information.

The complexity of the business environment is also increasing, creating the need for more information. In the days of the local economy, consumers chose from a rather small array of products, whereas they now choose from a tremendous number of products. This means that companies now face stiffer competition, and, in the global economy, competitors come from all parts of the world. In order to compete effectively in this environment, companies need increased amounts of information about which markets to enter and about which items to produce. Moreover, automation has driven up the number of new products introduced each year, and it has reduced the lag between conception and production. As a result, there is an increased premium on the speed with which products are designed, produced and marketed. The pressure for moment-by-moment information regarding the environment fuels the trend toward knowledge intensification.

Computers play a dual role in the current knowledge-intensive economy. They are powerful information tools, enabling people to manage information and to cope with an environment of staggering complexity. On the other hand, they increase the complexity of the economic environment by facilitating the growth of a global economy and by supporting the telecommunications network that binds it together. In addition, computers enable people to undertake immensely complex projects such as the Appollo flight to the moon and the current flights of the U.S. Space Shuttle. These generate staggering amounts of information, producing in turn the need for even more complex information tools such as supercomputers. The result is an upward spiral of complexity in which computers manage existing complexity and create new complexity, increasing the importance of information as an economic resource in the global economy.

These developments give added thrust to Francis Bacon's famous dictum that "Knowledge is power." It has always been apparent how this dictum applies to military affairs since military advantage is often achieved through superior intelligence operations. The breaking of the German code in World War II, for example, contributed to the success of the Allied Forces by allowing them to predict Hitler's next move and to counter it effectively. But Bacon's dictum also applies to economic affairs. Through research and development activities, companies acquire knowledge useful in analyzing markets and in developing new products, escalating them into a position of economic power. Further, intelligence operations may also contribute to the economic power of companies and entire nations.

Because information is now an economic resource as significant as gas, coal, and steel, many nations seek to enter the computer market in order to increase their information resources and economic power. Although the U.S. has dominated the computer market since it opened, other nations are mounting a significant challenge for technological and economic supremacy. Japan is leading the charge, and her initiative has profound implications for the shape of the global economy.

The Japanese Challenge

At the end of World War II in 1945, Japan lay in ruins. All of her major cities except Kyoto had been bombed heavily, and Hiroshima and Nagasaki had been devastated by atomic weapons. Her industrial capacity shattered and her food supply depleted, Japan's inflation rate ran so high that previously wealthy families were forced to exchange priceless family heirlooms for small bags of rice. Her once proud streets swelled with disease, hunger, and prostitution (Pempel, 1986).

No one expected Japan to rise out of the ashes, much less to become a major economic power again in the twentieth century. Yet Japan has risen so high that she now challenges the U.S. The Tokyo stock exchange is now the world's largest, exceeding the New York exchange by one trillion dollars (Shapiro, 1988). Selling highly successful items such as automobiles, computers, and video recorders on the world market, Japan has seen her exports skyrocket. This has resulted in a massive trade surplus in which she brought in $102 billion more than she paid out to other countries in 1986. In the same year, the U.S. ran a trade deficit of $134 billion, which meant that the U.S. had spent much more on imported goods than it had earned through exporting its own goods. Fifty-two billion dollars of that deficit stemmed from trade with Japan (Ozaki, 1988). By 1985, Japan had become the world's largest creditor nation, whereas the U.S. had become the world's largest debtor nation. The plight of the U.S. economy was made even worse by a towering national debt, which reached $2.6 trillion in 1988 (Berry, 1988).

Japan's economic challenge to the U.S. has been particularly strong in the realm of computers. In 1970, the U.S. was the undisputed world leader in the computer industry, including the memory chip market. Since 1978, however, Japan has captured fifty percent of the $30 billion chip market, while the U.S. share has dropped to forty-four percent. Furthermore, in 1975, U.S. companies controlled ninety percent of the market for dynamic random access memory (DRAM) chips, which allow computers to store and change data. But by 1986, the U.S. share had dwindled to five percent, largely as the result of competition from Japan (Dallmeyer, 1987). Equally ominous is the fact that the Japanese computer production is growing much more rapidly than is American production. From 1984 through 1987, for example, Japanese electronics production rose seventy-five percent, whereas U.S. electronics production rose only eight percent (Elmer-DeWitt, 1989).

The threat of Japanese dominance of the computer market concerns U.S. policy makers because computers have a powerful influence in both the economic and the military realms. Because computers are used so widely to increase productivity, new developments in computers ripple throughout the entire economy. And because computers are essential in designing new technology, advances in computers help to drive the overall pace of technological development. In the military, there is increasing reliance upon "smart weapons" that are guided by computers. To become a second rate power in the realm of computing is to risk becoming a second rate economic and military power.

This is why the U.S. and other Western nations have shown so much concern over Japan's imaginative new computer project. Called the Fifth Generation Project, it is intended to usher in a new era in the relation between people and technology.

The Fifth Generation

The Japanese Fifth Generation Project is an attempt to develop by the early 1990s an entirely new generation of computers, intelligent computers that can learn, solve diverse kinds of problems, and understand ordinary speech and pictures. This ambitious project, if successful, would render obsolete the current fourth generation computers that are, for the most part, unintelligent and in need of precise instructions written in a technical computer language. Further, it would establish Japan as the undisputed leader in computer technology, conferring substantial advantages in many areas of the knowledge-intensive economy. Even if the project were only partially successful, it would nonetheless boost Japan's economic power.

The key to the Fifth Generation Project is knowledge processing (Feigenbaum and McCorduck, 1983; Wood, 1988). Fourth generation computers are excellent tools for information storage, retrieval, and dissemination. But information is not knowledge—it is the raw data upon which knowledge is built. In order to develop knowledge, information must be selected, interpreted, and transformed into meaningful patterns. These activities require greater intelligence than has been achieved using any fourth generation system. They also require significant developments in hardware, software, and interfacing.

Fifth generation systems consist of three layers: hardware, software, and human interface. Ideally, they will allow nearly spontaneous conversation between people and computers, and this will require hardware of great complexity. An intuitive grasp of the order of complexity required can be achieved by considering that the human brain—the central piece of hardware in the human processing system—contains over ten billion neurons (nerve cells), each of which communicates with hundreds or thousands of other neurons. Since complexity of this order is required for human speech, vision, and other ordinary human capacities, it seems very likely that an extremely complex computer architecture will be required for the development of significant speech and vision capabilities.

The Japanese expect to develop hardware that is nearly 1,000 times more powerful than the most powerful computers available now. Current computers can perform from 10,000 to 100,000 logical inferences per second, where a logical inference is the equivalent of 100 to 1,000 conventional machine instructions. In contrast, fifth generation systems must be able to perform 100 to 1,000 million logical inferences per second (Bramer, 1984).

In order to achieve this dramatic increase in the speed of processing, the Japanese plan to develop chips containing 10 million transistors, an improvement of one hundredfold over current chips. Further, the Japanese plan to move beyond the current von Neumann hardware, named after John von Neumann, who was instrumental in the design of the computer. Von Neumann machines are serial processors that process instructions sequentially, one at a time. The Fifth Generation Project calls for the development of parallel-processing architecture. Parallel processing has the potential for dramatic increases in speed by having many processors work on different parts of a problem simultaneously, in parallel, much as different groups of people might work simultaneously on a complex problem (Dertouzos, 1987). If efficient parallel processors are developed, the current computer architecture will soon be as outmoded as manual typewriters.

In order to solve diverse problems and interact easily with people, fifth generation systems need highly sophisticated software. In particular, they require intelligent software that can reason, make inferences, and interpret the incomplete and inexact requests made by users. Artificial intelligence capabilities are also needed for the construction of a sophisticated human interface that can speak to users and that can respond appropriately to spoken and written requests. This is a tall order since the meaning of what people say varies tremendously depending upon the context. For example, the statement "That's very funny" can mean many different things depending upon the situation and the speaker. The ability to understand language in its natural context will require systems of much greater sophistication than current ones, which are limited to recognizing hundreds of words and very simple sentences spoken in an unambiguous context.

Critics charge that these expectations are unrealistic since artificial intelligence is still in its infancy and since the Fifth Generation Project requires that much greater advances in AI occur in ten years than have occurred in the entire thirty-five years that the field has been in existence. In addition, very little is known about parallel processing, which is the heart of the hardware improvements that are called for. These criticisms may be partially correct, but they miss the significant point. Even if the project fails to deliver the technological breakthroughs that are intended, it will still be highly significant because it has focused the attention of both government and industry on the hundreds of smaller problems that must be solved before sophisticated AI becomes a reality. By stimulating collaboration between government and industry, the project is creating a national framework for producing and commercializing parallel processing systems (Wood, 1988).

A National Project

In free market systems such as that of the U.S., the desire for profits, together with the laws of supply and demand, generates a tremendous diversity of research and development activities. These are not linked into a coherent national plan. In fact, strict antitrust laws prevent companies from collaborating in their research and development activities. Typically, these activities are designed to produce relatively immediate gains. Under ever increasing pressure from stockholders who demand profits in nearly every quarter, many companies deemphasize costly long-term research, even though it can lead to substantial long-term profits.

Japan offers a stark contrast to this situation (Feigenbaum et al., 1983; Lynn, 1988; Pempel, 1986). The Japanese Ministry of International Trade and Industry (MITI) is a powerful government agency that systematically analyzes and directs the long-term economic development of the country. In the late 1970s, MITI announced that "Information is the future," and it launched the Fifth Generation Project in 1982, providing $500 million dollars to support it over a ten-year period. Taking the group-oriented approach that pervades Japanese work, MITI has formed a consortium of eleven companies such as Hitachi, Fujitsu, Nippon, Mitsubishi, and Toshiba. Each company sends some of its best young talent to the newly established Institute for New Generation Computer Technology (ICOT), which is funded partly by matching funds from the participating companies. In essence, ICOT is a brain trust that allows bright, innovative thinkers to collaborate on the development of fifth generation computers and software.

This approach is unique because it utilizes the collective strength of different companies, which, if located in most countries, would work independently and secretively. The hope is that this pooling of talent will generate diverse ideas that are much more powerful and imaginative than those that could be achieved independently. These ideas become the property of all of the participating companies, which may then use them to manufacture products of their own choice. While the companies collaborate in the design and development processes, they still compete with each other in the production process, which is where the Japanese have consistently achieved competitive superiority relative to other countries (Moritani, 1982).

This approach is unique also because of its vision and long-range planning. MITI officials rotate regularly among the various departments of the ministry. This practice enables them to gain a broader perspective on the organization and its projects and also to develop a sense of teamwork. Because MITI officials are lifetime employees, they are free to ponder the future and to take risks without fear of the repercussions of the next elections or round of budget cuts. This lifetime employment policy generates deep loyalty and creates a degree of continuity of government that is all but unattainable in other nations.

MITI, however, is not the entire impetus behind the Fifth Generation challenge. MITI itself and the philosophy it embodies is rooted in a broader cultural matrix that underlies Japan's strength.

The Japanese Way

Japan has a population of 120 million, approximately one-half that of the U.S., yet most of her people are squeezed by a mountainous terrain into a space roughly the size of New Jersey. In addition, Japan relies extensively on imports for such necessities as food and energy. For example, she obtains over ninety percent of her oil, iron, aluminum, and nickel from other nations, which makes her vulnerable economically (Pempel, 1986).

Being poor in natural resources, Japan has made her people her primary resource. Her people are remarkably well educated, as the Japanese illiteracy rate is only one percent, far below the twenty percent rate of the U.S. The Japanese are also very intelligent, enjoying an average I. Q. of 111, 11 points higher than the U.S. average of 100. Ten percent of Japanese children have an I. Q. of 130 or more, compared to only two percent of American children (Christopher, 1983). They also have a passion for learning. Japanese publishers release 35,000 new titles each year, twice the number released in the U.S. Nearly every classroom contains a television set in order to take advantage of the regular instruction in five different languages, health, farming, and other subjects. As a result, the Japanese workforce ranks as one of the best educated and most intelligent in the world, and it is well equipped to deal with high technology and the rapid changes in the global economy.

The Japanese also have a strong national identity and group loyalty. Japan's national identity grew out of long periods of geographical isolation, together with over two hundred years of self-imposed social isolation during which all Christian missionaries and foreigners were banned (Reischauer, 1970). Japan also carved her identity out of a long history of struggles with China, her powerful neighbor. This national identity was intimately connected with a powerful sense of loyalty to the group. Under the prevailing Confucian system of ethics, each person's main moral obligations were to his or her family. This sense of family obligation extended beyond one's immediate relatives. For hundreds of years, Japan was a feudal society that demanded total loyalty to one's territorial lord. Even after the feudal system had ended, the Japanese felt a powerful obligation to the Emperor, who was viewed as a divine being worthy of sacrificing one's life for. Even today, the Japanese have such a strong collectivist attitude that they value group service over individual accomplishment. This is one reason why the Japanese typically work much longer hours than Westerners and pass up vacations which they have clearly earned (Christopher, 1983; Vogel, 1979).

The Japanese style of management, many aspects of which were borrowed initially from the U.S., embodies the sense of family that pervades the Japanese company (Vogel, 1979). Managers encourage employees to identify with the company, providing elaborate ceremonies for the induction of new employees. Companies typically have their own uniforms, insignias, and songs, and they often provide housing and athletic facilities for the workers. Larger companies often provide permanent employment, hiring workers from the time they leave school until they retire, typically at fifty-seven or fifty-eight years of age. The permanent employment system creates a sense of belonging that generates deep loyalty to one's company and fellow workers. Although unions exist, they are organized around companies, making for a Toyota union, a Nissan union, and so on. Having permanent employment and steady pay increases to look forward to, they typically develop a cooperative, nonadversarial attitude toward management.

Japanese managers also excel in the human aspects of management. In contrast to U.S. managers, Japanese managers start at the entry level and work their way up. Having worked at all levels of the company, they know the concerns of the workers, making it easier to communicate with them. Furthermore, Japanese managers often seek input from their workers. It is not unusual for managers to invite employees to participate in a quality control circle, a group of eight or so workers and managers who collectively analyze company problems in a democratic atmosphere. This approach has produced remarkable improvements in quality control since it is often the workers who are most sensitive to production problems and aware of alternate ways of machining, designing, and so on. It also builds a sense of participation in the company and of teamwork with management, boosting morale significantly (Moritani, 1982).

Japanese Superiority—Myth and Reality

Descriptions of the Japanese way and of challenges such as the Fifth Generation Project can create an aura of inherent Japanese superiority and invincibility. An accurate assessment of the Japanese challenge requires sober appreciation of Japan's economic problems, which are by no means few in number.

For one thing, Japan has a rapidly aging workforce, and the government predicts that twenty-one percent of the population will be sixty-five years or older by 2020 (McAbee, 1985). If this occurs, Japan will have a higher percentage of elderly citizens than any other industrial nation, imposing severe burdens on the social security and national health insurance systems. Because Japanese companies increase salaries on the basis of seniority, the rapid aging of the workforce produces spiraling labor costs, which may erode competitiveness. Further, Japan's choice to focus on high technology will rapidly increase the need for capital investment funds, for high-technology facilities rapidly become obsolete. Yet these funds may become increasingly scarce because the government engages in extensive deficit spending, and debt financing already claims twenty percent of the national budget. And although large Japanese companies have received extensive publicity for their lifetime employment policy, nearly three fourths of the Japanese workforce works in relatively small companies that do not guarantee lifetime employment. In fact, employment in these small companies rises and falls according to how much demand there is from large companies for their products.

These economic problems are compounded by social problems such as the highest adolescent suicide rate in the world, acutely clogged expressways, the chronic shortage of living space, and the lack of sewer connections and flush toilets in one-third of Japanese homes (McAbee, 1985). It goes without saying that most of these problems have parallels in the U.S.

Japan's economic strength also owes partly to historical factors rather than to systematic planning and collaborative action. For example, many of her heavy industrial plants were destroyed during World War II. In rebuilding these plants, Japan made improvements and modernizations that allowed her to ascend rapidly in the steel and shipbuilding industries. Furthermore, Japan has not been allowed since the war to rebuild her military forces. Unlike her Western competitors, Japan has been free of a heavy burden of defense spending, permitting her to channel money away from defense and into projects having direct commercial applications.

Japan's success also stems in part from her trade practices, which are not always consistent with a free market philosophy. For example, in 1980, the Cray supercomputer, which was made in the U.S., was the most powerful and least expensive in the world and attracted Japanese customers, particularly since Japan made no supercomputers at that time. But when MITI announced in 1981 its plans to develop a Japanese supercomputer, Cray's Japanese customers seemed to disappear (Prestowitz, 1988). Once the government made its wishes clear, Japanese companies fell in line, creating an unstated import barrier. On other occasions, the Japanese government attempts to limit the production of items such as memory chips, causing shortages for U.S. computer manufacturers that are as harmful as they are frustrating (Lewis, 1988). Practices such as these have triggered numerous proposals in the U.S. Congress for protectionist legislation.

It would be unfair, however, to attribute Japan's successes to historical advantages and biased trade practices. If the Fifth Generation Project catapults Japan into a position of superiority, it will be because of Japan's vision and organization as well as her high quality of technical training and culture of intense corporate loyalty. Myths aside, this powerful combination presents a challenge to which other nations must respond if they are to retain their technological and economic power.

The U.S. Response

Responding effectively to the Japanese challenge requires attention to many problems. For example, the U.S. computer industry suffers from a shortage of well trained engineers, as three fourths of the students in American Ph.D. programs in engineering and physical sciences are from foreign countries. In addition, the industry has become fragmented because many talented entrepreneurs continue to split off from large companies to start up their own businesses (Castro, 1988). But startup ventures cannot do the large-scale research that is needed to compete effectively with Japan and other nations in the Pacific Basin. Furthermore, American industry has been somewhat chauvinistic about its own technology and has paid too little attention to Japanese science and technology (Greenberg, 1986). These problems, coupled with the huge U.S. budget and trade deficits, necessitate coordinated movement on many fronts.

In 1983, the U.S. took an important first step toward solving these problems by creating an innovative research cooperative called the Microelectronics and Computer Technology Corporation (MCC), located in Austin, Texas. The MCC is a consortium of 21 American computer firms such as Digital Equipment Corporation, Honeywell, Motorola, RCA, and Control Data. As in the Japanese model, these companies will donate researchers and funds to MCC for up to four years. The researchers will collaborate on research projects and generate new ideas. Then the companies will use these ideas to compete on the production of items of their own choice (Marbach, 1985).

The MCC will have a budget of approximately 75 million dollars a year, a relatively modest sum when one considers that IBM alone spent $3.5 billion on research in 1985 (Budiansky, 1986). Nevertheless, the MCC has already succeeded in getting large computer companies to look beyond immediate results and to invest in long term research. Under the leadership of retired Admiral Bobby Inman, the MCC attracted 390 top scientists. Their work will be augmented by the decision of the University of Texas to establish thirty-five chairs in computer science, each endowed for one million dollars. This kind of collaboration between university and corporation may be exactly what is needed to increase the competitiveness of U.S. computer firms in the international market. Already the MCC has completed its first products, which include artificial intelligence software that aids the development of microcircuits (Elmer-DeWitt, 1989).

Antitrust legislation, however, presents a significant obstacle to ventures such as the MCC. Fearing charges of violations of this legislation, IBM chose not to join the MCC (Marbach, 1985). This is unfortunate since IBM is the industry giant, and it commands a powerful arsenal of research resources that would add immensely to the MCC. As a result, some executives in the industry see the current antitrust laws as blocking rather than facilitating the success of American business. Further, IBM, operating alone, has not contributed maximally to the development of the microelectronic circuit technology (Ferguson, 1985). Although it has designed some highly advanced circuits, it has produced them in relatively small numbers intended to service its mainframe computers. Other companies have therefore had difficulty obtaining these highly sophisticated chips. At the same time, IBM has purchased relatively outdated chips from other firms, which has encouraged them to produce chips that are somewhat less than state-of-the-art (Ferguson, 1985).

Groups similar to the MCC have also formed in other parts of the country. In the Research Triangle Park in North Carolina, for example, 13 chip and computer manufacturers formed a nonprofit research consortium called the Semiconductor Research Corporation (SRC). Established in order to pool talent and to distribute the financial burden of long-range research, it includes companies such as Digital Equipment Corporation, Intel, and Hewlett-Packard. Like MCC, the SRC is expected to benefit from the talent in nearby universities, which include the North Carolina State University, the University of North Carolina, and Duke University.

The U.S. government has, for many years, supported projects and agencies that have helped the U.S. to establish its leadership in the arena of computer technology. The primary agency is the Pentagon's Defense Advanced Research Projects Agency (DARPA), which sponsored projects leading to the first supercomputer and to systems for time sharing. Currently, DARPA supports much of the research for the development of a new supercomputer that would compete effectively with that planned by Japan. It is also the top supporter of research on artificial intelligence, one of the key components of the Fifth Generation Project. But many of the products that evolve out of research supported by DARPA are best suited to military applications. Yet these products and their spinoffs have consumer applications as well, and this should contribute to the economic viability of American business.

It is impossible to tell whether these responses will enable the U.S. to meet the challenges it faces in the world computer market. For one thing, this market is rapidly changing. Already, Asian countries such as the "Four Little Dragons" of South Korea, Taiwan, Hong Kong and Singapore are becoming powerful players in the technological arena (Shapiro, 1988). Moreover, other Western nations are also rising to the occasion. For example, 19 European countries have formed a $5 billion joint research project called EUREKA. One of EUREKA's main projects, the PROMETHEUS project, aims to design smart cars and traffic control systems that automatically detect any risk of collision and that increase communication between drivers (Dickson, 1988). These endeavors, like the Fifth Generation Project, are destined to produce rapid changes in technology and in the global economy. By increasing the intensity and the time scale of research and development activities, they will have a powerful impact on Third World countries that wish to compete in the technology market.

Impact on the Third World

In Bombay, which was once colonial Britain's gateway to India, A. W. Swamy lives in the slum of Dharavi, where over 500,000 people cram into only 80,000 huts. Water shortages plague the slum since there are only 162 public water taps. Sewage is also a problem, and children play beside pools of fetid water and piles of garbage. Earning an above average salary of approximately seventy dollars per month working on tires, Swami bought his family of five a home, a six-by-ten foot hut on the edge of a stinking sewer. There, they will live amidst a sea of squalor, hunger, and illiteracy, with little hope that things will improve. In fact, life may get much worse in the ghetto, as Bombay is expected to swell to thirteen million people and India's population is expected to reach the one billion mark by the year 2000 (Weintraub, 1988).

The Wealth Gap

Swami's lifestyle is not atypical of that of the 3.5 billion inhabitants of the Third World, which includes the less economically advanced nations of Asia, Africa, and Latin America. Although the more than one hundred nations of the Third World are diverse both culturally and economically, they tend to exhibit a common pattern of poverty and of low material standards of living. For example, in developed nations, the average Gross National Product (GNP), expressed per capita, is just over nine thousand dollars per year. But the per capita GNP in the Third World is barely over eight hundred dollars (Sivard, 1987). Even in relatively wealthy countries such as Iran and other oil-rich nations of the Middle East, there remains a tremendous gap between the wealthy few and the masses of the poor.

The crippling poverty that besets much of the Third World exacts high human and social costs. For example, a child born in Nigeria in 1982 could expect to live only forty-nine years, whereas a child born in the U.S. could expect to live nearly seventy-three years. In the poorest countries such as Ethiopia, tens of thousands of people may die annually of starvation, and malnutrition is pervasive. Lack of housing, sanitation, sewage control, and health care also cause widespread problems. For example, there is one physician for approximately 387 people in developed countries, but in the Third World, there is one physician for approximately 2,000 people (Sivard, 1987).

Explosive population growth amplifies most of these problems. From 1972 to 1982, the population of Egypt increased by over 40 percent, and high rates of population growth occur throughout Africa and Latin America. This growth is fostered by the high rates of illiteracy and by the traditional religious and social sanctions against birth control. Because many Third World countries have agricultural economies that place a high premium on human labor, families tend to be large in order to ensure a plentiful supply of labor. This creates a vicious cycle in which poverty fosters population growth, which in turn imposes heavier demands on existing resources, increasing the burden of poverty even further. Attempts to break this cycle through borrowing have only aggravated the problem. For example, Latin American countries now carry the crushing burden of a $400 billion debt (Garcia, 1989).

Viewed against this background of poverty and lack of industrial capacity, computer technology holds the lure of gold for many Third World nations. They sense that this technology is itself a lucrative business item and that it is the key to success in many traditional areas of business and industry. Some countries even hope that, by developing their own information technologies, they will be able to "leapfrog" the industrial revolution through which developed nations passed on their route toward success in the realm of high technology (Rada, 1985).

At the same time, many Third World countries fear the effects of not developing significant computer capabilities. Traditionally, low labor costs have made Third World products economically competitive. But the advent of computers and robotics is eroding the advantage of inexpensive human labor, and this in turn is reducing the competitiveness of Third World countries. For example, the cost of producing electronic devices by hand in Hong Kong, where labor is very cheap, is three times less than it is in the U.S., where labor is relatively expensive. With automatic production, however, it costs approximately the same amount to produce the items in either the U.S. or Hong Kong (Rada, 1985). Further, automated production often tends to reduce the overall production costs, giving the U.S. a particularly strong incentive to automate the manufacture of electronic components. As a result, countries such as Hong Kong believe that they too must automate in order to remain competitive economically.

Third World countries also worry that computer and information technology may increase the gap in wealth and industrial capacity that already exists between wealthy and poor nations. The basis for these concerns is apparent in the growing disparity between developed countries and Third World countries with regard to computer technology.

The Technology Gap

In the past, geographic location and historical circumstance were the dominant determinants of wealth. Increasingly, though, it is technology that determines wealth, and technology is distributed among nations no more equally than physical resources such as oil and iron. In 1980, for example, the U.S., Japan, and Western Europe produced over ninety-five percent of all integrated circuits (Bessant, 1984). Similarly, in 1979, developed nations owned eighty-three percent of the available data processing equipment, and they controlled approximately 90 percent of the world telecommunications market (Rada, 1985).

In addition, a small number of multinational corporations control large portions of the computer market, and these corporations are based in developed countries. For example, IBM, which has its headquarters in the U.S., controlled approximately sixty-five percent of the world computer market in 1978 (Bessant, 1984). Because of the increased importance of information and computers in business and industry, this technology gap between developed and Third World nations may make a bad situation worse.

It is difficult to overcome this technology gap because there are numerous obstacles to technology development in Third World countries. Developing sophisticated computers requires extensive research and development, which in turn requires an ample supply of skilled scientists and engineers, not to mention research funding. But Third World countries face a serious shortage of both skills and research funding. In the mid-1970s, all of the Third World countries combined had less than thirteen percent of the scientists and engineers in the world (Sigurdson, 1983). Being poor, they spend relatively little on research and development, accounting for only three percent of world expenditures in this category (Sigurdson, 1983). Worse yet, these problems interact and amplify each other. Lacking research funding, these countries have difficulty attracting first-rate scientists and engineers, who command high salaries and require the latest, most expensive equipment. In turn, the shortage of first-rate engineers increases the failure rate of research and development projects. This discourages investment, creating a vicious circle.

In addition, very high capital expenditures are required for developing and producing computers. Recently built plants for the production of chips in France and the United Kingdom, for example, cost approximately 100 million dollars (Bessant, 1984). This high price tag stems partly from the high costs of skilled labor and of state-of-the-art equipment. But it also reflects the importance of economies of scale in the technology market. For example, by doubling the number of items produced, manufacturers can slash the costs of producing each item by as much as thirty percent. This factor encourages the construction of large plants, which require capital costs that are too high for many Third World countries. It also contributes to the success of large, multinational corporations which can afford the high capital costs.

Many Third World countries lack the educational and scientific infrastructure needed to develop computer technology. Typically, they do not have many institutions of higher learning, which impedes their ability to produce well trained scientists and engineers in sufficient numbers. Having high rates of illiteracy, they are often forced to use their educational resources to educate the masses rather than to train a handful of scientists and engineers. Moreover, they have a shortage of information resources such as electronic data bases and telecommunications equipment (Rada, 1982), yet these resources are increasingly important in scientific and technological activity. These obstacles lead many countries to consider importing computers rather than making their own.

Technology Transfer

Talk of transferring technology evokes images of one country buying a complete computer system "off-the-shelf" from another country and putting it to use immediately. Usually, though, the situation is far more complex. An Argentine company, for example, that wanted to buy a computer to control the meat packaging process would rapidly discover the need to buy peripheral equipment such as heat sensors and meat cutters in addition to the computer. Peripheral devices are seldom available in a ready-to-use package, and they must be developed through an arduous process of research. Yet they can account for fifty percent or more of the price of the overall system (Bessant, 1983). Furthermore, many business applications of computers require local software modification that increases the overall system cost far above that of the computer alone. Software costs, which include the costs of programming, checking and documentation, often account for up to eighty percent of the cost of the system (Bessant, 1983). These hidden costs make it very difficult for relatively poor countries to import computer technology and to use it effectively.

The shortage of skilled labor also makes it difficult to import computer technology. After a computer system has been purchased and installed, skilled personnel must be available to keep the system running effectively, to modify the system for new applications, and so on. The development of new applications that can meet the emerging needs of the business requires skilled system analysts, programmers, and project managers. Typically, skilled technical personnel are in short supply in most Third World countries.

The effective use of information technology also requires a high level of commitment from management. But many managers in crucial Third World industries such as the garment industry lack expertise in the realm of computers and resist the introduction of the new computer technology (Hoffman and Rush, 1983). These problems of labor and of management provide significant barriers to the transfer and use of computer technology.

Computers and Sovereignty

Wanting to overcome the obstacles described above, governments in the Third World have often invited multinational corporations to set up operations in their countries. Ideally, a multinational computer firm could establish a plant in a developing nation such as India and staff it by bringing in a core of well-trained engineers and managers from other countries and by training new workers from India. In this scenario, the multinational would shoulder the startup costs and provide advanced technology and engineering expertise, taking the burden off of India.

The trouble with this type of arrangement, however, is that it risks both dependency and foreign interference. If, for example, India became highly dependent upon the multinational in the realm of computers, which are essential to Indian business, then India would relinquish control over her economic destiny. Decisions by IBM to withdraw its operations or to increase its prices could have profound effects on India, yet India would have little control over the decisions.

Furthermore, there are often hidden strings attached when a multinational corporation based in the U.S. enters a developing nation. For example, in 1970, the International Telephone and Telegraph Corporation (ITT) had strong economic interests in Chile, a nation in which Salvador Allende, a proponent of democracy, was poised to become President. Knowing that Allende promised to curtail the involvement of U.S. firms in Chile, ITT and other firms contributed large sums of money to Allende's conservative opponent. Prominent U.S. business executives also proposed a covert action to defeat Allende. Meanwhile, President Nixon had ordered the CIA to help organize a military coup to keep Allende out of office. In 1973, a coup occurred, ushering in the military dictatorship of Pinochet. Although Pinochet allowed the free market policies favored by U.S. businessmen, he was a brutal leader who abolished political liberties, executed nearly 30,000 Chileans, and arrested and tortured thousands (Parenti, 1989). Cases such as this make many Third World countries fear that they may lose their sovereignty by bringing in companies from other countries.

Wary of foreign involvement and seeking to control their own destiny, some Third World nations are establishing their own national computer industry, despite the obstacles to doing so. Brazil, for example, has decided to nurture its own computer industry by restricting imports. In 1984, Brazil passed its National Informatics Law, which states that the Brazilian computer market is open to microcomputers, minicomputers, and peripherals made only by companies having a minimum of seventy percent Brazilian ownership. This policy has succeeded in turning over the Brazilian computer market to national companies. Whereas foreign companies controlled the entire Brazilian computer market in 1974, Brazilian companies now control fifty-five percent of the $2.7 billion market. Furthermore, the industry now employs 16,000 people, many of whom hold university degrees, and it produces computer equipment that costs less than its U.S. counterparts (Botelho, 1987). Impressed by this success, other Latin American countries such as Mexico and Argentina plan to follow in Brazil's footsteps.

India is also restricting imports in order to protect its fledgling computer industry. By subjecting computers that cost under $10,000 to heavy import duties, India hopes to increase the chances that its domestically produced microcomputers will be competitive with foreign products. Because India does not plan to compete in the mainframe computer market, she leaves the door open for the import of IBM mainframe computers, which are used in oil and gas exploration. It is in the software industry that India has the highest ambitions. In fact, India plans an annual production of $100 million worth of software. Already, her software exports have risen by forty percent per year (Botelho, 1987). Building an independent computer industry also allows developing nations to decide which technologies and how much of them are appropriate to their own cultures. As seen in the Industrial Revolution, the entry of new technology into a society can disrupt traditional patterns of working and living. So it is with computers. By making deliberate choices about whether and how to use computers, and by controlling their own computer industries, Third World countries put themselves in a position to make key decisions about patterns of employment and production. They also enable themselves to preserve elements of their cultural heritage while advancing technologically and adjusting to the global economy.

Conclusion

The wheels of power in the global economy turn increasingly around computers. Information technology is itself a major source of business worldwide, and spiraling cost reductions, coupled with steady advances in miniaturization, are increasing its applications and appeal. In addition, computers are essential tools for handling the resources of information that grow ever more important in the competitive international arena. Whoever leads the way in information tools and resources gains a strong competitive edge in the global marketplace.

This realization has triggered a technology race pitting the U.S. against Asian countries such as Japan. Following a strategy of coordinating the efforts of government and business, Japan has launched its ambitious Fifth Generation Project, which is intended to create a new generation of intelligent computers. The U.S. and other Western nations have responded with their own cooperative initiatives to develop new computers. Although it is too early to tell whether these efforts will live up to their promise, even partial successes will thrust computer technology to new heights of speed and complexity.

The computer revolution poses difficult dilemmas for the relatively impoverished nations of the Third World. On one hand, they want to acquire computers in order to increase their standard of living and to avoid increasing the technology gap that already exists. On the other hand, they often lack the resources and the scientific infrastructure to develop their own computers, and they are wary of becoming dependent on foreign investors and multinational corporations that are guided by self interest. Yet, with some success, countries such as Brazil are pursuing strategies of developing a national computer industry that does not compete directly with heavyweights such as the U.S. and Japan but that protects national sovereignty.

The connection between computers and sovereignty is not restricted to the economic realm. Because computers have become fundamental tools in the military, they are vital to the protection of national security.

5

National Security

The year is 1997, and a second wave of Islamic fundamentalism has swept through the Middle East and Asia, rekindling ancient conflicts. In June, Iranian fanatics, seeking to purge the area of the Satanic infidel, invaded neighboring Iraq with gunboats and troops. Iraq retaliated using Soviet made smart missiles that were launched from French-built jet fighters and that identified and homed in on Iranian gunboats. At the same time, Israel and Syria were locked in combat again. Using American-made pilotless aircraft, which are controlled remotely by computers, Israel attacked a Syrian airfield in hopes of catching the Syrian fighters on the ground. The Syrians awaited them with a battery of surface-to-air missiles designed to shoot down attacking aircraft. But when the Syrians switched on their radar to attack the Israeli planes, Israeli smart missiles aboard the planes picked up the rays and locked in on them. The computers that guided the Israeli aircraft automatically fired the smart missiles, destroying the Syrian complex and striking a heavy blow for Israel.

As June ended, both the U.S. and the Soviet Union acted to protect their interests. Worried about its precious supply of oil, the U.S. issued a large contingent of aircraft carriers and rapid deployment forces to the

Persian Gulf on the one hand and the Mediterranean Sea on the other. The Soviet Union, fearful that the fundamentalist revolution might spark an uprising among its own Muslim population of 50 million people and wanting to constrain U.S. force in the region, mobilized its troops along its troubled borders with Iran and Afghanistan.

Tensions flared in July as Iranian gunboats shot down two unarmed U.S. reconnaissance planes using smart surface-to-air missiles, leading the U.S. to retaliate by shooting down two Iranian boats and bombing an inland route used to supply other gunboats. Shortly after, Syrian fighters suddenly began blasting Israeli jets out of the sky with surprising frequency, apparently by using smart missiles recently acquired from the Soviet Union. Worried that its mighty airforce was vulnerable and that Syrian victory was imminent, Israel unleashed its long suspected nuclear might, decimating two Syrian airfields and killing tens of thousands of civilians.

Both superpowers had resolved initially to work to limit the conflict and not to use nuclear weapons. But this resolve evaporated in August when Soviet tanks invaded Afghanistan and northern Pakistan, which had previously been the source of aid to the Afghanis during their resistance to the Soviet invasion of the early 1980s. By late August, the U.S. responded to increased Iranian mine attacks on its patrol boats by sending its rapid deployment forces onto Iranian soil. Stating that it would not tolerate U.S. troops in Iran, the Soviet Union dispatched several powerful tank divisions into Iran. Shortly afterward, the computers that are the heart of the U.S. early warning system flashed a gut-wrenching message—the Soviets had launched a major missile attack on the U.S. American officials considered the possibility that it was not a real attack but a false alarm. Not wanting to be caught unprepared, however, they sent U.S. nuclear bombers into the air. When frightened Soviet leaders saw U.S. nuclear bombers going airborne, they too sent their nuclear bombers aloft and prepared their long-range missiles for launch. The world tottered on the brink of World War III.

This hypothetical scenario illustrates several very disturbing things about the international security environment. First, it is a highly militarized environment. In 1986, the Year of Peace, global military expenditures reached $900 billion (Barnaby, 1988). Because of the global arms trade, which does a booming $50 billion dollars of business each year, practically any country can obtain a ready supply of powerful weapons (Barnaby, 1988). The U.S. and the Soviet Union are by far the biggest suppliers, accounting jointly for sixty percent of this global arms trade. Secondly, nuclear weapons have spread to conflict-ridden nations in highly turbulent parts of the world. In 1950, only the U.S. and the Soviet Union had nuclear weapons. Now, Great Britain, China, and France also have substantial nuclear arsenals, and nations such as Israel, India, and South Africa either have nuclear weapons or the capability to assemble them very quickly. And other nations such as Pakistan and Argentina are working to get the bomb.

What is most disturbing about the international environment, however, is that the threat of World War III is very real. Most strategists and policy makers believe that World War III will not begin with a surprise attack, a bolt-from-the-blue by the U.S. on the Soviet Union, or vice versa. Most likely, the next global war will begin through the escalation of a regional conflict that begins in hot spots such as the Middle East (Carnesale et al., 1983). Once the superpowers begin fighting, the chances of escalation are very high, and many authorities believe that escalation to large scale nuclear war is inevitable.

Because of the immense size of global nuclear arsenals, an all out nuclear war would be a catastrophe of such horrifying proportions as to be incomprehensible. Today, a single B-52 bomber carrying nuclear-tipped missiles packs awesome firepower equivalent to all of the explosives used in World War II. Any one of the approximately twenty nuclear submarines that the U.S. keeps on patrol at any moment can wipe out most major cities in the Soviet Union in approximately twenty minutes. Further, global arsenals contain some 55,000 nuclear weapons (Arkin et al., 1988), and the U.S. and Soviet arsenals each have nearly 25,000. If the superpowers unleashed even fifteen to twenty percent of their nuclear arsenals on each other, they would each kill over 100 million people in the other country. Millions of people would die immediately from intense heat, which at the point of detonation reaches the temperature of the sun. Many would die from the immense blast of the bombs, which creates winds of over 200 miles per hour, shatters buildings, and turns fragments of wood and glass into deadly projectiles. Many others would die a slower death from radiation and from the combined effects of burns, wounds, and radiation poisoning. Huge fires and radiation would spread, crippling agriculture and unraveling the very fabric of the ecosystem (London and White, 1984).

Computers play a key role in the military systems that could precipitate a global war. For one thing, computers have ushered in an era of smart weapons and computer guided vehicles—the era of the automated battlefield. These deadly but relatively affordable weapons sharply increase the military firepower and regional capabilities of small countries. Smart weapons also enable the superpowers to launch surgically precise strikes against the military targets of the other side. In addition, computers have become the nervous systems of military operations, monitoring enemy movements, communicating commands to troops, and even making decisions about whether and how to attack.

These and other developments raise profound issues regarding national security and global survival. Will computerized weapons be used for offensive or defensive purposes? Will they make the world a safer or a more dangerous place? To what extent should we rely upon computers for our security? The answers that we give to these questions will help to determine the fate of not only our nation but also our planet.

Computers and Weaponry

In World War II, as in many previous wars, firepower often held the key to victory. Attacking a well-entrenched enemy meant shelling their position relentlessly by aircraft, by ground artillery and perhaps by battleship. After the heavy bombardment had softened up the position, ground troops moved in for the conquest. This approach, however, uses tremendous numbers of bombs and other explosive devices, the vast majority of which never hit their targets. It would be much more effective to use a smaller number of deadly accurate weapons that have a higher success rate or kill probability.

The advent and the miniaturization of computers has spawned a new generation of highly accurate weapons called smart weapons. They use electronic sensors and small microprocessors to detect and to home in on their targets. Their effectiveness became apparent in the U.S. war in Vietnam. For example, in a long effort to destroy the Thanh Hoa Bridge, the U.S. Air Force flew 800 bombing sorties, losing ten planes without destroying the bridge. Using laser guided bombs, four Phantom F-4s destroyed the bridge in a single pass (Chapman, 1987). Because of their pinpoint accuracy and their ability to penetrate defenses successfully, smart weapons have made it possible for relatively small, inexpensive weapons to overcome much larger, more powerful devices.

The spread of smart weapons across the globe has increased the military power of relatively small countries such as Afghanistan. Indeed, the Afghanis' use of smart "Stinger" missiles against Soviet forces in the 1980s played a significant role in thwarting the Soviet invasion. Because of their military effectiveness, smart weapons are used today on land, at sea, and in the air.

Smart Weapons at Sea

In 1982, the United Kingdom and Argentina went to war over control of the Falkland Islands, off the southeastern coast of Argentina. Having a powerful navy and air force, the U.K. was much more powerful than Argentina. Using smart missiles, however, the Argentine Air Force inflicted severe damage on the British fleet.

On May 14, the *HMS Sheffield*, a British destroyer, was patrolling north of the Falkland Islands, an area also being guarded by the Argentine Air Force. An Argentine pilot detected the presence of the *Sheffield* and fed the coordinates into the computer of a French-made Exocet missile, which stands 15.5 feet high and travels at a speed of 500 miles per hour. At a safe distance of over 20 miles, the pilot launched the Exocet, which dove nearly vertically until it came within six or eight feet of the water. Then it flattened out and, guided by its own computer, it sped towards the *Sheffield*. It struck six feet above the waterline, ripping open a gaping hole that left the *Sheffield* crippled and buried under dense smoke.

What is remarkable about this incident is that the *Sheffield* was a 4,000-ton, modern destroyer that cost approximately $50 million a decade before the war. In addition, it carried highly advanced defense systems designed to protect against missile attacks. Nevertheless, it was destroyed by a relatively small missile that cost only $250,000. Using relatively inexpensive smart missiles, then, it is possible to defeat much larger and more powerful, not to mention costly, forces.

The British lost the *Sheffield* to a smart weapon, but they too used smart weapons to advantage in the Falkland Islands conflict. For example, the *Conqueror*, a British nuclear-powered submarine, fired a Tigerfish torpedo on the Argentine cruiser *General Belgrano*. As the Tigerfish sped beneath the water at 60 miles per hour, it spooled out tin wires that allowed it to communicate with the submarine's computer. Tiny electrical impulses sent through the wires guided the Tigerfish silently until impact. A second Tigerfish also hit the *General Belgrano*, opening a hole and shooting a wave of burning oil across her deck. A short time later, the *General Belgrano* lay at the bottom of the sea. The British went on to win the war, which killed some 750 Argentines and 256 British.

This incident, like that involving the *Sheffield*, shows that computerized weapons have changed combat at sea. Although the sheer amount of firepower is still important, the advantage now lies increasingly with the side that marshals a combination of firepower and computerized weapons. Because smart missiles such as the Exocet are both powerful and relatively inexpensive, they are used by many countries. As a result, even small countries have the ability to inflict serious damage upon much larger opponents.

The use of smart weapons, however, does not necessarily mean safer seas. On July 3, 1988, for example, the *SS Vincennes*, which patrolled the explosive Persian Gulf area, detected the approach of a plane the *Vincennes* crew members believed to be a hostile F-14 Tomcat fighter. The crew wanted to avoid a repeat of a 1987 disaster in which the frigate *SS Stark* did not fire on an Iraqi plane, mistakenly launched two missiles which damaged the *Stark* and killed 37 people. The *Vincennes* fired two SM-2 missiles that electronically detected and homed in on the approaching aircraft, blowing it to bits before it had moved close enough to do significant damage. But the aircraft turned out not to be a fighter but a commercial Iran Air Airbus on a regularly scheduled flight. All 290 civilians aboard Iran Air Flight 655 died.

In the aftermath of the tragedy, many eyes turned to the *Vincennes'* Aegis system, a $600 million battle system that combines radar, radio, computer processing, and missile tracking and firing systems. Used on eleven different U.S. cruisers, the Aegis had been hailed as a miracle of modern technology and as a single-vessel shield for an entire fleet. Using sophisticated radars, Aegis can track over 100 aircraft, ships, submarines, torpedoes, and missiles simultaneously. For each type of threat, Aegis computers pick out appropriate weapon and coordinate the firing at multiple targets. But Aegis is designed to operate in the open seas, not in the close quarters of the Persian Gulf. In fact, the Aegis radar cannot distinguish the size and shape of an aircraft reliably, and this contributed to the failure of the crew to distinguish a 62-foot fighter from a 177-foot commercial airliner (Church, 1988).

Subsequent investigations revealed that the Aegis system has not been tested fully. For example, in tests conducted through 1984, the Aegis system hit only seven of twenty-two targets. Yet the U.S. launched the first ship that carried the full system in 1983. Other ships carrying Aegis have also encountered problems. Off the coast of Lebanon, the commander of a U.S. destroyer spotted a small "Cessna type" aircraft approaching, but the Aegis system on a nearby ship repeatedly failed to spot the plane (Hilts and Moore, 1988). Furthermore, it is extremely difficult to test complex systems such as Aegis since combat situations are often laden with ambiguity and surprise. It is relatively easy to program a system to respond correctly to expected events. But even the programmers do not always anticipate the unexpected events, and they therefore cannot program the system to respond in ways that the commanders want.

The tragedy of Flight 655 provides a grim reminder that the high technology that we increasingly rely on for our security carries in itself very serious risks. There is no such thing as a technological fix that guarantees total security.

Cruise Missiles

One of the most devastating of all smart weapons is the cruise missile, a small, light vehicle that can be launched from land, air, or sea. Cruise missiles are powerful weapons in part because of their pinpoint accuracy. For example, the Tomahawk missile developed by the U.S. can fly 1,500 miles and impact consistently within 300 feet of its target, which is sufficiently accurate to destroy even a hardened military target using a nuclear bomb. In an impressive test, a Tomahawk missile was fired from a submarine off the coast of California toward a target in the Nevada desert. It arrived 45 minutes later, splitting a piece of cloth stretched between two poles.

The Tomahawk's accuracy owes to a computerized guidance system called TERCOM, an acronym for Terrain Countour Matching system. TERCOM contains a high-resolution map of enemy terrain made by sophisticated reconnaissance satellites (Range, 1986). As the missile speeds along close to the ground, the computer compares radar readings with its internal map, making necessary flight corrections to keep the missile on target. In addition to being highly accurate, the cruise missile is very difficult to defend against. Because it is small and flies only 30 feet off the ground, following the contour of the terrain with great precision, it is difficult to detect by radar. Thus it is likely to reach its target, delivering a substantial payload of either nuclear or conventional bombs.

Cruise missiles are attractive also because of their small size and low cost. They can be hidden in unlikely places such as shoddy trawlers or trucks that can come very close to enemy borders without evoking suspicion. Because the cruise missile is so concealable and mobile, it cannot be easily targeted and destroyed by the enemy. It is also highly cost-effective since it costs under one million dollars yet can destroy vessels such as large warships that cost over one billion dollars. Because of these many advantages, the U.S. has retrofitted most of its aging B-52 bombers with cruise missiles which can be launched beyond enemy borders.

Unfortunately, the small size and the mobility of the cruise missile impair efforts toward arms control and arms reductions. In order to establish an effective arms control agreement, the parties to the agreement must be able to verify that the other side is not cheating by building additional weapons secretly. For most purposes, we can achieve adequate verification using on-site inspectors, as provided by the 1987 INF Treaty, in which the U.S. and the Soviet Union agreed to destroy all intermediate-range nuclear missiles. Or we can use satellites so powerful that they enable reconnaissance experts to read the license plates of cars and to discern small changes in military and industrial activity. But cruise missiles are so small that they could be produced and transported without being detected by either inspectors or reconnaissance satellites. In fact, it is difficult to imagine any procedure that would provide an exact count of the number of cruise missiles that a potential enemy has. Even a team of one thousand inspectors stationed throughout a country could overlook a hidden underground production facility located in a remote region.

This is a significant problem because arms reduction is an important part of our effort to achieve national security. Previous arms control agreements such as SALT I have helped to limit the production and the deployment of destabilizing weapons that upset the balance of power, that make one country feel unusually threatened, or that increase the chances of a nuclear war which will destroy both superpowers and many other nations as well. Although cruise missiles add to our stockpile of effective weapons, they make it difficult to slow or to halt the dangerous arms race.

The Automated Battlefield

Using blitzkrieg tactics reminiscent of World War II, the commanders sent three tank divisions forward at top speed, hoping to catch the enemy off guard and to acquire new territory. As the tanks moved forward, a swarm of pilotless aircraft appeared suddenly. The tank gunners quickly took aim at the enemy aircraft, but the drones flew a difficult zig-zag pattern and then swooped in close enough to launch their smart warheads. Guided by tiny microprocessors, the warheads struck many of the tanks at exactly their most vulnerable points—the turrets and engine covers—sending red hot pieces of metal ricocheting inside the tank. Most of the tanks were destroyed, but the remaining ones turned to run away. But each retreating tank gave off an 800-degree exhaust, an easy target for the infrared sensitive missiles that appeared next over the horizon. In a matter of moments, the retreating tanks became burning heaps (Barnaby, 1986).

This scenario is futuristic, but the Pentagon is already planning for it. The Defense Advanced Research Project Agency (DARPA), the main sponsor of research for the Department of Defense, unveiled in 1983 a ten-year plan called the Strategic Computing Initiative (Jacky, 1987; Stefik, 1985). This program aims to produce an autonomous land vehicle, a pilot's associate system, and a battle management system. Controlled by computer, the autonomous land vehicle can be used for purposes of reconnaissance and weapons handling and delivery. The pilot's associate, on the other hand, is designed to assist pilots by responding to spoken commands, interpreting radar, and selecting appropriate weapons systems, thereby reducing the severe information overload that besets pilots in combat situations. Rather than typing in a long string of commands, a pilot could, for example, say "Show me all of the Tomahawk-capable cruisers," and the computer would immediately provide the requested information. The battle management system would provide a commander with a comprehensive picture of enemy capabilities, terrain, weather, and available troops. It would also try out various courses of action via simulation and propose actions to the commander.

Advances in computers lie at the heart of these three projects. For example, an effective autonomous land vehicle must be capable of performing nearly 100 billion operations per second, which is one thousand times the speed of current computers (Barnaby, 1986). DARPA plans to achieve this whopping increase by developing parallel processors, much as in Japan's Fifth Generation Project and the U.S. projects that it elicited. Both the pilot's associate and the battle management system require processing speeds of the same magnitude.

Fighting tanks effectively is a high priority in the Pentagon's thinking about the automated battlefield. In Europe, the site of the first two world wars, the Soviet Union and other Warsaw Pact nations have twice as many tanks and armored personnel carriers as the U.S. and its NATO allies. In order to thwart a Soviet ground attack, the Pentagon has developed sophisticated antitank weapons that are guided by computers. The Apache Attack Helicopter, for example, carries up to sixteen Hellfire missiles that can be launched in a salvo. These are "fire-and-forget" missiles that can be launched while out of sight of the attacking tanks. Each missile climbs to a point where it can "see" a laser beam that a ground designator has focused on a tank. Then the missiles swoop down, each following a different laser beam. This system is relatively cheap, since each $40,000 missile can destroy a $3 million tank, and it is rapidly making tanks obsolete (Barnaby, 1986). Also under development is a system called TACIT RAINBOW, an air-launched antiradar missile. TACIT RAINBOW can fly above the enemy for up to an hour, waiting for an enemy radar beam. When it picks up a beam, its computer homes in on the source and swiftly guides the missile to the target (Barry and Morganthau, 1989).

The Pentagon plans to use these advanced technologies to develop a new strategy called the Airland Battle doctrine for fighting war in Europe. This doctrine calls for deep strikes against advancing enemy columns. By attacking the second echelon of follow-on forces, the U.S. hopes to gain the advantage of surprise and to disrupt the flow of supplies to the front line. The Airland Battle doctrine embodies a shift toward offense, taking the battle deep within enemy territory (Barnaby, 1986; Chapman, 1985). In addition to raising the question whether this offensive shift would encourage a U.S.-Soviet battle to escalate, it raises broader issues concerning the role of smart weapons in protecting U.S. security.

Smart Weapons, Deterrence, and Limited War

Deterrence is the main policy guiding U.S. military activity. The basic concept behind deterrence is to prevent or deter war by threatening unacceptable damage to an aggressor. Applied to the nuclear arena, the idea is that by having a large nuclear arsenal, the U.S. deters attack by promising to answer attacks with a devastating retaliatory attack.

Smart weapons enhance deterrence in numerous ways. According to Pentagon officials, they deter Soviet aggression in Europe by neutralizing the Soviet advantages in troops and armored personnel carriers. They also strengthen our defense of Europe by reducing the need for large standing armies there. This is significant because there is a rapidly shrinking number of people who are in the ages at which they are eligible to serve in the U.S. military.

Smart weapons also answer the need for the U.S. to respond to attacks in a flexible manner. If, for example, another country attacked a U.S. patrol boat using conventional (non-nuclear) weapons, it would make no sense for the U.S. to respond with an all out nuclear attack. Following the doctrine called flexible response, the U.S. seeks to tailor its response depending upon the nature of the attack (Freedman, 1981). Using smart weapons, the U.S. can respond effectively to limited attacks without going nuclear.

On the other hand, smart weapons create a host of difficult problems. Because of their proliferation, nations around the world now have more powerful weapons at their disposal, which will undoubtedly increase the destruction wreaked by war. In addition, smart weapons have sparked a new round in arms races worldwide. Opponents such as Iran and Iraq, India and Pakistan, or the U.S. and the Soviet Union struggle to avoid falling behind the other, fearing that inferiority in computerized weapons will weaken them. The acquisition of each new weapon system twists tensions up a notch, as nations see that their adversaries have acquired new tools with which to destroy them.

Furthermore, many smart weapons are highly provocative since they are well suited to offensive use. For example, if Iraq acquires a new smart missile that has a range long enough to allow it to reach the Iranian capital, then the Iranians feel very threatened. Eventually, perceived threat levels could rise so high that the Iranians believe that they must destroy the Iraqi missiles, leading to war. Similarly, the highly accurate U.S. missiles such as the MX and the Trident II submarine-launched missiles have a powerful offensive capability, which threatens the Soviets and encourages them to strengthen their offensive capability. In choosing to buy or to develop smart weapons, nations should think carefully about what kinds of weapons enhance their security. And they should pay close attention to whether they are developing an offensive or a defensive posture.

But the greatest danger posed by smart weapons is the ever-present risk of escalation. There are so many hot spots in the Third World that war can erupt practically anywhere. And once it does, it is all to easy for the superpowers to become involved. If nuclear weapons were the only weapons available to the superpowers, they would be very reluctant to fight each other since no one knows whether a nuclear war can be limited or will inevitably escalate to mutual destruction. But superpower commanders who are reluctant to use nuclear weapons might be very willing to use non-nuclear, smart weapons in hopes of fighting a limited, conventional war.

The trouble is that in the nuclear age, any conflict between the superpowers can escalate into a nuclear war. For example, a commander who sees that his forces will certainly be defeated unless he authorizes the use of a more powerful weapon would be tempted to use tactical nuclear weapons launched by field artillery or delivered by cruise missile. Indeed, nuclear weapons have been integrated extensively with conventional forces, increasing the likelihood that they will be used in an ostensibly conventional war (Bracken, 1983). Once a nuclear weapon has been used in a battle, the chances of nuclear retaliation and escalation are high. Soviet defense analysts, like many of their U.S. counterparts, reject the idea that nuclear war can be limited (Freedman, 1981). It is unrealistic to think that smart weapons will keep us below the nuclear threshold. In the final analysis, it must be people, not smart weapons, that prevent nuclear war.

Command, Control, Communications, and Intelligence

A central component of contemporary warfighting capability is called C^3I (pronounced *"see cubed eye"*), short for command, control, communications, and intelligence (Carter, Steinbruner and Zraket, 1987). To see what this means, consider what the U.S. would need to do to respond effectively to a massive nuclear attack. The first step would be to detect the incoming missiles, assess their probable or actual damage, and communicate this information to the President and the Joint Chiefs of Staff. In order to retaliate, the President would then issue commands to the launch control stations that fire the U.S. nuclear weapons, which are located in ICBM (intercontinental ballistic missile) silos in the Midwest, on submarines patrolling various parts of the world and on bombers stationed in the U.S. and abroad. These commands would trigger battle plans stored on computers. All this would have to occur very rapidly, preferably within the approximately twenty-five minutes that it takes for the intercontinental ballistic missiles to reach their targets. In all of these events, computers play a key role.

Intelligence

Strength alone does not win battles—the successful commander must have effective intelligence operations that indicate how strong the enemy is, where enemy forces are, and when to attack. Intelligence operations today seldom involve the double agents and crafty spies who are featured in movies. In fact, technical devices such as computers, telecommunications, satellites, and various kinds of sensors perform a large number of intelligence operations. It is estimated that the U.S. intelligence network, which includes large organizations such as the CIA (Central Intelligence Agency) and the highly secret NSA (National Security Agency), spend approximately 20 billion dollars annually. Over eighty-five percent of this money is devoted to technical means of collecting and analyzing information (Harwood, 1985).

Through technical intelligence operations, the U.S. government intercepts and analyzes military communications in order to learn about an enemy's deployments of weapons and troops, its military strategy, and its battle tactics. Using a system of computers, satellites, and ground-based listening posts, the NSA can intercept virtually any telephone conversation or any radio or Telex transmission in the world (Harwood, 1985). Because most secret transmissions are coded or encrypted in order to make them unintelligible to outsiders, the NSA uses computers to decipher these secret codes.

At sea, computers are the center of naval operations aimed at locating enemy forces and military targets. For example, the U.S. Navy has established numerous data fusion centers called Fleet Ocean Surveillance Information Centers (Bracken, 1983). These centers receive information from satellites, ships, and aircraft regarding the locations of Soviet naval forces. They analyze the information in order to detect patterns of activity that enable the U.S. to predict the normal locations of Soviet ships and to identify deviations from the customary patterns, which might signal impending military operations.

Computers also allow the Navy to identify the distinctive sound of Soviet submarines, which are noisier than U.S. submarines (Ford, 1985). Thirty-six underwater listening posts feed information to very large computers in Monterey, California, which then determine the locations of Soviet nuclear submarines. Largely because of its computers, the U.S. has more advanced submarine-detection capabilities than the Soviet Union. This is widely regarded as a significant advantage for the U.S. since it is relatively easy to attack nuclear submarines effectively after locating them.

Effective intelligence entails knowing about the extent of the damage inflicted and suffered in a war. In a nuclear war, for example, the President and other military leaders will need damage-assessment information in order to decide how to respond to an attack and to select targets that have not been destroyed already. Accordingly, the U.S. government has begun construction of a new damage-assessment system called the Integrated Nuclear Detonation Detection System (Bracken, 1983). It detects the flash of nuclear explosions using sensors mounted on satellites located in deep space where they cannot be destroyed quickly by antisatellite weapons. The satellites transmit the information to computers that integrate the information and provide a report of what has happened to both the U.S. and the Soviet Union.

Computerized intelligence systems are used not only for combat-related purposes but also for purposes of arms control and arms reduction. In particular, computers play an important role in the verification processes used to ensure that the parties to an agreement are not cheating. For example, the U.S. and the Soviet Union have agreed not to test nuclear weapons having a yield greater than 150 kilotons, the explosive equivalent of 150,000 tons of TNT. In order to verify that the Soviets have not violated this treaty, the U.S. collects vast amounts of data from seismic sensors and then analyzes it by computer. For example, a team of U.S. computer scientists has recently begun using expert systems to analyze data collected from a bank of seismic sensors in Norway, which is close enough to the Soviet Union to accurately register underground nuclear tests (Mason, 1988).

In a similar project, the Natural Resources Defense Council, working with scientists from many countries, has placed a ring of seismic sensors around the areas where the Soviets conduct their underground nuclear tests, allowing detection of explosions as small as one kiloton. This highly effective verification opens the door for further negotiations to ban nuclear testing, and it exemplifies the manner in which computerized intelligence systems can be used for peaceful purposes.

Problems With Intelligence

The use of computers, however, does not guarantee the accuracy of intelligence information. The intelligence derived from computers is only as good as the data that are fed into the machines and as good as the programs used to analyze the data. In Vietnam, for example, the U.S. relied on computers to identify targets for bombing. The U.S. Air Force dropped hundreds of thousands of sensors on the Ho Chi Minh trail that detected sound, body heat, motion, and even the ammonia from human urine. Data from the sensors was transmitted to computers that created computerized maps of the region, selected targets for bombing, and directed strike aircraft to the targets. Both the sensors and the computers, however, were unreliable and led to many unnecessary and ineffective bombing raids. On numerous occasions, the Air Force bombed peasant convoys, empty jungle, and even herds of animals. The end result was that the U.S. dropped three times the bomb tonnage on Southeast Asia than was used in all of World War II (Chapman, 1987).

Computerized intelligence systems sometimes contribute to intelligence failures by creating a glut of information. Because they make it very easy to collect and store vast amounts of information, they tempt the intelligence community to collect much more information than can be analyzed effectively. The result is an increase in the quantity of information and at the expense of the quality of information. Yet it is the quality of information that makes for effective intelligence. For example, the discovery of a Soviet brigade in Cuba in 1980 aroused much public attention and also raised the question of why it had not been discovered earlier. It turned out that information on the brigade had been available for years but had been overlooked due to the lack of quality analysis (Harwood, 1985). Ironically, the collection of more and more information can lead to less intelligence.

In fact, the existence of an intelligence information glut has been recognized for years. In 1966, a study by the inspector general of the CIA concluded that the CIA does not collect enough of the right kinds of information and that the quantity of information is degrading the quality of information. The report also pointed out that technological advances in the collection of information can do more harm than good in the absence of high standards guiding the storage and retrieval of information (Bracken, 1983). It is unfortunate that by the mid-1970s, over seventy percent of the intelligence budget was spent on the collection of information, whereas only nine percent was spent on analysis (Harwood, 1985). This problem continues today because of the increasing capacity of technical systems for collecting and storing information.

Another intelligence problem is that it is difficult to safeguard computers from counter-intelligence operations. As computers operate, they produce radio waves that could be detected by foreign intelligence agents using highly sophisticated equipment (Schrage, 1985). By listening to what is happening inside government computers, foreign agents would obtain information that they could use to threaten our national security. In order to overcome this problem, the government has created a special security program called Tempest, which aims to prevent radio-frequency emission from traveling beyond computers by encasing them in copper sheaths and by developing software that masks the operations of an intelligence program (Schrage, 1985). The fact that the government is spending one billion dollars a year on Tempest indicates just how important computers are to our intelligence operations.

Early Warning

In the nuclear age, early warning of an actual attack is crucial, for it takes only 10 or so minutes for SLBMs to reach their targets, and it takes approximately 25 minutes for ICBMs to reach theirs. The U.S. has constructed an elaborate network for the rapid detection of an enemy attack and for the rapid issue of commands for counterattack. Computers are the nervous system that connects and coordinates the various elements of this network.

The heart of the network is NORAD, the North American Air Defense Command, which is buried in concrete-hardened structures deep within Cheyenne Mountain outside Colorado Springs. NORAD receives a continuous stream of information from many early warning radar systems from various stations in such locations as North Dakota and the Arctic perimeter. At NORAD, computers integrate and analyze the incoming information to determine whether an attack is about to be made or is actually under way. Depending upon the information received, the commander at NORAD can increase the level of alert through several steps and he can also put the station on full alert. As the level of alert increases, various forces are mobilized. If there were a relatively high level of alert, for example, the bombers controlled by the Strategic Air Command (SAC) would take off, preventing their destruction on the ground.

On full alert, the President rushes from the White House to a specially-equipped Boeing 747 called the National Emergency Airborne Command Post, also called the NEACP or "Kneecap." Because of the short response time available while under a nuclear attack, various attack plans have been prearranged and stored on the computers at NORAD, allowing the President to simply select a particular plan, which is then executed mostly by computer. The U.S. plan, then, is to rely upon an airborne command post and communications and computer technology in responding to a nuclear attack.

But this early warning system does not always work as intended. For example, on June 3, 1980, the computer display at the SAC base near Omaha indicated that SLBMs had been launched at the U.S. Shortly after, the National Military Command Center in the Pentagon also indicated an SLBM attack. SAC ordered its bomber crews to board their B-52s and start their engines, and ICBM crews were put on a higher level of alert. Fortunately, the attack turned out to be false alarm caused by the failure of a 74175 integrated circuit chip in a Data General computer (Borning, 1987). The chip cost approximately 46 cents. Similarly, in the 1950s and 1960s, the early warning system mistakenly interpreted innocuous events such as the passage of a flock of Canada geese and meteor showers as

Soviet attacks (Bracken, 1983). Between 1979 and 1981, there were over one hundred false alarms issued by the early warning system.

These episodes have received extensive attention in the press and in films such as *War Games*, perhaps inflating the public perception of the risks of accidental nuclear war. In fact, however, it is highly unlikely that an isolated technical problem could cause a war (Carter, 1987). Each warning must be confirmed by numerous stations, and an error made by one part of the warning system may be detected by another part. Further, elaborate procedures exist for the authentication of orders and for the authorization to launch nuclear weapons. Ideally, the President must authorize the use of nuclear weapons, and he is never very far from the Black Bag, a locked briefcase containing the codes that must be used to authorize the use of nuclear forces. In addition, the launching of ICBMs requires the coordinated actions of two people who must simultaneously insert a special key and enter a series of secret codes into separate stations located too far apart to be operated by one person.

This does not mean, however, that the risks of accidental nuclear war are negligible. When a false alarm occurs in isolation, it is relatively easy to detect and to negate. But matters may be quite different when a false alarm occurs in the middle of a political crisis that has already put forces in a state of alert. For example, in 1961, the U.S. detected the construction of Soviet missile bases on Cuba, precipitating the Cuban missile crisis. During this crisis, the U.S. blocked the passage of Soviet ships and demanded the immediate removal of the missiles. Many leaders agree that this highly charged confrontation could have resulted in a nuclear war. It is sobering to think what might have happened if, at the peak of the tension, the NORAD computers had issued a warning that the U.S. was under attack by Soviet ICBMs. In such an extreme crisis, false alarms might be misinterpreted, and there might not be enough time to detect and to correct the error.

This problem is amplified by the tight coupling of both U.S. and Soviet forces with warning systems that has occurred since World War II (Bracken, 1983). For example, an early warning leads the U.S. commanders to launch aircraft in order to avoid destruction on the ground. But the Soviets could interpret the takeoff of U.S. bombers as a signal of an impending invasion, causing them to increase the level of alert of their forces. This in turn could fuel the U.S. response even further, generating an upward spiral of alerts on both sides that make for a hair-trigger situation.

Command and Control

The establishment of an effective command and control system is an important part of deterrence since an enemy would be less willing to attack if he were certain that the victim would successfully detect the attack and command the release of strong retaliatory forces.

The performance of the U.S. system has been impressive overall, but it is far from perfect. In the 1967 Middle East war, six urgent messages to move away from the battle area were sent to the *USS Liberty*, which was operating in the eastern Mediterranean. Yet two messages went to the Philippines, another went to Greece, and still another went to Germany. The *Liberty* never received the message, probably because of the unavailability of a top-secret communications channel for transmitting such an important message (Bracken, 1983).

It is sobering to think that this type of communication failure played an important role in the initiation of World War I (Tuchman, 1962). On August 3, 1914, Kaiser Wilhelm II and his advisors awaited a response to the ultimatum that had been issued to Britain and France. Plans had already been made to have the 16th Division invade Luxembourg at 7:00 P.M. if no response had been received. At the last moment, the German Chancellor insisted that Luxembourg must not be invaded, whereupon the Kaiser ordered his aide to telephone and telegraph the 16th Division to cancel the invasion. Had it gotten through on time, this order would have stopped the opening move of the war. Yet the order was not received until 7:30, leading to four years of horrible fighting in a war that is widely regarded as pointless.

Over the last twenty years, the Pentagon has worked to establish a World Wide Military Command and Control System (WWMCCS) that would allow computers at various major command posts to exchange information directly. In 1977, however, the Pentagon tested the effectiveness of the system, and the results were disturbing. There were 54 failures in 124 attempts to transmit messages from the U.S. European Command, and there were 132 failures in 300 attempts to transmit or to receive data from the Atlantic Command (Ford, 1985). The high incidence of failures is unsurprising in light of the complexity of the system, which is governed by a program said to be 17 million lines long. These disappointing results serve as a poignant reminder that it is unwise to attribute a high degree of credibility to a computer system just because of its complexity and sophistication.

In order to be effective in a war, the C^3I system must be survivable. The ability of the system to survive a nuclear attack has increased in importance since defense analysts and policy makers in the 1980s have talked seriously about fighting a limited or a prolonged nuclear war. Fighting a limited nuclear war would require a continuous stream of information about the amount of damage that had been inflicted and sustained, about which forces remain to be used, and so on. In the absence of this information, particularly in a state of total communications darkness, it would be extraordinarily difficult for commanders to assume that the enemy was limiting its use of nuclear weapons, producing an irresistible pressure for escalation.

Whether the U.S. C^3I system could survive a nuclear strike is uncertain, owing in part to the fact that nuclear detonations produce a damaging electromagnetic pulse or EMP. In 1962, the U.S. performed an atmospheric nuclear test by detonating a bomb 248 miles above Johnston Atoll in the Pacific. The flash was visible 800 miles away in Hawaii, and it was followed about a second later by multiple power failures, ringing burglar alarms, and dead street lamps (Broad, 1983). Scientists determined that the cause of these problems was an EMP produced by the nuclear blast. The blast knocks electrons out of air molecules in the upper atmosphere, and the electrons are deflected downward by the Earth's magnetic field, transmitting an invisible burst of EMP energy in 10 to 20 billionths of a second.

The EMP created by nuclear blasts is believed to be so intense that a single Soviet warhead detonated 200 miles above Nebraska would enshroud the entire nation with an EMP on the order of 50,000 volts per meter. This EMP would not harm most people, but it would destroy unprotected computer circuits and other electromagnetic devices such as automobile starters. The result could be a massive power failure and communications darkness in which it would be impossible for citizens to communicate by telephone, radio or television. Just how extensive the damage would be is uncertain since the atmospheric detonations that produce the largest EMPs were banned by the 1963 Limited Test-Ban Treaty before extensive research had been conducted.

The power of the EMP makes it an ideal first-strike weapon. By detonating several large nuclear warheads at high altitude, an enemy could begin a nuclear war by disabling the C^3I system of the victim. This warfighting strategy, called a decapitation strategy, aims to eliminate the command capabilities—the head—of the opponent. Having knocked out the opponent's ability to retaliate and to communicate with their forces, the attackers would have a powerful advantage. Thus vulnerability to a decapitation strike poses a serious threat to national security. Further, C^3I vulnerability invites attack and is destabilizing since it gives the enemy the opportunity to fight and to win a nuclear war without suffering the consequences of retaliation.

Some defense analysts believe that the C^3I system of the U.S. is excessively vulnerable to the effects of the EMP. For example, the system relies heavily on the use of common carrier lines supplied by AT&T, which are vulnerable to EMP (Bracken, 1983). In addition, few of the airborne command posts that would be used in a nuclear war are sufficiently hardened to withstand a very large EMP (Broad, 1983). Even satellites in deep space are vulnerable, for radiation from nuclear blasts in space causes a damaging surge that resembles a terrestrial EMP (Broad, 1983).

The system is also vulnerable because it consists of a relatively small number of command and communication centers that an enemy might be able to destroy quickly using a small number of weapons. A detailed study in 1981 revealed that fewer than 50 Soviet nuclear weapons could disable the entire system (Ford, 1985). Other experts believe that the system would survive but would be disrupted (Carter, 1987). Even a disruption would be very dangerous since it would delay a U.S. retaliatory strike, giving an attacker added time to launch a second strike or to prepare itself better for the retaliatory strike from the U.S.

Recently, the U.S. has made the protection of the C^3I system a high strategic priority. Government officials plan to protect the system from EMP by encasing the computers in screened steel shelters or by placing them deep underground. They also plan to replace metal communication cables with fiber-optics transmissions lines that are resistant to EMP effects. The Air Force will build a backup ground system (called the Ground Wave Emergency Network or GWEN) for communicating with SAC missile and bomber bases. This system will transmit very low frequency signals that are difficult to jam and that are less disrupted by nuclear blasts than are standard radio signals. The Pentagon also plans to use the space shuttle to deploy in the latter 1980s a network of military satellites for purposes of global communications and missile guidance. Called the Military Strategic, Tactical and Relay (MILSTAR) network, the system will consist of satellites having sensors and small motors that enable them to detect antisatellite weapons and to take evasive action (Blair, 1985).

Even these improvements, however, cannot ensure that the system will perform as intended under attack. Since no one has ever made a nuclear attack on the U.S., the system remains untested in important respects. The system has been tested repeatedly via simulation, but there will always remain an uncomfortably large gap between simulation and reality. Furthermore, military technology is developing rapidly. For virtually every new measure that one country develops, skilled opponents will develop a countermeasure. Because intelligence information is imperfect, it is always difficult to know for sure exactly which countermeasures U.S. opponents actually have and how they will use them. Despite all their precision, computers will not take uncertainty out of war.

Strategic Defense Initiative

In the 1980s, the doctrine of deterrence came under fire from policy makers, including President Reagan, and citizens alike (Caldicott, 1984; Schell, 1982). Critics argued that although deterrence has succeeded since World War II in preventing another global war, it has also left the world hip-deep in weapons of mass destruction, as global arsenals now contain the equivalent of over six thousand pounds of explosives for every person on earth. It is extremely unlikely that any human strategy, deterrence included, is entirely perfect. If deterrence fails even once, the result would be an unparalleled catastrophe that would kill millions of citizens and unhinge entire societies. Living under a nuclear sword of Damocles, people in many nations have experienced psychological problems ranging from anxiety to resignation and chronic denial (Greenwald and Zeitlin, 1987; Lifton and Falk, 1982; Mack and Snow, 1985).

Having a powerful faith in technology, Americans often turn to technology to solve their most difficult problems. This is exactly what President Reagan did when he proposed a radical alternative to deterrence in his nationally televised speech on March 23, 1983. Praising U.S. accomplishments in science and technology, he called upon technologists to develop a shield in space against attacking nuclear missiles, thereby rendering nuclear missiles "impotent and obsolete." He called his new approach the Strategic Defense Initiative (SDI), but, because of the futuristic space weapons it proposed, it also became known as the "Star Wars" defense.

Reagan's proposal calls for the development of the most sophisticated computer software ever designed. This software would be the brain that guides and coordinates an immensely complex battle management system. Reagan's proposal brings to a head a question that cropped up repeatedly in the discussions of the Aegis and the Airland Battle systems—how reliable will complex battle management software be? Because this issue is vital to our survival in the nuclear age, we shall examine it in detail in the context of the SDI proposal.

A Layered Ballistic Missile Defense System

Attacking ballistic missiles such as Soviet ICBMs travel through four flight phases in route to their targets. A fully developed SDI system would have four layers, enabling it to attack enemy missiles in each of their four flight phases. The rationale for having a four-tiered system is that a large Soviet attack would involve thousands of ICBMs and SLBMs. It might be impossible to destroy so many missiles using a single-tiered system, but in a four-tiered system, missiles that leak through the first tier will still be attacked by the second tier, and so on. Even if each layer were only 70 percent effective, the overall effectiveness of the system might exceed 90 percent (Fletcher, 1984).

The first phase of ICBM flight, which lasts for approximately seven minutes, is called the boost phase since the missile is lifted out of its silo and through and out of the atmosphere. There are substantial advantages to attacking enemy rockets during the boost phase (Fletcher, 1984). For three minutes, each missile has a burning rocket, which produces a plume that space satellites equipped with sensors can easily detect. During the boost phase, the missiles have not yet released their multiple warheads, so the number of targets is much smaller. Nor have they released the large numbers of decoys that they may use in later stages in order to fool the defense.

During the boost phase, the SDI system would fire space-based lasers, highly concentrated beams of energy, at individual enemy missiles, penetrating their hulls and rendering them ineffective (Graham, 1983). As shown in Figure 5.1, ground-based laser weapons would also be used by generating the beam on the ground and aiming it at a laser mirror in space, which in turn focuses the beam on enemy missiles. These laser weapons require vast amounts of energy, which could be generated by controlled, nondestructive nuclear detonations. In addition to laser weapons, the system would use space platforms that fire hypervelocity guns at the missiles. These high powered guns would fire smart bullets that home in on enemy missiles and that can destroy a target on impact (Fletcher, 1984).

Following the boost phase, the ICBM enters the post-boost phase, during which it releases its multiple warheads (multiple independently targetable reentry vehicles or MIRVs), directing them toward different targets. It might also release large numbers of decoys, making it more difficult to shoot down the real missiles. The SDI system would attack these targets using a second layer of lasers and hypervelocity weapons. Yet another layer of lasers and hypervelocity weapons would attack the missiles during the midcourse phase of flight, which offers the advantage of a relatively long engagement time of twenty minutes. The disadvantage, however, is that the defense must discriminate the warheads from as many as hundreds of thousands of decoys (Fletcher, 1984). During the final phase, at which the warheads are only two minutes away from their targets, the SDI system would fire ground-based interceptor rockets that destroy missiles on impact.

This full scale SDI system would be fantastically expensive—over one trillion dollars. This exorbitant cost, coupled with doubts about the feasibility of developing all of the powerful lasers and hypervelocity guns, has led the Pentagon to consider a limited SDI system that could be deployed as early as the mid-1990s (Bunn, 1988; Smith, 1988). Because the SDI program is currently a research program, it is impossible to predict exactly what form the proposed system would eventually take. Whatever its form, however, it will require complex battle management software to guide it.

Battle Management Software

An SDI system would have to be run by computers since the events in a nuclear attack unfold very quickly and since the missiles that the system is intended to destroy will be travelling at a blinding speed of over 10,000 miles per hour. Using the input from sensors mounted on space satellites, the computer would detect enemy missile launches, discriminate between decoys and actual missiles, target and fire at enemy missiles, and keep track of which ones had been destroyed. The system would probably include a local computer in each layer to instruct the weapons of that layer to attack particular targets. Each local computer will relay information to a central battle management computer about which targets still need to be attacked.

This battle management system would have to be extremely fast, and it would need extensive artificial intelligence capabilities (Ornstein, Smith, and Suchman, 1984). During an attack, for example, it would have to detect the attack immediately, sort out the decoys, and identify and target enemy missiles.

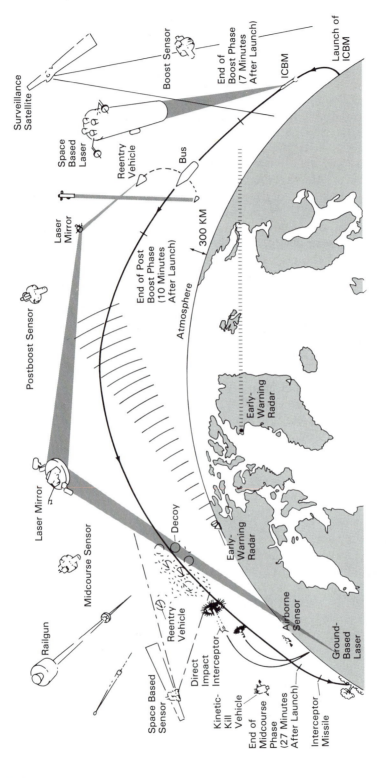

Figure 5.1. A four-tiered defensive system would, under the SDI proposal, defend against ballistic missile attacks. From "The Development of Software for Ballistic Missile Defense," by H. Lin. Copyright © 1985 by SCIENTIFIC AMERICAN, Inc. All rights reserved.

118

Ideally, it would identify the position and the velocity of each missile, determine its future trajectory and command a particular weapon to fire at it. And it would have to do this for thousands of missiles in a very short period of time.

The battle management software would be immensely complex. It would probably consist of at least 10 million lines of code, although estimates range as high as 100 million lines of code (Roberts and Berlin, 1987). This is much longer than the highly sophisticated programs used for projects such as the space shuttle, which has an in-flight control program approximately 100,000 lines long. To produce a program of the magnitude required in an SDI system would probably require 3,000 programmers and analysts working for ten years (Lin, 1985). Further, the system will probably require fifth generation architectures that allow parallel processing (Jacky, 1985).

The SDI proposal calls for nothing less than a quantum leap in computer technology and in weapons systems. Extensive research is needed to determine whether the system could be developed, and $4.1 billion dollars have been allocated for research in 1988. The entire proposal, however, assumes that it is possible to produce reliable battle management software. Among computer scientists, there is growing doubt that this is possible.

Debugging and Fault Tolerance

Anyone who has written even simple computer programs knows that errors often turn up unexpectedly. The process of correcting these errors is called debugging, and it involves testing the program repeatedly and making the necessary modifications.

Attempts to debug the proposed battle management system would encounter serious problems. For one thing, programs that are millions of lines long are the product of tens of thousands of hours of labor, and they evolve over time as errors are discovered and remedied. As a result, no single person or team of programmers comprehends the entire program (Borning, 1987; Weizenbaum, 1976). Debugging this type of program is unlike the task of debugging a small program that can be comprehended in its entirety by a single person (Parnas, 1985). What typically happens is that a team of programmers, having discovered an error, makes a change that seems to remedy the problem. But the changes made in fixing one problem often introduce other problems, which may ripple throughout the program. Some of the created problems may be more serious than the original one, and they may be harder to locate and to remedy (Lin, 1985).

For this reason, computer scientists agree that it is unrealistic to expect very large programs to be purged completely of errors (Ornstein, 1987; Parnas, 1985). Instead, they attempt to keep errors at a low but tolerable level and to build in safeguards that will prevent devastating errors from occurring. The best way of determining whether a program has in fact achieved a particular level of fault tolerance is to test it repeatedly, preferably under the circumstances in which it will actually be used.

The trouble is that the SDI system cannot be tested under fully operational conditions. It would be impossible to stage a test of an all out nuclear attack on the U.S. And the stakes are too high to permit an actual attack to be the first operational test. Simulation testing helps to ensure that software works as it was intended to. But simulated environments never match the real environment exactly. No matter how well the system performs in a simulation, serious questions remain as to how well it will perform in actual combat with the element of surprise added (Lin, 1985).

The severity of this problem is increased by the fact that some errors turn up in programs that have been used successfully in the field for an extended period of time. For example, the complex program that guides the space shuttle had performed well in numerous flights prior to the end of 1985, so it seemed to have passed the requirement of operational testing. Yet a shuttle launch in December of that year had to be postponed at the last minute because of software problems. Even minor errors can have devastating consequences. In fact, the U.S. lost control over its Mariner space probe because of a minor but undetected software error—a period that should have been a comma (Ornstein, 1987). One wonders how many errors might turn up at a fatal moment in the SDI battle management program. If even a single error allowed several missiles to pass through unscathed, millions of people could be killed. Errors in the SDI system could also provoke war. If, for example, an error led the U.S. system to begin shooting at Soviet satellites, this act would almost certainly be taken as an act of war that demanded retaliation.

Specifications and Surprises

Computers are literal-minded machines, and many a programmer has been frustrated by the fact that computers do exactly what they have been told to do rather than what the programmer had wanted it to do. Even when a programmer has eliminated all errors of syntax and logic in a program, it may still fail to work as intended. In fact, the most difficult errors to spot and to correct often occur in the initial stage of designing software, the stage of specifying exactly what the program must be able to do.

To illustrate the difficulty of making adequate specifications, consider the task of designing a program that enables a hypothetical robot to perform an utterly ordinary task such as hailing a cab on a city street. Initially, the specifications appear simple since all one has to do to hail a cab is to move to the edge of the sidewalk, raise one's hand, and wait for a cab to pull over. But things start getting complex quickly from there. It would be inappropriate for the robot to walk into people on the way to the corner, so it must be programmed to recognize and to avoid bumping into people. If it is raining and the robot is susceptible to rust, it will need to use an umbrella. If other people are also hailing a cab, it will need to queue up or to develop a strategy for getting a cab. If the streets are empty, it will need to try another method of getting a cab, and so on. The point is that there are countless contingencies that could arise in performing an everyday task, and it is vexingly difficult to foresee all of them. This makes it correspondingly difficult to identify all of the specifications required for an effective program.

The problem of inadequate specifications has reared its ugly head repeatedly in military affairs. An embarrassing example is the previously mentioned sinking of the *Sheffield* by an Exocet missile in the Falklands war (Jacky, 1985). The detection equipment on board the *Sheffield* picked up the approaching Exocet missile. But the defensive computer program, failing to recognize the Exocet missile as hostile, took no defensive action. The problem was that the programmers had expected to fight against Soviet weapons, not against the Exocet, which is French made. Specification errors have also been the source of problems in the U.S. early warning system. As mentioned earlier, what the NORAD computer once responded to as a major missile attack turned out to be the rising moon. Who could have foreseen that the system would respond to its own radar signals bouncing off a heavenly body?

With regard to the SDI, the problem is that it is virtually impossible to predict what will happen in a nuclear war. No one can claim to know exactly what will happen since there has never been a nuclear war. It is extremely difficult to predict the numbers and kinds of decoys that the Soviets might use in a large-scale attack. It is equally difficult to predict what other countermeasures they might use to thwart the SDI system (Ornstein et al., 1984; Parnas, 1985). Consequently, it will be extremely difficult to program the battle management system to respond effectively to all of the possible contingencies that it might have to respond to, and the reliability of the system will remain uncertain.

Furthermore, this problem is not entirely technical in nature. Computer scientists have developed sophisticated methods for making sure that programs meet the stated specifications. But there are no algorithms or proven methods for making sure that the specifications themselves are correct (Borning, 1987; Ornstein, 1987). In writing specifications, we shall have to rely on two distinctly human and fallible qualities—human judgment and experience.

In light of this fact, it is ironic that an SDI system would leave little room for immediate human judgment. If a reliable SDI system were constructed, it would probably have to operate automatically because of the very rapid response times required for an effective defense. This means that computers would make the key decisions without direct human intervention (Jacky, 1987; Ornstein, 1987). This is a radical change since, throughout the nuclear age, humans have remained in the decision loop which could unleash nuclear weapons.

Advocates of SDI might argue that computers make better decisions in crises than people do and that humans really make the decisions anyway since it is people who program the computers. This view, however, overlooks the unpredictability of nuclear war and the possibility that the preprogrammed decisions that we make now might not be the ones that we would want to make in the heat of an actual nuclear crisis. In an extreme crisis, the human feelings and intuitions of the moment, which cannot be programmed into computers, might be all that could prevent an all-out nuclear war.

The Limits of SDI

These problems of software reliability are crucial, but there are many other problems that deserve mention here. The main one is that an SDI system would not live up to its promise of providing a peace shield. Even if the system were ninety-nine percent effective, eighty or so warheads would penetrate through, causing one of the greatest disasters of all time (Drell and Panofsky, 1985). No one now expects the system to be ninety-nine percent effective, as most current estimates range from thirty to seventy percent. In addition, the SDI would not defend against low-flying cruise missiles, and other nonballistic weapons, of which there are thousands. Stated bluntly, the SDI system would not render nuclear weapons impotent and obsolete, but it would cost over one trillion dollars. Further, the vision of an SDI system has been watered down significantly because of technological and budgetary obstacles encountered since 1983. Pentagon officials now envision a limited system of interceptor rockets that, at best, would destroy only 1,500 of 5,000 incoming missiles. Yet even this limited system, which would be designed to protect missile fields instead of people, would cost approximately $150 billion per year (Smith, 1988).

To implement an SDI system would be destabilizing since it would give the U.S. something that the Soviet Union did not have. Deploying the system would also trigger a new round in the arms race, extending it into space (Drell et al., 1984). For example, the Soviets might develop countermeasures such as fast-burn rockets that reduce the time in the boost phase during which the defense would be able to take aim at the attacking missiles. Or they could develop anti-satellite weapons that could knock out the U.S. sensors and communications satellites. Indeed, these countermeasures would cost the Soviets much less than it will cost the U.S. to build an SDI system.

The SDI system would also deliver a heavy blow to arms control by violating three important arms control treaties, for example, the 1972 ABM Treaty (Drell et al., 1984). The ABM Treaty allows the defense of one site, such as a national capital or a missile field, but it prohibits regional or national defense, which is exactly what the SDI proposes. In addition to damaging U.S.-Soviet relations, a treaty violation would lead many countries to question the credibility of U.S. agreements. It would also call into question the U.S. commitment to world peace, since in the current Gorbachev era of troop cutbacks and arms reductions proposals, there is a rare window of opportunity for making significant new treaties.

But the greatest limit of the SDI proposal is that it attempts to provide a technological solution to a political problem. New technology alone will not overcome tensions between nations that are locked in conflict. It is these tensions, which stem from economic rivalry, clashing ideologies, and historical events, that fuel arms races and provoke war. In the final analysis, it is people who decide to build nuclear weapons, and only people can decide to decrease the chances that they will be unleashed.

Conclusion

The accuracy of weapons has taken a quantum leap because of tiny computerized guidance systems that have ushered in an era of smart weapons. Smart weapons provide a highly cost effective means of destroying much more powerful weapons such as tanks and battle cruisers. Weapons such as smart missiles can be fired at a distance, thwarting attacks before they penetrate deeply into one's homeland. These weapons, however, also have offensive uses, allowing nations to launch attacks with surgical precision. The possession of a large arsenal of smart weapons can be highly threatening to other countries, and the acquisition of smart weapons by one country often triggers a risky arms race with its rivals. Perhaps the greatest risk is that commanders who have smart weapons will be more willing to fight what is intended to be a conventional, non-nuclear war but which escalates into a nuclear catastrophe. In order to protect security, nations must think carefully about the possible consequences of acquiring and using various kinds of smart weapons and of maintaining an offensive or defensive military posture.

Automated battle management systems are also revolutionizing military activities. On the contemporary battlefield, events unfold too quickly and too many things happen simultaneously to allow effective management by unaided humans. Accordingly, the U.S. military increasingly uses computers to manage combat by land, sea, and air. President Reagan's proposal to build a space-based defense against ballistic missiles calls for a highly sophisticated computerized battle management system. But the feasibility of developing such a system is questionable since it is impossible to iron all of the bugs out of battle management programs, which can be millions of lines long. Undetected errors can lead to tragedies such as the destruction of Iran Air Flight 655. Developing reliable battle management software is not entirely a technical matter. Many of the most significant program errors arise from failures of the program designers to foresee everything that could happen in combat, which by its very nature is full of uncertainty.

The ancient Greeks pointed out that humans suffer from excessive pride or hubris. This point remains valid today, only now we are particularly prone to technological hubris, which leads us to believe that we can create error-free technology to solve all of our problems. But even relatively well tested technology remains error prone. In January, 1986, the Space Shuttle *Challenger* exploded shortly after launch, killing all of the astronauts on board and providing a grim reminder that errors can arise all too easily in technology that is generally considered safe. In order to ensure our survival in the nuclear age, we must avoid the trap of technological hubris. This same trap must also be avoided in dealing with problems of computer crime and security, the subject of the following chapter.

6

Crime and Security

Business hummed along as usual on Arpanet, a busy network which connects 60,000 computers and which provides the primary communications channel for scientists working on unclassified military research projects nationwide. Suddenly, in November, 1988, some 6,000 computers in the network jammed mysteriously, causing massive shutdowns and launching computer security teams into action.

The cause of the shutdown was a computer virus that had been injected into the network by Robert Morris, a 23-year-old graduate student at Cornell University. A computer virus is a program that propagates itself from computer to computer via disks or networks and that can, depending upon its design, either reside quietly in computer memories or destroy precious information and files. Morris had apparently intended his computer virus to disguise itself as an ordinary piece of electronic mail and to copy itself slowly and harmlessly throughout Arpanet. But a design error caused it to replicate wildly out of control, capturing much of the computers' processing resources and grinding the computers to a halt (Elmer-DeWitt, 1988).

Morris' virus caused extensive damage in the form of lost time for both computers and security personnel. But this virus had been relatively friendly. What security analysts fear more is that malicious pranksters or high-tech terrorists will infect computer disks and networks with hostile viruses that will garble or destroy files. It is sobering to ponder what could happen if vandals or thieves penetrated the massive EFT networks that make transactions worth hundreds of billions of dollars every week.

As electronic networks have proliferated nationwide, we have created an effective information infrastructure, weaving ourselves into an ever tighter web with computers. Although this dependence has born many fruits, it has also increased our vulnerability. For this reason, computer security has become a vital concern at every level, from individuals to corporations and even entire societies.

Threats to computer security come in many forms, both external and internal. External threats include floods, fires, earthquakes, tornadoes, and other so called acts of God, which do extensive damage every year to computers worldwide. External threats also stem from human malice, which can lead to acts such as sabotage and arson. Yet the most pervasive threat is computer crime, which the U.S. Department of Justice has defined as "any illegal act for which knowledge of computer technology is essential for its perpetration, investigation, or prosecution" (Parker, 1983, p. 23). Typically perpetrated by insiders, computer crimes match the diversity of traditional crimes, coming in forms such as fraud, theft, and embezzlement.

The first step in protecting the security of our computers is to become aware of the threats and risks associated with computer use. But awareness by itself is not enough, particularly when the security of our information infrastructure is at stake. Safeguarding computers also requires active measures such as using secret passwords, limiting access to carefully screened personnel, and coding data so that they are not readily intelligible and useable.

A particularly important facet of computer security is the protection of intellectual property. The computer age has brought with it new forms of property such as computer hardware, software, and algorithms. In addition, information itself has become an increasingly important commodity, one that underlies the scientific and technological developments that are essential for our economic success. The strength of nations turns increasingly on their ability to stimulate the production of new information and new forms of intellectual property. In order to do this, society must protect intellectual property rights and allow individuals and corporations to reap the economic fruits of their labors. In deciding how to protect intellectual property, societies are doing more than protecting economic investments. Ultimately, they are deciding their future and actively choosing what kind of society they want to be.

Crime by Computer

Computer crime has attracted extensive public attention in part because of the large amounts of money involved. Whereas the average burglary yields just over $300, and a bank embezzlement nets approximately $20,000, the average loss in a case of embezzlement by computer is approximately $450,000 (Logsdon, 1985; Parker, 1983). One of the reasons why the figure for embezzlements by computer is so large is that most computer embezzlers are insiders, people who know the system very well and who are trusted by the bank or company for which they work (Bloombecker, 1986). Computer crime is predominantly white collar crime, although there are some reports that organized crime uses computers to keep track of stolen auto parts or of prostitutes in a ring involving many cities.

Lack of controls that make for a high chance of detection may also account for the large size of computer crimes. Ordinary accounting controls such as audits hardly ever uncover clever computer crooks since computerized systems do not leave a sufficient audit trail to track accurately, and a complete paper trail is seldom available. Furthermore, computers make it difficult for the auditors to work independently since, in order to get into the system and retrieve the information they need, they have to rely on the workers whom they are auditing (Parker, 1983).

We know very little about the extent of computer crime. Most computer crimes go unreported, and the ones that are known are usually discovered by accident. Although computer crime is believed to account for less than one percent of the total annual crime losses to government and business each year, the known annual losses from computer crime still run in the hundreds of millions of dollars (Logsdon, 1985). There is simply no way of knowing how much is lost because of software piracy, the widespread practice of making illicit copies of commercial software or of software owned by someone else. It is also impossible to know how much is lost as the result of workers using company computers illicitly for personal purposes or for playing games. What we can be relatively sure of is that computer crime will continue since the stakes are large. And, as indicated in the cases described below, most of which were compiled by Norman (1983), there are countless opportunities for computer crime.

Embezzlement and Fraud

Bob was the owner of a computer firm which kept accounting records for a fruit and vegetable shipping company in California. Having noticed that the company had an incomplete audit operation, Bob arranged a swindle that antedated computers by many years. First he created accounts for seventeen dummy vendor companies, which presumably provided services to his employers. He inflated the accounting records to show higher payments made to real vendors than were actually made. If, for example, a real vendor sent a bill of $1148, he would record in the computer a bill of $1248. Then he would pay the actual bill and credit the difference of $100 to one of the dummy accounts. Whenever he wanted money, all he had to do was to record an imaginary bill from one of the dummy vendors and issue a payment, which he would keep for himself.

In order to avoid getting caught, Bob developed a computer model that told him how large to make his payments to the dummy accounts. For example, if the model indicated that sales that were five percent of the total inventory were relatively common, then Bob knew he could probably get away with making phony orders and payments that did not exceed five percent of the total inventory. So successful was this scheme that Bob embezzled $1 million overall and $250,000 in one year alone. He did not get caught until a bank became suspicious of large checks being made to a labor organization. Like many embezzlers, however, Bob expressed relief at having been caught, as the mounting pressures of making sure he had covered everything up were getting to be too much.

Bob's crime pales by comparison to some of the fraud schemes that have been reported. For example, in the Equity Funding scandal, which was discovered in 1973, employees of an insurance company created some 64,000 bogus life insurance policies and sold them to other insurance companies, using computers to mask this reinsurance scheme (Parker, 1976). The value of the fake policies was estimated at a staggering $200 million. In another case, a group known as the Harris gang had its trainees gain jobs among large customers of TRW Credit Data, a service company that provides credit information about millions of people to businesses all over the nation. When police raided the ringleader's home, they found 300 falsified TRW credit-reporting forms ready to be entered into the computer (Norman, 1983). It is sobering to think how easy it would be to use such false credit information to milk banks and loan agencies for loans to fictitious people.

Perpetrators of computer fraud and embezzlement use a variety of techniques, but none is more difficult to detect than the Trojan horse. In a Trojan horse attack, a programmer creates computer code that appears to be part of a familiar, trusted program when in fact it is designed to allow unauthorized activity to occur interspersed with the normal activity of the program. For example, J. McCloud was a thirty-year-old programmer who, like many computer crooks, opted for fraud in order to make up for his recent business failures and spiraling gambling debts. Working for a money order company, he claimed that he was debugging the computer program that kept account of all the credits and debits of the company. But he was really planting a Trojan horse that consisted of only six additional statements in the BASIC language.

Using those statements, McCloud was able to enter fictitious requests for money orders marked with an "E" in a particular column into the computer without having the computer print out a corresponding money order. That allowed him to steal money order blanks, mark them with an "E" in the appropriate place, and cash them himself. But the more loot he collected, the more out of balance the books became. By the time he had filched $100,000, McCloud's luck ran out and he was apprehended (Parker, 1983).

What worries security analysts is that many Trojan horses will go undiscovered and will penetrate systems ranging from bank programs to election programs used to tally votes. Buried within long programs tens of thousands of lines long, Trojan horses can be extremely difficult to detect, particularly if the programmer has been very clever in hiding the horse. Hiding inside a program such as one used to create bar charts showing election results, a well designed Trojan horse could change an election outcome by manipulating the vote counting procedure and turning off the computer's audit trail (Leonard, Strauss and Edwards, 1988).

Not everyone can use the Trojan horse technique, which requires extensive knowledge of programming and of how a system works. Many frauds use much more mundane techniques such as manipulating data before they have been entered into the computer. Sarah, for example, was a timekeeping clerk, and her job was to fill out data forms on 300 employees, listing the number of regular and overtime hours for each. On the forms she filled out, she listed both the name and the employee number for each person. While watching how key punch operators typed the data onto computer cards, she noticed that the operators used only the employee names and disregarded their numbers. A programmer friend, however, told her that the computer program that generated the payroll used only the employee numbers. She immediately recognized the possibility of giving the key punch operators forms with someone else's name but with her own number on it, which would lead the computer to record additional hours for her and to issue her a larger paycheck.

Sarah soon began recording someone else's name and her own identification number on forms listing overtime hours, thereby collecting unearned overtime for herself. That year, she managed to take home several extra thousands of dollars. But she got caught when an auditor who examined employee W-2 income tax forms noticed that Sarah had drawn an exceptional salary for a timekeeping clerk. When she was confronted, she confessed and showed relief over ending her life of fraud, which she said had become addicting and worrisome (Parker, 1983).

Theft

The aphorism "Time is money" has taken on new meaning in the computer age, as precious computer time has become highly sought after by straights and thieves alike. In Philadelphia, for example, two computer programmers used their company's UNIVAC computer to generate sophisticated musical arrangements. Over a period of three years, they developed, printed, and distributed their musical scores under the name Camps, Inc. But this turned out to be expensive music, as they were eventually charged with misusing $144,000 worth of computer time (Norman, 1983).

One way of stealing computer time is to employ a widely used technique called a trapdoor. A trapdoor is intended to be a point in a computer program where one can insert special testing aids for purposes of debugging. In debugging a large program, for example, it is common practice to insert a trapdoor that suspends the normally operating restrictions on system access, allowing the programmer to move freely throughout the system in order to make sure it works properly. But trapdoors make programs vulnerable to computer criminals. In one case, a programmer discovered a trapdoor that enabled him to transfer control from his program into a region of computer storage where data were kept. By feeding programming instructions into that region of storage, the programmer made the system bypass normal control procedures, allowing him to steal valuable computer time from a time-sharing system (Parker, 1983).

Computer thefts involve not only computer time but also products such as data and software. At Encyclopaedia Britannica, three computer operators copied computer tapes that contained the names and addresses of two million customers. The value of the tapes was estimated to exceed $3 million. Fortunately, the company recovered the stolen tapes before competitors had used them (Norman, 1983). In another case, an ambitious programmer sought to get his company ahead of the competition, a company called ISD, in producing a program to drive graph plotters. Naturally, he wanted to know ISD's programs. Working by phone and using his own computer to impersonate one of ISD's clients, he dialed into the ISD computer and filched a copy of their plotting program. The discovery of this theft led the civil court to award ISD $300,000 in damages (Parker, 1976).

Piracy

Neither professional programmers nor deranged crooks, however, carry off most computer thefts. Ordinary citizens are largely responsible for the most widespread form of computer theft: software piracy. Tim, for example, was a student at a large university in the northeast, where he had become an avid computer user. After hours, he spent much of his time playing computer games with friends, who were part of a PC users group that frequently exchanged the latest games and programs among themselves. The way the exchange worked was that whenever a group member acquired a new piece of software, he or she passed a disk to other group members, who would then make their own copies for free. This was a harmless practice when the software was a homegrown game or a public domain piece that had not been produced for purposes of commercial gain. But most of the group members had stacks of floppy disks containing such popular programs as Lotus' *1-2-3* or Ashton-

Tate's *d-Base III*, both of which are copyrighted and initially cost over $300. Tim boasted that his own collection had a face value of over $10,000, yet all he had paid for were a few floppy disks that cost fifty cents apiece. When asked how he could justify violating copyright laws by making illicit copies of those programs, Tim replied that everyone does it and that, by overcharging for their products, the companies had attempted to "rip him off." He also rationalized that what he did is no different from what everyone else did in taping albums and making copies of books.

It is impossible to tell how widespread software piracy is since piracy is a clandestine activity. But the general rule of thumb in the software industry is that for every sale of a piece of software, there is at least one unauthorized copy of that software (Branscomb, 1988). The size of this wave of piracy is indicated by a clever experiment begun at the editorial headquarters of *Macmag* magazine, which many Macintosh users read. Richard Brandow, the magazine editor, deliberately placed a virus-infected program on a computer system at the headquarters. Although office rules prohibited copying any of the programs on the system, Brandow knew copying would occur, and he sat back for six months to see how far it would go. On March 2, 1988, the first anniversary of the Macintosh II computer, Macintoshes from Montreal to Melbourne lit up with the message "Richard Brandow, publisher of *Macmag* and its entire staff would like to take this opportunity to convey their universal Message of Peace to all Macintosh users around the world." This message, which had been caused by Brandow's virus, had spread to some 350,000 computers in a span of only six months (Bloombecker, 1988). When Brandow publicized the results of this experiment, software sales in Canada increased by 13%. Apparently, the fear of picking up a virus by copying software had led users to buy the software instead.

Although it is very difficult to estimate how much damage software piracy causes, most authorities say the annual losses are between $20 billion and $60 billion. The Lotus Corporation claims that it loses approximately $160 million annually because of illicit copying of *1-2-3* (Branscomb, 1988). These large financial losses translate into lost jobs, as piracy may have cost the computer industry some 750,000 jobs over the last five years (Howe, 1986). Extensive losses also occur through the gray market. For example, shops in places such as Hong Kong and Korea often sell bootleg copies of commercial software such as *1-2-3* for approximately five dollars. This tempts some companies to go outside of the country to buy the software that costs so much more in the U.S. Of course, Lotus never sees profits from these sales.

Piracy also causes indirect damages in the form of lost creativity and autonomy. By reducing the profits associated with developing software, piracy reduces the incentives for companies to develop new software, encouraging them to leave the software field for more lucrative ventures. If many large software producers elect to stop developing software, an important national source of new ideas about software will be compromised. American firms could look to countries such as Japan for new software, but this would make them ever more dependent upon foreign products and strengthen the economic power of their Japanese competitors. Ultimately, piracy threatens not only individual companies but also the vitality of our national software infrastructure.

Hackers

In September, 1986, an intruder in the San Francisco area broke into a large number of computer systems, including those of nine universities, three government laboratories, and fifteen Silicon Valley companies. But he did no damage. Apparently, his goal was to see how many computer systems he could crack into (Denning, 1988).

In a similar case, a West German used his home computer to tie into a public library network, through which he gained access to a defense contractor's computer in Virginia, which in turn connected to a military network. Searching his way through the military network, he penetrated the computer system at the Lawrence Berkeley Laboratory, where a great deal of classified weapons research is done. From there, he invaded computers in Japan, found his way into defense computers in Nebraska and Texas, and took a convoluted route back to a computer in West Germany (Chandler, 1988). Fortunately, he erased no files.

The perpetrators of these escapades are hackers, a new breed of intellectual thrill seekers who are strongly committed to open information access but who also love ingenious pranks. Some of these pranks have nothing to do with computers. At MIT, for example, a legendary hack occurred in the 1982 football game between Harvard and Yale. In the second quarter, a black ball with "MIT" written on it popped up suddenly at the 40-yard-line and grew rapidly until it burst, leaving a cloud of smoke and a set of dismayed fans (Specter, 1988).

In the realm of computers, hackers abhor barriers to free information and entry onto systems, which they spend a lot of time cracking. Many of the hackers are students, who center their lives around computers and who form groups with other hackers. Using electronic mail and computer bulletin boards, hackers often share information about how to break into the computers of many different organizations. In Richmond, Virginia, for example, two bulletin boards called Fatland and Dark Side openly listed phone numbers and detailed instructions for breaking into Walter Reed Army Medical Center and the Taylor Naval Ship Research and Development Center, which is a testing site for submarines and aircraft carriers (Epstein, 1985).

Ideally, hackers seek to be creative but harmless. Yet their exploits often turn out to be harmful. The West German hacker described above caused roughly $100,000 damage in lost computer time and the time required of staff and consultants to track him (Stoll, 1988). His exploits also caused extensive nonmonetary damages. The trespasser had invaded others' property, conducted espionage, and violated people's privacy by reading confidential information and personal electronic mail. In the end, he probably did more damage by violating the standards of trust and cooperation that encourage the free flow of information and that are taken for granted on many computer networks. Similarly, Morris' virus on the Arpanet system, which was described at the beginning of this chapter, has been called "the hack heard around the world" since it challenged users' trust that anything said via a computer network can be kept confidential (Specter, 1988).

Furthermore, what begins as a relatively harmless prank can escalate and get out of control. In 1980, a group of four thirteen-year-olds who became known as the Manhattan school gang broke into a large subscriber service network used by companies such as Pepsi Cola. Initially, the group caused no damage to files or information. But as the days passed and their appetite for adventure increased, they began playing rough. First they penetrated into the computer of Canada Cement La Farge in Montreal and deliberately crashed or shut down several 80-megabyte disks used to handle everything from payroll to shipping. La Farge notified the police of the problem and agreed to work with a fraud investigation team, which planned to allow the youngsters to break into the computers again and to track them as they did. Over the following eight days, the hackers broke in forty-two more times using unauthorized passwords. Wanting to stay in business while the investigation continued, La Farge restricted the hackers' access via the unauthorized passwords to only a few hours a day. Apparently angered by this restriction, the hackers killed the jobs being done by the computer, and they erased nearly ten million bytes of memory. By the time they had been caught, the hackers had broken into systems at the University of Toronto, Bell Canada, Honeywell Information Systems, and many others. To the chagrin of their headmaster, they had done all of this from school (Parker, 1983).

The exploits of hackers awaken in many of us a desire for adventure and for asserting the power of individuals over large corporations and government agencies. Yet it is easy to romanticize hackers, who have been called "heroes of the computer revolution" (Levy, 1984). In addition to causing unintended damage while breaking into systems, hackers have caused serious security headaches and have run up large bills for the time invested by computer staff and investigators. Although some would argue that the way to solve this problem is to grant the open access to information that hackers seek, open access to information is by no means the only value or the most important one in using computers. Many computer users cherish the value of privacy, which gives them the opportunity to carry on confidential discussions and to develop ideas out of the public eye. More-over, open access to information would make government and business agencies more vulnerable than they already are to thieves, spies, and saboteurs who do not embrace the lofty values of pure hackers. This puts society in a dilemma of how to respond to hackers. On one hand, most hackers are not dangerous criminals, but on the other hand, their activities may pave the way for very harmful exploits by people of evil intent.

Viruses and Vandals

F. J., a financial reporter for the Providence *Journal-Bulletin*, put in her disk drive a floppy containing six months of notes and interviews. Eager to crank out a newspaper story, she tried to call a file to the screen. But all she got in return was the warning "disk error" flashing on the screen. Worried that the contents of the disk had somehow been erased, she said "I got that sinking feeling...Every writing project of mine was on that disk" (Elmer-DeWitt, 1988, p. 62). J. M. took her disk to a systems engineer, who examined the disk's contents line by line. Probing through what had become a garbled mess of data, he discovered a chilling message that left no doubt this was an act of sabotage: WELCOME TO THE DUN-GEON...CONTACT US FOR VACCINATION (Elmer-DeWitt, 1988).

A malicious computer virus caused the destruction of J. M.'s data. The message above was accompanied by the name and telephone number of a computer store run by two brothers in Pakistan. When interviewed, the brothers admitted they had placed the virus program on disks they sold to tourists at extremely low prices. Their motive was to punish computer users for buying bootleg software that deprives merchants of potential sales. Revenge was also a motive, as one of the brothers was angry at having developed customized software himself that had been copied and used all around the city in which he lived (Elmer-DeWitt, 1988).

Estimates are that some 250,000 computers were infected with a computer virus in the first nine months of 1988. Whereas some of these viruses were relatively playful, others were downright vicious. One of the worst viruses deleted everything stored on the infected computer and printed the word GOTCHA! on the screen. Another one called "rck.video" presents interesting animation featuring Madonna. Then it erases whatever files are present and leaves the degrading message "You're stupid to download a video about rock stars" (Elmer-DeWitt, 1988, p. 66).

Computer viruses have also been used for purposes of sabotage. In 1988, a Fort Worth security officer who had been fired from his job with a financial services company allegedly implanted a time bomb virus on the company's mainframe computer. The programs were designed to lay dormant and then spring to life once each month, gobbling up masses of data. After that, they were to replicate themselves and move to new locations in the computer memory, from which subsequent attacks would be launched. But the saboteur never allowed the time bombs to go off. Instead, he manually destroyed electronic records of 168,000 sales transactions. Having been tried and convicted, he was sentenced to seven years of probation and forced to pay $11,800 in damages (Burgess, 1988).

Incidents such as these have generated widespread fears of computer viruses. Many computer users are thinking twice about copying software from bulletin boards and about putting borrowed disks into their computers. Although these fears can grow out of proportion to the threat that actually exists, there is legitimate cause for concern. A cleverly designed but malicious virus could wreak havoc on large computer networks such as the ones used by large banks to transfer hundreds of millions of dollars daily. Such a virus could potentially threaten national security if it were implanted onto military networks used for purposes of command and control. If vandals implanted malicious viruses in popular commercial software, millions of computer users could suffer serious damage. For these reasons, computer security is an increasingly vital concern.

Protecting Security

Threats to computer security come in many forms. Every year, floods, fires, earthquakes, and other so-called acts of God cause many millions of dollars in damage to computers. Extensive hardware damage also stems from disgruntled employees, vandals, and saboteurs, who have done such things as set computers ablaze, wrecked the heads of disk drives using screwdrivers, and blown up entire computer facilities. As discussed above, however, threats to hardware barely scratch the surface of computer crime, as, every year, thieves steal software or distort it for their own perverse use in embezzlement and fraud. Computer abusers also steal valuable computer time, snatch or destroy data, and infect systems with potentially lethal computer viruses.

Because these threats are so diverse, it is necessary to employ a variety of security measures. Some of the most basic measures are designed to protect the physical integrity of the system. For example, computer managers typically house their computers in temperature-controlled and humidity-limited environments in order to guard against malfunctions and damage caused by excessive heat and moisture. They are also careful to make backup copies at frequent and regular intervals of the programs and data used on the system, and they typically store these copies in vaults protected against floods, excessive magnetism, and most physical calamities. These secure backup copies enable them to avoid major losses and to recover relatively quickly even if there has been serious damage to software and data due to vandalism or fire.

In addition, most managers place physical barriers to unauthorized entry into vulnerable computer centers. Although they use traditional means such as posting security guards and keeping doors locked, they also use computer-aided techniques to identify authorized users. Some systems, for example, require people to look into an eyepiece and then use the computer to analyze the pattern of the blood vessels at the back of the eye, which is as distinct as a person's fingerprint. Other systems require prospective entrants to speak, and the computer then analyzes whether the voice pattern matches that of an authorized user.

These methods, however, cannot stop misuses by people who are authorized to be in vulnerable areas. Nor can they thwart hackers who operate at a distance using their home computers and telephone lines to break into computers. For these reasons, managers often employ measures internal to the computer system for limiting access to valuable resources and information.

Limiting Access

Most computer systems limit access to authorized users by means of a secret password system, which is the software equivalent of a lock and key system. Typically, each user selects or is assigned his or her own secret password, a sequence of eight or so randomly arranged letters, numbers, or combinations thereof. When users attempt to sign on to the computer, the system asks them for their password and lets them on only if they type in a password that matches one on an authorized list.

Although password systems are useful, their effectiveness is often compromised by sloppy practices. The system works only so long as users keep their passwords secret. But users occasionally tell their passwords to someone else or write them down, giving unauthorized users a chance to find them. These potential problems lead many computer managers to issue new passwords to users periodically so that crooks cannot make use of any old ones that they have discovered. Furthermore, passwords are effective only if they cannot be easily guessed or figured out. Yet many users choose passwords that are simple to guess, as in the initials CSW or the abbreviated name MIKET. A simple way to protect against guessing is to use passwords that are randomly constructed, such as 70Y9TF72.

Password systems are vulnerable if they allow users an unlimited number of tries to sign on. Hackers often exploit this error by programming their home computers to dial up a computer system and to try out probable passwords. By trying out a very large number of possible passwords, they often stumble onto one that works. In order to guard against this type of invasion, many systems are designed to hang up or to cut users off after they have made two or three unsuccessful tries to give a valid password.

Because many security violations involve authorized users, a secure system must also have internal checks against activities such as data theft and file tampering. Here again password systems are useful. For example, the computer manager can partition the computer's memory into a hierarchy of sectors that are graded according to level of security. All users may access the information, programs, and files contained in the less secure sectors of memory. But additional secret passwords are required to move up the hierarchy and access the more secure sectors of memory. In many cases, only the computer manager and one or two trusted colleagues know the passwords that provide access to the most secure portions of memory, such as those containing accounting information.

Another way of limiting access is to place restrictions on what users can do with information, files, and programs. For example, a teacher could allow her students to use a program of computer-assisted instruction by giving them student passwords and the name of a file to retrieve. But she could limit their ability to change the program she had written by giving them read-only privileges, which enable them to display the program on their screens but not to modify or add to it. Software producers often use this technique also. By giving their customers read-only privileges, they hope to reduce the chances that the customers will inadvertently change or even erase the software. In addition, they try to limit software piracy by including on their disks a routine that allows the user to make only one copy for backup purposes.

No matter how well designed these access restrictions are, however, clever and determined invaders can eventually find a way of penetrating deeply into the system. For this reason, the system should provide a method of monitoring and tracking those who violate security. An automatic audit trail, for example, provides a complete record of the activities of everyone who signs on. By following an audit trail, a computer manager can often determine who is illicitly entering secure portions of the system and what methods they used to do so. By keeping a close watch on unsuccessful attempts to sign onto the system, the manager can tell whether an outsider is attempting to break in. The trouble is that the most sophisticated computer crooks may figure out how to alter or to bypass the auditing devices. This has led security analysts to develop methods of encryption that make it nearly impossible for criminals to use information even if they manage to steal or intercept it.

Data Encryption

Probably the most effective means of preventing the misuse of information, one that is widely used to transmit information over banking and military networks, is to code it in ways that are indecipherable to outsiders. This is done through the use of an encryption scheme, which uses rules to transform the original message or "cleartext" into a meaningless jumble of symbols called "cyphertext." In a very simple encryption scheme, each letter of the alphabet could be assigned random number as a code as follows:

A B C D E F G H I J K L M N O P Q R S T...
13 26 19 4 10 1 14 8 2 5 20 16 22 6 11 3 7 12 17 9...

In order to send a message such as "It is raining hard," the message sender would first create ciphertext by substituting numbers for letters. Using the key shown above, the cyphertext is as follows:

2 9   2 17   12 13 2 6 2 6 14   8 13 12 4

Having generated the cyphertext, the sender transmits it via electronic network or courier to the receiver, who also has a key that will decipher the message back to the cleartext. This method requires that both the sender and the receiver have a key for coding and decoding the message and that they not share the key with anyone else. If outsiders break the code by figuring out the key, they would be able to not only understand the messages sent but also to change data for their own benefit. If this happened on a large EFT network, the consequences could be disastrous.

Most banks, financial services, and government agencies use a top secret encryption scheme called the Data Encryption Standard or DES (Athanasiou, 1986). Created largely by the National Security Agency, a federal intelligence agency even more secretive than the CIA, the DES uses a complex and classified mathematical model to code and decode messages. Each user has a unique and secret key consisting of 56 binary digits (zeroes and ones). By applying this key to the cleartext, the message is scrambled into a jumble of zeroes and ones that is unintelligible to everyone except an authorized recipient, who also has a key. In order to break such a key by trial and error, a thief would have to try out 2^{56} different keys or about 70,000,000,000,000,000 possibilities. With so many possibilities, trial and error is not a highly effective method for breaking the code. Conceivably, more clever methods for breaking the code could be designed, but IBM is reputed to have devoted seventeen person-years to breaking it, and they failed to do so.

Although the DES enjoys wide usage, critics have charged that it is too short. The military routinely uses encryptions that consist of 128 binary digits, making them twice as difficult to crack as the DES by trial and error. It is not entirely clear why commercial enterprises should have shorter keys and less security than the military. In fact, the DES is a modified version of the Lucifer system developed by IBM, and the Lucifer system used 128-digit keys. Furthermore, the development of parallel processors and of faster super-computers could significantly reduce the cost and difficulty of breaking a 56-digit code through trial and error methods (Diffie and Hellman, 1977).

What is even more worrisome is that the National Security Agency, which initially promoted the DES, suddenly withdrew its support for the DES in 1985. Agency officials say that they are concerned because so many elements of the DES are publicly known. Yet the agency has kept classified evidence that would answer the question in the back of users' minds—just how secure is the DES? The lack of access to this evidence, coupled with the withdrawal of NSA support, has stimulated fear that perhaps the DES is really not as secure as it ought to be. In addition, NSA's involvement in the construction of the DES raises the possibility that NSA may have secretly concealed a trap door in the DES that enables them to break encrypted text without the key (Athanasiou, 1986).

Seeking to develop alternatives to DES that are publicly available but that do not come from NSA, many analysts have turned to encryption schemes based upon prime numbers, which are divisible by only themselves and one. The best known is an algorithm called RSA after the mathematicians Rivest, Shamir, and Adleman who developed it. RSA keys are based on the insight that it is very easy to find two large prime numbers and to multiply them together to form a long product number. But it is extremely difficult for someone else to factor it, that is, to figure out which prime numbers yielded that product. For even a small number such as 5,893, it can be difficult to figure out that it is the product of 71 and 83. To break an RSA cipher, one would have to factor a product number that is hundreds of digits long and that was produced by multiplying primes that were hundreds of digits long themselves (Athanasiou, 1986).

Factoring such long and complicated codes will require more than significant increases in computing speed. Breakthroughs in number theory are needed most, yet they are very difficult to make. For now, RSA methods provide effective means of encrypting messages. But significant advances in number theory could change this, creating the need for new encryption schemes. This qualifier reminds us that no means of protecting security is ever perfect. In a time of rapid advances in knowledge and technology, a method that is relatively effective one month may be highly vulnerable the following month. Protecting security means staying one step ahead of those who would violate it.

Computer Crime and Legislation

Despite the best attempts to stay ahead of criminals, determined wrongdoers can still find ways of violating security. Providing stiff penalties for security violations could serve as a deterrent against crime, assuming that the computer system includes effective means of tracking and apprehending violators. But one of the main reasons for the rise of computer crime is that the law has not yet instituted stiff penalties in this area.

Fears of the damage hackers and crooks could do stimulated the development of federal legislation to prevent unauthorized entry into federal records. The Computer Fraud and Abuse Act of 1984 outlawed unauthorized access to classified national security information and financial records covered by federal laws. The Act was extended in 1986 to cover a wider variety of computers used by the federal government. It makes it a misdemeanor to trespass in a federally-used computer or to use or disclose stolen passwords. It also makes it a felony to break into a federal computer in order to destroy or change data such as medical records or to steal amounts over $1,000. Depending on the nature of the crime and whether the criminal act is a first offense, the law provides penalties ranging from fines to jail sentences of up to twenty years (Reiss and Dolan, 1989).

This federal legislation, however, applies only to computers used by the federal government or in interstate commerce. In order to protect computers that are not used for federal purposes, most states have enacted legislation pertaining to specific computer crimes such as embezzlement via EFT systems. But the state laws vary widely in what they outlaw and in the penalties they impose for particular computer abuses (Bloombecker, 1984). For example, Utah and Virginia do not mention unauthorized computer abuse in their criminal codes, yet Ohio and Georgia consider unauthorized access a felony. Whereas some states make little effort to deal with nonmalicious hackers as a separate category, New Jersey defines as a disorderly person someone who gains unauthorized access into a computer but who does not alter or damage any property or services as a result (Reiss and Dolan, 1989). Until there is greater consistency in the law and stiff penalties for computer crimes, abusers will be tempted to broach security.

Yet it is also important to be realistic about how much laws can accomplish. Even stiff laws will be relatively ineffective so long as it is difficult to apprehend security violators. In fact, it is very hard to catch violators since most are not outside invaders but trusted insiders who know the system and who understand how to cover their tracks (Betts, 1985). Probably the best way of protecting a system against abuse by trusted insiders is to be very careful in screening and promoting employees. In the end, protecting security is as much a human problem as a technical one.

Security Dilemmas

Companies have often fallen into the trap of believing they have achieved perfect or nearly perfect security. Security specialists at Honeywell Information Systems, for example, spent six grueling years designing exceptionally tight security for their new "multics" system. The system included secretly encrypted passwords, strict limits on which users could access which portions of memory, and an automatic audit trail that allowed system managers to track the activities of all users of the system. The designers of the system were so confident of its security that they recommended that it be used to store and process classified information, and they issued a press release expressing their confidence in the system. Even their competitors admitted that it included the most elaborate security safeguards of any large computer marketed up to that time (Logsdon, 1985).

But Honeywell's security bubble soon burst. The morning following the press release, a Honeywell computer operator was shocked to see an insidious message lighting up the computer screen. After a long and derogatory tirade over the inadequacy of the multics system, the message ended with the statement "ZARF IS WITH YOU AGAIN!" Fortunately for Honeywell, ZARF was neither a sinister crook nor a Palestinian virus but a group of security experts from the U.S. Air Force and the Mitre Corporation, which handles many defense contracts. The group acted as a Tiger Team that worked tirelessly to penetrate even the most secure computer systems for the purpose of identifying security weaknesses and possible means of attack that intruders might use. So far, ZARF's Tiger Teams have successfully penetrated every new system that has been marketed, providing a poignant reminder that there is no such thing as perfect security (Logsdon, 1985).

The fact that perfect security is unattainable puts computer managers in a quandary. On one hand, this realization makes them aware of their vulnerability and encourages them to develop and implement better security measures. Calls for tighter security often come from users, who can become panicky over virus attacks, even if they have only heard about them. On the other hand, extremely tight security measures can limit the usefulness of the computer systems. For example, national computer networks such as Arpanet which allow the immediate exchange of scientific information are useful precisely because they permit the relatively free flow of information. If they contained too many layers of security measures, users would find it very difficult to exchange information readily with the broadest appropriate audience. Similarly, many educational networks such as BITNET, which interconnects hundreds of colleges and universities in the U.S. and abroad, enable educators to exchange ideas about scholarly work, teaching, computing, and many other topics. Too much security on BITNET would impede the relatively free exchange of ideas and would defeat the purpose of having the network.

Although this quandary has no easy solution, the wisest course is probably to strike a balance between too little and too much security. Network managers have found that relatively strong security can be achieved by using standard measures such as secret passwords, limited access to particular system processes and commands, and methods for identifying and dealing with multiple unsuccessful attempts to log on to a system (King, 1988). These precautions do not allow perfect security, but they do provide for moderate to high levels of security that simultaneously enable the relatively free flow of information that users need. Of course, the answer one gives to the question "How much security is enough?" depends upon the purposes of the computer system. A computer that is used routinely to store and transmit classified information requires much higher levels of security than one that handles unclassified information. Each group of users must ultimately decide how much security is enough for their system. In making these decisions, however, we ought to resist panic and remember that losses can occur from too much security as well as from too little.

Cost, too, is a significant issue in deciding how much security is enough. Increasing security is always an expensive proposition, but as additional security steps are taken, diminishing returns rapidly set in. Achieving the highest levels of security requires enormous sums of money. Usually it is consumers who foot the bill for security measures. If the user costs rise too high, many people will be unable to use the system. In addition, money spent on security could have been used to add new programs to the system, to upgrade the computer, or to hire additional staff. Buying security, then, involves making difficult tradeoffs. Which tradeoffs will be acceptable depends largely on one's goals and the uses to which one's computer are put. Here again, the wisest course for most users is to strike a middle course between too little and too much security.

Protecting Intellectual Property

Susan, a former teacher turned programmer, built an elaborate software system called REGISTRAR, a system that colleges and universities can use to automate the tasks of keeping student records and registering students for courses. In developing the system, she tested REGISTRAR at five colleges, asking both the registrars and the computer scientists of those colleges to give feedback and suggestions regarding the program via an electronic mail network. To her delight, the computer scientists and their students took an active interest, going so far as to send her subroutines and software tips anonymously that she eventually incorporated into REGISTRAR. Six months before she had completed REGISTRAR, a similar product hit the market, and she was concerned because this competitor was graphically exciting and easy to use. Wanting to avoid a total loss on her work, she modified REGISTRAR so that it had the same look and feel as the competitor program had.

Before marketing REGISTRAR, Susan wants to copyright it or to somehow protect her ownership of the program and her rights to the profits from selling it. But she worries that she may have stolen ideas from her competitor. And she is not sure who really owns the ideas in some of the subroutines she received anonymously from the computer scientists. Even if she obtains legal rights to REGISTRAR, she worries that software pirates will sap her profits anyway.

Susan's situation is indicative of the widespread concerns about protecting intellectual property. Protecting rights to intellectual property is vital for society since ideas and knowledge are increasingly important resources both economically and socially. Understanding this, the Founding Fathers developed a system of property law, the goal of which is to encourage the generation of new ideas without sacrificing the open flow of information that democracy needs in order to flourish. U.S. property law is based on the model that inventive people will continue to generate new ideas and products so long as they retain the rights to the economic gains that follow from their ideas. This model has been viable for hundreds of years, both in the U.S. and in the European countries from which it was borrowed.

Today, new technology in general and computers in particular pose serious challenges to the effective implementation of this model. Historically, the model was upheld through legal protection in the form of patents, copyrights, and trade secrets. These legal devices for protecting property rights, however, evolved long before computers did. The computer revolution has introduced many new forms of potential property such as programs, many of which defy the traditional categories. Moreover, technology changes much faster than the law, and this makes it ever more difficult for the law to keep up with computers. The result is that a great deal of uncertainty exists about how to protect intellectual property rights. Nevertheless, an entrepreneur such as Susan would still look for protection to the traditional protective devices of patents, copyrights, and trade secrets.

Patents

A patent, which can be granted by the Patent and Trademark Office, gives the patent holder the exclusive right to make, use or sell the patented invention in the U.S. for seventeen years. But this extensive protection is difficult to obtain. For one thing, an invention qualifies for a patent only if it is new, useful, and nonobvious in light of existing technology (Becker, 1981). In addition, only physical things and processes are eligible to be patented. Patents are not awarded for algorithms such as mathematical formulas and laws of nature. The Patent Office has long believed that anyone should be free to use them and that these ought to be kept in the public domain in order to promote scientific and technological advances. This restriction sharply limits the patentability of computer programs, which are not tangible items and which embody algorithms. So far, the Patent Office has granted patents to computer programs only when they have been part of a novel physical process such as a method of typesetting or of curing rubber. An even greater obstacle in a rapidly moving field such as computers is that it often takes two or three years for the Patent Office to do the research required to process patent applications, and no protection is provided during this period (Office of Technology Assessment, 1986).

Furthermore, there are many concerns about the adequacy of international patent law. Because the computer industry is global and many of the largest producers are multinational corporations, it makes little sense to have a product that is patented in the U.S. not be patent-protected in other countries as well. Yet nations differ widely in their legal systems and in how consistently and strongly they enforce their laws. Without a fully uniform system of international patent law, entrepreneurs will continue to worry that their inventions are vulnerable to theft and unwanted use by others. In general, patents do not provide the broad and immediate legal protection that most computer entrepreneurs seek.

Copyrights

Unlike a patent, a copyright protects a work from the moment of its creation, and it does apply to software. A copyright grants authors control over the copying of their work for the lifetime of the author plus fifty years. In order to copyright a piece of software, an author simply includes at the beginning of the program a statement such as this (Becker, 1981):

© [name of copyright owner]

[date of first publication]

© John Doe 1990

Copyrights, however, do not protect ideas. They only protect the original expression of ideas in a fixed and tangible medium (OTA, 1986). In a computer program, for example, a copyright would protect primarily the code, that is, the program itself, but not the algorithm on which it is based. In 1980, the Copyright Act was amended to cover programs in a variety of forms ranging from PASCAL programs to programs embedded on Read Only Memory (ROM) chips.

Although copyright coverage is relatively broad and easy to obtain, it is limited in numerous respects. For example, a copyright applies to the expression of ideas in a fixed medium. But it is not entirely clear as to what constitutes a fixed medium. Software products such as data bases are usually being refined on a continuous basis, posing a significant challenge to the "fixed medium" provision. This problem will become more severe as parallel processing becomes more common and as large programs are distributed over a system of networked computers and in which new computers are constantly added. In addition, the courts have not been consistent in interpreting the term "expression." Some decisions have limited the protectable expression to the literal code, the actual programming statements but not the structure and the logic of the program.

Other decisions, however, have said that the protectable expression includes the manner in which a program operates, the steps through which it controls the computer, and the form in which it displays information on the screen (OTA, 1986). Currently, Lotus is challenging imitators of its *1-2-3* system, arguing that the others have violated copyright by virtue of having a similar look and feel as *1-2-3* has. In March, 1988, Apple Computer launched a suit against Microsoft Corporation and Hewlett-Packard Corporation, contending that those firms created software that employs windows that are too similar to the Mac user interface system. These cases indicate that in the area of copyright law, there is very little black and white but a lot of gray area.

Even if copyright law were very clear, it would still be extremely difficult to enforce. Prosecuting the cases of software piracy, which probably number in the millions, would hopelessly overburden the courts. Catching software pirates would also require invading the privacy of homes and offices, and this would be very unpopular and could damage our individual freedoms.

Trade Secrets

Trade secrets offer a third means of protecting intellectual property. Trade secrets cover any confidential formula, process, mechanism, or compilation of information that is used by a business to gain a competitive advantage over its rivals. Trade secrets are highly advantageous in the computer industry because they cover ideas and algorithms, not just the expression of ideas. Whereas it is difficult to fit many computer products into the traditional copyright categories, all of the ideas and mechanisms one could generate in the realm of computers can potentially be covered by trade secrets. Unlike patents, trade secrets require no waiting time, no formal procedures, and no large processing fees. These features make trade secrets much more palatable means of protection than patents or copyrights.

An example of a successful trade secret is the Coca Cola formula, which has never been patented and is known to only a few personnel. The trade secret will last as long as it remains a secret. If other companies were to discover the formula on their own, then the trade secret would be lost. But the secret would not be lost if a competitor obtained the secret by unfair means such as espionage (Becker, 1981). This requirement of maintaining secrecy places heavy demands for confidentiality and loyalty within the company.

In the computer industry, maintaining secrecy can be much more difficult than in other industries. For example, once a chip that incorporates secret features becomes available on the mass market, other companies and individuals can analyze it carefully and discover the secret. They can also use what they have learned to make and to market similar chips themselves. This practice of reverse engineering is both legal and widely used, and it often thwarts attempts to maintain secrecy. A similar problem confronts software manufacturers. Once programs have been mass marketed, they no longer qualify as trade secrets since mass marketing usually results in disclosure of the programs. To get around this problem, some vendors have licensed their programs to users, who thereby agree to keep the programs secret (OTA, 1986).

Trade secrets also pose problems of public policy. The point of protecting intellectual property is to encourage the free flow of ideas. Yet if companies overrely on trade secrets for protection, too much information becomes inaccessible to the broader community. In the high technology arena, locking up too much information limits the rapid exchange of ideas that can benefit the entire industry. If the computer companies maintain too many trade secrets, it will be difficult for the entire industry to develop the broad array of new products in a timely manner, which will eventually erode the competitiveness of the U.S. computer industry. Furthermore, if industry giants such as IBM keep too much information secret, they may gain a very large edge over other companies, evoking complaints about unfair competitive advantage and fears of monopoly (Carlyle and Moad, 1988).

Alternatives to Legal Protection

The upshot of this discussion is that there are significant limits on the existing means of protecting intellectual property, and the law is continually playing a game of catchup with technology. Recognizing this, many manufacturers have sought alternative ways of protecting their investments.

One such method is to offer software as freeware. Under the freeware system, users obtain a copy of a program for free and try it out. They are encouraged to send a nominal fee such as thirty-five dollars to the producer if they like it. This system is based on the idea that high software prices encourage software piracy and that satisfied users will not mind paying a small fee, particularly after they have had a chance to try out a program and see that it does something that they need. In addition, marketing and distribution methods are built into the system. If one user tries out a piece of software and likes it, he or she may pass it on to a friend or even announce its availability on an electronic bulletin board. This makes freeware highly attractive to individual software producers who want to concentrate on developing programs rather than on marketing and distribution. But the freeware approach is risky because it depends ultimately on users' good will and honesty. Most large companies have been unwilling to entrust their survival to the good will and honesty of consumers.

A more viable method that many software developers are trying is to charge relatively low prices in hopes of obtaining a larger sales volume. Individuals and small businesses often cannot afford to pay several hundred dollars for a single piece of software such as *1-2-3*, and many individuals say that they feel cheated by companies that charge so much for their products. These feelings encourage software piracy and give the offenders a ready, albeit thin, justification for their actions. By charging lower prices, software producers bring their products in a more affordable range and defuse customers' bad feelings about the price. The result has been reduced rates of software theft without any changes in the law or in law enforcement.

Although this latter approach makes sense in view of the current problems in obtaining legal protection for intellectual property, it is little more than a pragmatic attempt to make the best of a difficult situation. It does little, however, to address the broader need of society for a coherent conceptual framework that recognizes the importance of intellectual property rights and that takes systematic steps to protect them. Addressing this need will probably require the formation of new laws and categories of legal protection that are better suited to high technology products than are the traditional categories of patents, copyrights, and trade secrets. But laws are neither formulated nor implemented in a social vacuum. Their genesis and enforcement stands ultimately on the awareness, the choices, and the collective will of the citizens.

Conclusion

Our steadily growing dependency upon computers, and the development of a national and international information infrastructure have made computer security a vital concern for individuals, corporations, and societies. Of the wide variety of threats to computer security, computer crime is potentially the most harmful. Using computers, determined embezzlers have siphoned off large sums of money and covered their tracks, and hackers and vandals have infected computer networks with computer viruses which have done shut down large systems or destroyed precious information. Yet some of the most extensive losses owe not to hardened criminals but to ordinary computer users who pirate their own copies of commercial software.

Computer managers employ a variety of methods to protect computer security. Through the use of locks, computerized identification procedures, and secret passwords, they restrict access to the system to only authorized users. In addition, they can encrypt data, coding it in a form that is unintelligible to everyone except the holders of a secret key. They can also use auditing procedures to track, catch, and prosecute offenders. But prosecution remains difficult since it is very difficult to catch clever computer crooks, most of whom are trusted insiders who succumbed to obvious temptations, and since the law is only beginning to come to grips with computer crime. No matter how tight one's security measures are, however, perfect security remains unattainable. The quest for high degrees of security must be balanced by a consideration of the high costs involved and by the understanding that too much security can inhibit the free exchange of information that is needed in order for democracy to flourish.

Technology is outracing the law, and this poses serious problems in protecting intellectual property. Traditionally, inventions and property were protected via patents, copyrights, and trade secrets. But computer products such as software packages do not conform readily to these categories. This results in limited protection, which in turn impedes the desire to create new products and information technologies. What is needed is a coherent national policy that adapts the legal system to the emerging needs for protecting intellectual rights to computers and computer-related products. This need for a coherent national policy regarding the use of information will also be apparent in the analysis of privacy.

7

The Challenge to Privacy

Lucky Kellener, a lawyer with a good credit record, wanted to move to a larger apartment. When he went looking for a new apartment, however, three different landlords refused without explanation to rent to him. Eventually and by chance, Kellener learned that his name had been placed on a secret computerized blacklisting service. But it was not because of anything he had done wrong. It turned out that several years earlier Lucky had paid his brother's rent. Several months later, Kellener's brother had been evicted, but Lucky's name had been inadvertently included in the court documents. Lucky's name subsequently appeared in a computerized list of undesirable tenants shown to many landlords. It was bad enough that he had been blacklisted incorrectly, but what was worse was that he had no way of even knowing about it (Burnham, 1980).

In another case, William Douglas Thompson III applied for credit cards with Gulf Oil and Montgomery Ward in 1978, providing his occupation, address, Social Security number, and wife's name. A Gulf computer operator requested Thompson's credit file from a local credit bureau, the San Antonio Retail Merchants Association. The bureau returned denigrating information about a man who had the same first and last names but a different middle name, occupation, address, and Social Security number. Gulf rejected Thompson's application for credit. Montgomery Ward also ran a credit check. But it received a file containing the wrong name, former address, and employer, and the wrong credit information, some of which was damaging. It too denied Thompson credit. Because he was unable to obtain credit, he and his wife and children lived for two years in a house with no furniture. Eventually, Thompson discovered the errors in his credit records and confronted the credit bureau. But the bureau did not correct all of the errors in his file, and it failed to notify the vendors who had rejected Thompson's applications that it had made the errors. Thompson sued and won $14,485 (Winokur, 1984).

Both of these cases illustrate that it has become routine in American society for large corporations such as credit agencies to collect and distribute extensive information about private citizens without their knowing exactly who keeps records on them and how the information is used. In fact, the five largest credit-screening companies keep computer records on more than 150 million citizens, and insurance companies maintain computerized health records on ninety percent of the working population (Marx, 1985). Furthermore, federal and state governments have a voracious appetite for information about citizens. Together, the Department of Education and the Department of Health and Human Services hold over one trillion files on U.S. citizens, and the federal government overall holds approximately fifteen files per citizen (Deitel and Deitel, 1985). Clearly, we are an information intensive society.

Computers have served as powerful catalysts in our quest for collecting and using information. For one thing, computers provide a relatively inexpensive means of storing vast quantities of data in a small space. But the greatest breakthrough that stems from the use of computers is in the use and distribution of information. The government, for example, has for many years kept vast mountains of information in the form of seemingly endless banks of file cabinets. But it has been too expensive and time consuming to search through much of this information by hand. Computers overcome this problem by providing the capacity for automatic searches conducted at high speeds. Once the sought-after information has been obtained, it can be transmitted across the country in a matter of moments.

Collecting and using so much information offers obvious benefits. The FBI, for example, can do a better job of fighting crime if it has extensive and readily accessible information about smuggled drugs, stolen firearms, and other crimes. Without computers, government agencies such as the IRS would probably collapse under the weight of the information they must process. Similarly, large insurance companies would rapidly get crushed by their heavy burden of customers and claims if it were not for computers. Citizens, too, enjoy benefits such as going to pharmacists who use computers to keep track of patients' medications and to avoid harmful drug interactions or overdoses.

But computers also open up new avenues for the abuse of citizens' rights. If the government collects too much information about private citizens, we drift toward a controlled society in which the government becomes a Big Brother that monitors the citizens and abridges their freedom. Computers also open new opportunities for invading the privacy of individuals. For example, if you had experienced a temporary bout of depression following the death of a spouse and had received psychiatric treatment, you might wish this information to be kept private. Yet insurance agencies typically require a complete medical history. Having this information disclosed to others is embarrassing, and it is also risky. If this personal information fell into the wrong hands, it could be used for undesirable purposes such as character assassination and blackmail. Of course, computers alone do not threaten citizens' rights. It is the people and organizations that use computers which pose the threat.

These examples point out that the need of organizations to know about individuals must be balanced against the need for privacy. They also raise a host of difficult questions. What is the optimal balance between the needs of organizations and those of individuals? Do agencies have the right to share their computer records on individuals with other agencies, or should individuals have rights of authorization? Should citizens be informed about who keeps information about them and with whom the information is being shared? As individuals and a society, what choices could we make to protect privacy?

These questions and related ones admit no simple answers. In addition to being inherently intricate, these questions arise out of social and technological changes that are too recent to have been analyzed fully. Further, rapid advances in information technology create new problems, frustrating one-shot solutions. Whatever answers are given to these questions must be grounded in an analysis of why privacy is important and of how the use of computers can threaten privacy.

Why Privacy is Important

The importance of privacy is not always appreciated. In a democratic society such as ours, privacy is such a pervasive and ingrained feature of life that we take it for granted. Moreover, many people question the need for privacy, arguing that those who have done nothing wrong should have nothing to hide. Although this view contains an element of truth, it overlooks the central role that privacy plays in the normal development of individuals, honest as well as dishonest. It also fails to recognize the social importance of privacy in the protection of liberty and the maintenance of a democratic society.

Individuation

Privacy plays an important role in individuation, the process through which people develop as unique individuals having their own values, beliefs, and personalities (Reiman, 1976). In public, there is almost always social pressure to behave in a particular manner. In a classroom, for example, you are expected to behave as a reflective student, whereas at a party, you are expected to behave as a cheerful and outgoing friend. Because of this social pressure, we all learn to wear a variety of social masks as various occasions demand.

Underneath these masks, however, is what may be called a core self, one's innermost identity. Within this identity, you experience unique feelings, cultivate your own values and beliefs, and interpret your life experiences in a personally meaningful way. Privacy is often required in order to develop this core self. At one time or another, most people have experienced an intense desire to be alone in order to think through what happened in an emotionally demanding situation or to make a decision. In this sense, privacy allows individuals to get to know themselves, to carve out their own identities and to make their own choices about how to act (Westin, 1967). By fostering individuation, privacy promotes the individuality that is an essential part of American culture.

Dignity

Privacy also contributes to a sense of personal dignity (Bloustein, 1984). Each of us has a sense of psychological space that is uniquely our own. This space includes your innermost thoughts and feelings, private events which you may not want to become public. Within this space, you have the freedom to do whatever you want when out of the public eye. Encroachments upon this psychological space, whether by a voyeur, a wiretap, or a lie-detector, can make you feel violated. This amounts to an invasion of your personality, which is ordinarily held to be inviolate, thereby decreasing your sense of dignity.

Violations of our psychological space can cause severe embarrassment. Few of us want to have details of our sex lives or our financial affairs made public. Although the public has a legitimate need to know about the personal affairs of people running for government office, it is doubtful that your neighbors need to know your intimate affairs. When personal information is publicized against the wishes of the individual, the resulting gossip and reputational damage can cause severe distress, impairing mental health.

Mental Health and Creativity

Societal pressures to conform to norms of expected behavior can be overwhelming, particularly when they conflict sharply with the needs of the individual. If, for example, you wanted to dress casually at work but your boss demanded that you wear a suit, this would create conflict. In turn, conflict causes anxiety, a state of psychological distress, physical tension, and worry. Similarly, the norms of behavior at the office may dictate deference to your supervisor, leading you not to say what you really think. If you were very angry about the supervisor's decisions but could not speak out for fear of losing your job, you would experience substantial amounts of conflict and anxiety. The buildup of anxiety over time can cause a variety of psychological disturbances ranging from panic reactions to obsessive or compulsive behavior (Davison, 1982).

For most people, privacy affords a convenient solution to this problem. In the privacy of your home, for example, you can speak your mind more directly and vent the frustration and anxiety that may have built up at the office without suffering adverse consequences. It is a rare person who has never felt the relief of venting anger and frustration in solitude or in private conversation with a friend. In a sense, privacy offers a psychological safety valve that prevents the accumulation of excessive anxiety.

Privacy also provides a fertile environment for the development of creativity. For one thing, it gives individuals time alone to work without distraction. Many writers, scientists, and engineers have commented that they need blocks of time free from disruption in order to do their best work. Further, privacy provides freedom from social censure, allowing people to take risks and to try out ideas that they might be reluctant to present in public. Inventors, for example, have often commented that most of their ideas fail and that society initially treats many of their best ideas as crackpot. If all of their ideas were subjected to uncontrolled public scrutiny, inventors might suffer heavy criticism, which could stifle their willingness to experiment with new ideas. In addition, privacy guards against the theft and exploitation of inventors' ideas, preserving the economic incentives for creative endeavors.

Personal Autonomy

One of the most important functions of privacy is to protect individual autonomy (Fried, 1984; Gavison, 1984; Westin, 1967). In public, there are tacit but strong demands to act in a particular manner, and departures from the norms of the group can lead to harsh criticism from peers. Under fear of criticism and rejection, people often conform to the demands of the group. In doing so, they become agents of the group, temporarily relinquishing their capacity to act freely and to make their own decisions. When this occurs, they no longer function as moral agents, for people can behave morally only if they are free to choose. Aside from strict conformity, the presence of others almost always exerts some influence on our behavior. Typically, people are less likely to act fully as themselves when they know they are being watched or listened to.

Privacy provides an effective antidote to group pressure by giving us a secure psychological space within which we can act freely. In the privacy of your home, for example, you are free to think and to say what you want. And in the privacy of a voting booth, you are free to vote as you please, without fear of reprisal for your choices. This protection of individual autonomy is crucial for the effective functioning of a free society.

The Social Value of Privacy

Privacy is essential in the development of many of our most cherished interpersonal relationships. People can be friends or lovers without privacy, to be sure. But privacy allows people to share ideas and feelings that they might not express in public. In private, we can take others into close confidence and establish unusual levels of trust that could not be established easily while in the public eye. Without privacy, we would probably have no confessors, no one with whom we could bare our souls. Similarly, privacy allows two people to experience the intimacy of a love relationship without fear of embarrassment through public exposure. In a sense, privacy provides fertile soil in which intimate relationships can grow (Gerstein, 1984).

Privacy is a precious commodity for organizations, just as it is for individuals. Large corporations often need to keep their new ideas secret in order to prevent competitors from stealing and capitalizing on them. If they could not maintain privacy, corporations might be forced to decrease the amount of research and development they do, and this would reduce both the quality of their products and the competitiveness of the national business enterprise.

Diversity

Privacy also fosters the social diversity and the tolerance that have been important throughout our history. Many of the early settlers of the U.S. sought to escape religious persecution, and the right to practice the religion of one's choice is still cherished today. Privacy allows different sects, particularly controversial ones, to pursue their religious practices without the fear of having the details of their services or doctrines exposed to unwanted public scrutiny. As long as they break no laws through their religious practices, they are free to do as they choose.

This protection of social diversity is particularly apparent with regard to unusual life styles. In the private sanctuary of our homes, for example, we are free to engage in behavior that most people find atypical and even bizarre. One person might live as a nudist at home, whereas others might engage in homosexual relationships. Without privacy, social pressures would discourage these activities. Although some people have argued that society has no place for nudity and homosexuality, others have pointed out that a society that does not tolerate diversity is one that limits personal freedom. In essence, privacy safeguards individual and social diversity in areas in which no societal consensus has been achieved (Gavison, 1984).

Privacy and Democracy

Perhaps the most important function of privacy, however, is to limit the power and control of the government (Gavison, 1984; Westin, 1967). What could happen when a government violates the privacy of the citizens was portrayed vividly by George Orwell in *1984*, the chilling story of a totalitarian govern- ment that dominated citizens by watching them constantly and by persecuting those who disagreed with government policies. In Orwell's scenario, there were no individual freedoms—the citizens had become mere pawns of the government. Orwell's story is a sobering reminder that in order to maintain the freedom of choice that is the cornerstone of democracy, the government must allow its citizens their right to privacy.

It is tempting to think that the U.S. government would collect information only for benign purposes such as taking the census and prosecuting criminals. Once collected, however, data can be used for other purposes, including political ones, that are difficult to foresee. During World War II, for example, data from the Census Bureau, which are not supposed to be used for political purposes, were used to locate over 100,000 Japanese Americans living in California. By order of the President, they were forced out of their homes and into guarded relocation centers. This act horrified and confused the Japanese Americans, many of whom had been born in the U.S. and who were strongly committed to its government. J. Edgar Hoover, the head of the FBI at that time, said later that his agency could have watched closely the small number of serious Japanese spy suspects and that the forced evacuation of all Japanese Americans had been a response to public political pressure (Burnham, 1980). In times of crisis, then, seemingly harmless information can become a potent political weapon.

Democracy requires a delicate balance between the needs of the govern- ment for information and the right of individuals to act freely, without fear of censorship or political retaliation. Because it limits the information that governments can collect about citizens and protects the right to freedom of choice, privacy is a prerequisite for democracy.

Computer Threats to Privacy

Before computers had been invented, it was possible to violate individuals' privacy by listening to their phone conversations, peering into their windows, or obtaining written financial and medical records. Privacy invasion is not new and is certainly not unique to the era of computers.

By the same token, however, there are significant new threats to individ- ual privacy that stem from the widespread use of computers. For example, computers produce tremendous increases in the amount of information that can be stored and transmitted concerning individual citizens. This has resulted in a quantum leap in the threat to individual privacy.

This increased threat stems in part from the vast increases in the ability to collect and store information. In the past, the collection of large amounts of information required armies of workers, enormous amounts of paper, and vast amounts of storage space. The paper-and-pencil method of collection was both inconvenient and expensive. In contrast, computers make it possible to collect vast quantities of information automatically and to store it in a small space and at a lower cost. Using magnetic tape, for example, the information kept in a multistory university library can be stored in a single room. Furthermore, the technology of information storage and retrieval is advancing at a rapid pace. It is safe to predict that the development of such devices as compact disk players, which can be integrated into computerized systems, will improve storage and retrieval capabilities as much as the development of the silicon chip did.

Possessing the means of collecting vast amounts of information and having the need to do so, many agencies and corporations are inclined to ride the momentum of the information wave and collect more and more data on citizens and customers. Since collecting information has become such a common and accepted practice in our society and since there are real demands for more information, this inclination is understandable. With more information stored and available, however, the opportunities for misuse have expanded. But the problem lies not only in the availability of more information but also in the routine collection of different kinds of information than were stored traditionally.

Transactional Data

Transactional data consist of records of activities such as buying or selling that are common features of daily life. The automatic collection of transactional data is rapidly becoming routine. When customers use their credit cards to buy something in a store, for example, information is automatically sent to their files, identifying what they bought and indicating the price, the date, and the identity of the merchant. Similarly, when you use a credit card to make a phone call, information is automatically sent to your file concerning the time, the date, the number called, how long you talked, and the price of the call. As a result, the computer data banks of credit institutions contain masses of information regarding personal transactions. In earlier days of cash and check transactions, this kind of information was either collected on a much smaller scale or not collected at all because of the high costs involved in manual recording and record keeping.

Significant risks attend the collection and storage of so much transactional information. By examining all of the transactions someone has made using a credit card, it is possible to obtain a relatively complete picture of where he goes, of his habits and values, and of his style of living. A record of someone who had used a credit card to pay for a business trip would provide a surprisingly complete account of his activities, down to the details of where he had eaten, what kind of car he had driven, and whom he had called. If this information fell into the wrong hands, such as those of a corrupt government, it could be used to spy on dissenters or to pressure them into conformity.

Errors

The collection of more and more information makes it progressively harder to make sure that the information is correct. And as is often said by people who work with computers, "Garbage in, garbage out." This means that if errors are made in putting information into the computer, then the output of the computer will also contain errors. In some instances, ludicrous errors have cropped up. Richard Brudzynski, for example, was a lawyer who frequently advised his clients to check their credit records to see if they contained erroneous information. One day he decided to take his own advice and check his own records. To his surprise, his records indicated that he was married to Florence Brudzynski, who was really his mother. The records also indicated his occupation as stockboy, a position he had not held in over five years. Understandably, he felt strange over his new identity as a 28-year-old lawyer-turned-stockboy who was married to his 63-year-old mother. Not wanting this incorrect and Oedipal identity, he had his records corrected (Winokur, 1984).

Errors in computer records, however, are not always so benign. Shirley Jones was a law-abiding citizen and mother of three who was mistakenly arrested in 1982. When she told the arresting officers that she had not done anything wrong, they said that they had been trying to catch her for four years. To her shock, she was jailed for eighteen hours. It turned out that "Shirley Jones" was an alias that had been used by a wanted criminal whose real name was Vera Davis. When police computer records showed the name "Shirley Jones," officers moved in on the innocent Ms. Jones for the arrest. The computer records had been more than a little off. Whereas Shirley Jones was five feet seven inches tall and weighed 220 pounds, Vera Davis was six inches shorter and weighed only half as much (*San Francisco Examiner*, Oct. 7, 1984).

The chances of this kind of error occurring are uncomfortably high, owing largely to the creation by the FBI of a National Crime Information Center (NCIC). The NCIC provides a computer network that links together federal, state, and local criminal justice agencies. NCIC files contain over 17 million records and provide information on everything from stolen vehicles to criminal histories. Using the NCIC, a police officer in virtually any state can pull a motorist for a traffic violation and issue a computer check to determine in a matter of minutes whether the car is a stolen vehicle or whether the driver is wanted on other charges by either the FBI or some other state agency. Although this system has been useful in fighting crime, it contains large numbers of errors (Dahl, 1988). In 1985, the FBI has reported a six percent error rate, which translates into roughly 12,000 erroneous reports and warrants issued each day. And some of the errors are howlers. In Mobile, Alabama, for example, 338 out of 453 warrants inexplicably listed the height as seven feet eleven inches, the weight as 499 pounds, and the hair color as "XXX" (Burnham, 1985). Very high error rates also occur in state records (Laudon, 1986).

Poor data quality in data bases such as the NCIC can damage the reputation and the job prospects of millions of citizens. Half the state governments and over three-quarters of the city governments ask on employment forms whether the applicants have a history of arrest. Laudon (1986) estimates that 15 million government workers at various levels are subject to criminal history employment checks. But the high error rates in the data bases question the validity of these checks. Furthermore, computerized arrest records tend to follow people permanently. In the days of manual records, one could move to a new location in order to get a fresh start. By contrast, computerized records tend to circulate through-out networks and to remain accessible on a long-term basis. As a result, someone who was arrested for disorderly behavior as a result of drinking too much at age eighteen may carry the burden of that arrest for an entire lifetime. This becomes particularly serious in light of the fact that roughly one fourth of the labor force—over 25 million people—has an arrest record (Laudon, 1986). All of these people are at risk of being denied jobs or privileges, even if the offenses were minor or if they had served time and turned over a new leaf.

Errors can also consist of saying too little rather than too much. A medical record, for example, might indicate that an individual received psy-chiatric treatment for depression, and this information could keep him from attaining certain kinds of positions and responsibilities. This would be inap-propriate if, in fact, the person had needed only temporary treatment because of profound grief over the death of a spouse. In general, errors of incomplete-ness and omission cannot be detected through simple accuracy checks of the sort that might identify typing errors and patently false information. The upshot is that it is vexingly difficult to achieve high levels of correctness or data integrity, particularly in very large data bases.

The Retrieval and Dissemination of Information

Tremendous amounts of information can be stored on paper, and countless government file cabinets and rooms are filled with information concerning individual tax records, medical records, and so on. Paper storage methods, however, suffer the obvious flaw that as more and more information is stored, the information becomes increasingly difficult and time consuming to retrieve. Imagine, for example, how much work it would require to retrieve a tax form submitted to the IRS by a particular person in 1940, before the advent of the computer. Long search times entail skyrocketing costs, and the high cost of retrieving the information by hand deters many searches. For practical purposes, stored information becomes unusable when it cannot be retrieved efficiently.

The computer reduces this problem by providing a fast and cost efficient means of retrieval. Using a computer, only a few quick key-strokes will retrieve a tax record for a particular individual. The person doing the search never leaves his or her desk, and the computer provides access to the stored information in a matter of seconds. In addition, computers make it possible to transmit this information immediately over long distances, using the vast network of telephone lines and global telecommunications links that now exist. With regard to retrieving and disseminating information, the computer is truly a revolutionary tool.

The power of the computer in retrieving and transmitting information answers the need of people such as prospective employers for information. But this increased accessibility of information also creates new avenues to abuses of privacy. Networks such as the NCIC make it so easy to distribute information widely that it is increasingly difficult to keep information private. With respect to arrest records, this makes it difficult to enforce the principle that one is innocent until proven guilty, a fundamental precept of our criminal justice system.

The distribution of information via computer can also increase the longevity of information, the amount of time during which the information will remain stored and usable. For example, Maryland might send a piece of information to neighboring states, which then release it to private employment and credit agencies. In turn, the latter distribute it to individual employers, who share it with their business associates. In many cases, there is no complete record of where or to whom the information has been sent, making it very difficult to call back the information or to correct it. Buried in the recesses of many different computers, the information will remain retrievable and usable for long periods of time.

The widespread distribution of information makes it difficult for citizens to know who has information about them and to restrict access to it. In one case, a store decided not to grant credit to a man and would not explain why (Arbib, 1984). When he went to court to find out the source of his bad credit rating, he discovered that a credit-information bureau had a record of a different man who had the same name and who had actually lost a court case involving the failure to pay a debt. Having had this information removed from his file, he thought he had restored his good credit rating. To his chagrin, he discovered later that other credit-information bureaus had stored the same false information under his name since they had all obtained the incorrect information from a common source. In the age of computers, each of us needs to know who keeps records on us, and we also need to be able to correct errors that are in our files.

The increasing ability of corporations to distribute information raises the question of who controls the information kept in a file—the holder of the file or the individual whom the file pertains to. In one highly publicized case, U.S. Treasury officials suspected Mitchell Miller of producing and distributing untaxed whiskey. Without notice to Miller, grand jury subpoenas were sent to the two banks where he had accounts. The banks then showed Miller's financial statements and checks to Treasury officials even though the subpoenas did not require immediate disclosure. Miller subsequently challenged the subpoenas on the grounds that his bank records had been improperly seized since they belonged to him. But in *United States v. Miller*, the Supreme Court ruled that a customer's records are in fact owned by the bank and that the customer is therefore entitled to neither a notice of the subpoena nor an opportunity to challenge it (Office of Technology Assessment, 1986).

This decision undoubtedly contradicts the expectations of most citizens that their financial records will not be disclosed without their consent. More important, it empowers banks and, by implication, other record-keeping agencies to distribute confidential information about customers. This opens the door to widespread abridgments of privacy. Although computers did not play a role in the *Miller* case, the use of computers can severely amplify the risks to privacy that are allowed by the Supreme Court ruling.

Record Matching

Several records are kept on nearly every citizen today. Increasingly, state and federal governments are using computers to compare and match different records in order to identify cases of fraud. The usefulness of record matching is particularly apparent in the highly publicized case of Jose Martinez. Jose's mother had been receiving welfare payments for her son for over four years. But federal investigators became suspicious when they compared welfare records against federal Medicaid records. Jose's name never appeared in the medical records, yet it seemed highly unlikely that a little boy would never have been treated for common problems such as earaches or viral infections. Further investigation revealed that Jose was a fictitious person who resided solely in the welfare records. Louis and Angela Lopez, having created him and an entire family in order to collect welfare benefits, had taken in $60,000 in illegal welfare payments (Early, 1986).

It has always been possible to match records from different sources by hand, but the high costs of manual matching render it impractical in all but a small number of cases. Computers, however, make it possible to do record matching on a mass scale at only a fraction of the cost of manual searches. The federal government is using this capability of high speed record matching on a widespread basis. In its initial project, Project

Match, the Department of Health, Education and Welfare compared welfare files to its own payroll on the idea that no one should simultaneously
be employed by HEW and collecting welfare.

Since Project Match, the government has expanded its record matching programs dramatically. Between 1980 and 1985, the number of federal
computer matches tripled, and the federal inventory of microcomputers
rose from a few thousand to over 100,000 (OTA, 1986). Today, there are
more than 1,200 state matching programs and over 200 federal matching
programs. In addition, the government is collaborating with private businesses in some matching programs. In 1983, for example, the IRS matched
the income statements on tax returns against private companies' computerized lists of income estimates for particular households in order to
identify cases of tax evasion (Laudon, 1986).

Unrestrained record matching, however, poses serious threats to civil
rights. Many matching projects amount to fishing expeditions aimed at
detecting cases of fraud and criminal behavior. Yet the courts have
generally ruled in other areas that fishing expeditions violate the Fourth
Amendment right to be free from unreasonable searches. Record matches
conducted in shotgun fashion may also violate citizens' Fourth Amendment rights (Shattuck, 1984). There is also a danger that individuals will
be prosecuted without due cause. In one case, a woman quit nursing school
and signed onto the welfare rolls after she had been diagnosed as having
cervical cancer. Having received cobalt treatment, she went to work for a
federal agency and notified the welfare department to stop the payments.
When the welfare checks kept coming, she wrote the welfare office again.
But the welfare payments continued, and the woman used the money to
pay her medical bills. As the result of Project Match, the woman lost her
job and was charged with welfare fraud. Eventually, her case was dismissed from court when the judge learned that she had notified the welfare
department twice that she had returned to work (Early, 1986). As record
matching is used more frequently, this type of case and the personal
problems it creates will probably become increasingly common.

In addition, many government matching programs have not followed the
initial guidelines, which require that cost-benefit analyses be conducted before
a matching program begins. But few programs have actually met this requirement, in part because it is difficult to measure the successes and the drawbacks
of matching programs. The available data on costs and benefits, however,
provide conflicting evidence regarding the cost efficiency of matching projects
(OTA, 1986). The Department of Health and Human Services (HHS), for
example, estimated that record matching helped it to identify $1.4 billion in
savings in 1983 (Kusserow, 1984). On the other hand, some studies indicate
a rather poor yield for record matching projects. For example, in the original
Project Match, there were 33,000 "hits," that is, computer matches that

warranted investigation. These were narrowed down to 638 serious cases, but only 55 of these were actually prosecuted (Clarke, 1988).

Another matching project compared the employee records of the Department of Health and Human Services (HHS) with the welfare rolls of counties surrounding Washington, D. C. The computer turned up 638 cases of possible fraud, but seventy-five percent of these were dismissed after further investigation. In the end, only 15 welfare mothers were indicted. Five of these cases were dismissed, four had charges reduced to misdemeanors, and six others plead guilty. Despite all its work, HHS recovered a meager $2,000 (Laudon, 1986).

The Balance of Power

The extensive use of record matching also presents grave dangers at the societal level, for it could give the government and corporations a frighteningly complete dossier on individual citizens. Carried to an extreme, government officials could very rapidly learn how individual citizens live, including the details of their political contributions, reading preferences, financial transactions, credit histories, and medical conditions. To see the dangers posed by this situation, consider how much more powerful and effective Hitler would have been if a Third Reich computer network had been in place in the Nazi era. In nations such as the U.S., most information is probably collected with benign intent. Even so, information collected with benign intent at one time can be misused at a later time, setting the stage for a Big Brother state in which the government monitors and controls its citizens. Those who view this type of misuse as impossible in the U.S. would do well to remember the McCarthy era of the early 1950s, when a public panic over communism ignited a series of political witchhunts.

The threats posed by unrestricted record matching are remarkably similar to those posed by the establishment of a centralized information agency. In 1965, the Social Science Research Council proposed the formation of a National Data Center for the purpose of consolidating the multiple records that the federal government keeps on each citizen. The benign intent was to eliminate redundant files, conserving storage space and cutting costs. Having created a single file for each citizen, one would have to access only one file in order to obtain information concerning a person's taxes, medical records, social security, or draft status. Under this arrangement, a citizen would carry a single card that serves as the key to all of the information held on that individual. Recently, Australia has considered adopting such an arrangement (Clarke, 1988).

The advantages of a National Data Center, however, are vastly outweighed by the potential losses in individual freedom and privacy. If the federal government had a relatively complete, central file of information on all citizens, it could exercise an inappropriate degree of political control over them. In fact, this type of arrangement has long been used in South Africa to keep blacks under the thumb of the reigning apartheid regime (Conrad, 1986). Moreover, if citizens believed that the information they supplied would be used against them, they might be less willing to cooperate with the government. Recognizing these problems, many U.S. citizens, including computer experts, took a strong, vocal stand against the establishment of the Center, defeating the proposal. For similar reasons, Australians voted down the proposal to establish an "Australia card" (Clarke, 1988).

Nevertheless, the pressures to collect information on individuals remain very strong, particularly since computers offer a relatively fast and efficient means of doing so. In fact, the Office of Technology Assessment (1986) and many advocates of civil liberties worry that a *de facto* national database covering nearly all Americans already exists. For one thing, the federal government enacted the 1984 Budget Deficit Reduction Act, requiring that all states participate in matching programs in order to receive federal funds for welfare (Clarke, 1988). In taking this step, Congress demanded that all states allow the matching of millions of files concerning possible recipients of Medicare, Food Stamps, and Aid to Families with Dependent Children (AFDC) to files concerning Social Security, federal taxes, and medical and employment histories.

What is now being matched is not a carefully selected handful of records but a mammoth collection of files that are truly national in scope. Indeed, at last count, there were 50 million Social Security beneficiaries, 95 million individual taxpayers, 21.2 million food stamp recipients, 61.8 million people covered by private health plans, 21.4 million recipients of Medicaid, 154 million registered motor vehicles, and 140 million licensed drivers (Laudon, 1986). The U.S. is a networked nation, and the eye of the government is upon each one of us.

The extensive use of record matching has gone unchallenged by Congress and the American public, in part because of the desire to reduce fraud and government waste. This state of affairs, however, could give the government excessive power and erode the privacy of individual citizens. In fact, nearly half the American public believe that computers actually pose a threat to their privacy (OTA, 1986). What we need are systematic ways of protecting our privacy.

Legal Safeguards Against Privacy Invasion

The law is the most obvious channel through which privacy might be protected. Unfortunately, the U.S. Constitution does not specifically guarantee a right to privacy. The right to privacy, however, is closely related to several rights covered by the Bill of Rights, particularly by Articles I and IV. Article I guarantees freedom of speech and of the press, the right to petition, and the right to assemble. Without privacy, these freedoms would be difficult to maintain since people are not free to say what they want when they know that they are being overheard by others who may use what is said against them. Article IV protects the right to keep one's home, papers, and possessions from unreasonable searches and seizures conducted without a warrant. By safeguarding the right to keep one's possessions private from unauthorized searches, this Article seems to recognize a limited right to privacy.

Most likely, the Founding Fathers did not address privacy in the Constitution because in their time, there were many fewer organizations and government agencies collecting detailed information about citizens. In addition, they did not live to see the rise of electronic technologies such as electronic wiretaps and computers that pose severe threats to privacy. They may also have assumed that privacy is a precondition for the rights that they enumerated in the Constitution, but we will probably never know for sure.

Even though privacy was not addressed explicitly in the Constitution, it has been the subject of legal analysis following the drafting of the constitution. In 1890, Samuel Warren and Louis Brandeis published an influential paper entitled "The Right to Privacy." They argued that citizens have a right to privacy that is part of their right to their own personality and to immunity from personality invasion by others. Writing as a Justice on the Supreme Court thirty years later, Brandeis stated that the right to privacy is part of the right to be let alone, among the most comprehensive and highly valued of all rights.

It was not until 1965, however, that the Supreme Court explicitly recognized a general right to privacy. In *Griswold v. Connecticut*, the Court overturned a state law that prohibited the use of contraceptives, even by married couples. The Court pointed out that the only way of enforcing the law would have sacrificed the right to privacy of the residents of Connecticut. In writing the majority opinion, Justice Douglas referred to a right of privacy that is older than the Bill of Rights itself.

At present, there is substantial debate about whether the right to privacy is distinct in itself or is in fact derived from other rights such as the rights to ownership and to freedom of speech (Gavison, 1984; Thomson, 1975). There is also question about whether it means being let alone, as Warren and Brandeis stated, or having control of significant personal matters (Fried, 1984; Wasserstrom, 1984). It is clear, however, that privacy must be protected and that changes in the law must be made in order to meet the technological challenge. Although this challenge has been met only in part, virtually all states recognize the right to privacy either by common law decisions or by statute (Freedman, 1987). In addition, the federal government has enacted significant privacy protection legislation over the past twenty years.

The Fair Credit Reporting Act of 1970

Legislation designed to protect privacy must strike a balance between the need of agencies to collect information and the right of individuals to privacy. Credit agencies rank high on the list of institutions which have a legitimate need to collect information since so many people apply for credit cards and loans. But there need to be constraints on the actions of credit agencies if the individual right to privacy is to be preserved. For example, individuals should have the right to see the information used by an agency to deny credit, and they should also be able to correct errors in their records. In addition, there should be limits on whom credit agencies distribute information to.

These ideas are incorporated into the Fair Credit Reporting Act of 1970. This Act gives individuals the right to inspect the information in a credit agency's files that had been used to deny credit. Moreover, it gives individuals the right to challenge the accuracy of the information in their files and to insert their own explanation of the facts into the record. It also requires that agencies purge their records of obsolete items such as information concerning arrests and legal suits that are more than seven years old. These provisions aim to increase both the accuracy and the currency of the information.

The Act also limits the distribution of information about credit standing to organizations that need it for legitimate business purposes such as hiring, insurance investigations, or the granting of credit. In order to obtain information that falls outside the scope of ordinary business transactions that require credit checks, people or organizations must have either a valid court order or written permission from the consumer whose record is to be inspected. Organizations that fail to comply with these regulations must pay the damages sustained by the consumer and also the consumer's court costs and legal fees.

The weakness of this Act is that it places a heavy burden on the consumer. It does not, for example, require credit agencies to notify customers that records are being kept or to whom information has been sent. It also does not require that agencies show customers their complete records, only the portions that have been used against them so far. Further, the consumer bears the burden of correcting inaccurate information. These shortcomings have led to the development of additional legislation.

The Privacy Act of 1974

The Privacy Act of 1974 was designed to protect individuals from unconstrained information-handling practices of the federal government. The introduction to the Act noted that computers are essential for maintaining effective government operations but that their use has significantly increased the threats to individual privacy.

In order to limit the power of the government over individuals, the Act prohibits agencies other than the FBI from keeping secret files concerning particular individuals. At least once a year, each agency must publish in the *Federal Register* a description of each file that it keeps and what kind of information it contains. Instructions must also be provided on how individuals can obtain a copy of their files. The Act gives individuals the right to inspect their records and to demand the correction of erroneous information. An agency that refuses to make a correction must state its reasons in writing, and this statement can then be challenged in court.

The Act also imposes constraints on collecting and distributing information. It allows individuals to refuse to supply their Social Security number when it is not required by federal law, making it difficult to consolidate information from different sources. Furthermore, the Act stipulates that information can be used only for the purposes for which it was collected. In addition, information cannot be transferred from one agency to another without the written consent of the individual. Information can, however, be transferred between agencies in connection with a law enforcement action. Intentional violations of these provisions can lead to fines of up to $5,000 and to civil penalties equal to the damages incurred by the individual.

This Act ranks as one of the most comprehensive and significant pieces of privacy legislation. It is limited, however, since it applies only to the federal government. Approximately one-fifth of the state governments have implemented constraints on state agencies, but most states still lack clear standards for collecting and distributing personal information (Marx, 1985). The Act also lacks a powerful enforcement mechanism. The Office of Management and Budget (OMB) was given responsibility for enforcing the Act and developing guidelines for its implementation. Yet OMB was the very agency that encouraged the widespread use of record matching, which is probably the greatest threat to privacy today. The Act left a significant loophole by allowing "routine" information transfers between agencies such as the Treasury Department and the IRS, agencies that obviously need to transfer information on a regular basis. But the OMB watered the Act down by claiming that "routine use" consists of practically anything that government agencies say is routine (Laudon, 1986). For these reasons, the Act is best regarded as an initial step rather than a comprehensive solution to the problem of privacy invasion.

The Right to Financial Privacy Act of 1979

The power of the federal government could increase significantly if there were no checks on its ability to collect personal information concerning the finances of its citizens. The Right to Financial Privacy Act of 1979 is designed to limit the ability of the government to gather information about particular citizens from financial institutions such as banks.

This Act requires that a federal agency must demonstrate that the information requested pertains to a law enforcement operation. Having sent a subpoena for the information to the financial institution, it must send a copy of the subpoena to the individual whose records are sought. In addition, the agency must indicate how the individual could initiate a court challenge to prevent the release of the information. It must also notify the financial institution in writing that the individual has been informed of his rights and that the time during which a challenge could be made has expired or that the attempt by the individual to block the release of the information in court has failed.

Like the Privacy Act of 1974, this Act applies only to federal agencies, and most state agencies remain unconstrained. This is unnerving since the *Miller* case established that financial institutions such as banks are free to disseminate their highly personal information, even to government officials. This is not to imply that government officials are corrupt. But as Justice Brandeis once warned, the greatest dangers to freedom sometimes come not from the evil acts of tyrants but from the well-intentioned acts of overzealous leaders.

Keeping the Law Current

The legislation described above has taken significant steps in protecting individual privacy. But additional steps are needed, for the changes brought about by computer technology continue to outstrip the law. In 1967, the Supreme Court ruled in *Katz v. the United States* that wiretapping violates the Fourth Amendment, though in 1968 Congress legalized wiretapping that had been approved by court order. This protection against electronic eavesdropping, however, applies only to aural communications that can be understood by human ears. It does not cover messages transmitted by computer such as electronic mail, electronic documents, and even telephone messages transmitted in digital form.

In order to close this legal gap, the Electronic Communication Privacy Act was passed in 1986. This Act makes it a felony to intercept private messages sent through computer networks and requires that law enforcement officials obtain a search warrant in order to examine copies of digital communications that are stored on computer. Although this Act is promising, critics worry that it cannot guarantee adequate protection. Despite this Act, for example, the Reagan administration made several attempts to monitor the use of public data bases in an effort to limit access to unclassified but "sensitive" information (Elmer-DeWitt, 1987). These attempts failed, but they left few doubts that the government would continue pressing for more information on private citizens.

Similar problems exist in keeping the law abreast of changes in record matching capabilities and practices. As discussed above, there has been an explosion of record matching programs by federal and state agencies in the 1980s. Yet no significant new legislation has evolved to keep these practices in check (OTA, 1986). And this situation has no quick remedy.

In fact, as the pace of technology development quickens, it will become increasingly difficult to keep the law current. As the need for new laws increases, it is important to move beyond piecemeal legislation that puts out isolated brushfires without fighting the larger blaze. What is needed is a comprehensive framework for the protection of privacy, a national policy that will guide the collection and the use of information throughout society and that will shape the development of new laws.

Toward a National Privacy Protection Policy

In 1977, a national Privacy Protection Study Commission sketched the outlines of a comprehensive national policy in a report entitled *Personal Privacy in an Information Society*. It began by pointing out that government agencies and private organizations now store so much personal information that it is possible for the government to obtain excessive power over the citizenry. It also noted that record keeping has become relatively indirect. A century ago, individuals had direct, face-to-face contact with officials of record keeping organizations such as banks. Now, however, one seldom has direct contact with organizations such as credit bureaus. In addition, organizations often collect information about individuals from other organizations, and they attempt to verify their own information by comparing it with that held by other organizations. In effect, organizations pay more attention to what other organizations say about people than to what they say about themselves. This makes organizations too receptive to information that is incorrect, incomplete, or illegally collected.

The Commission also noted that neither the law nor computer technology now give individuals the tools they need in order to protect their interests in the records that organizations keep about them. Few people know who keeps records on them, much less what information those records contain, and few know what rights they have to inspect and to challenge information. In addition, many people feel helpless when confronting large organizations having vast power and resources. The irony of this situation is that organizations could use these resources to protect privacy. In the same way that an error in a record can be transmitted nationwide at the speed of light, so too can corrections. The same technology that threatens privacy could be used to protect it, if only there were laws or incentives for doing so.

Carefully avoiding laying the blame for these problems on any particular organizations or people, the Commission called for the achievement of three objectives, the first of which is to minimize intrusiveness. In order to give individuals the opportunity to avoid association with intrusive organizations, it recommended that individuals be informed more fully about the information needs and practices of a record-keeping organization before entering into a relationship with it. Because intrusion often occurs through the use of inappropriate information, the Commission recommended that organizations not collect information such as arrest records that employers might use to deny employment. It also proposed that record keepers be required to exercise reasonable care in choosing organizations to collect information for them. These reasonable care recommendations are designed to prevent the collection of confidential information under false pretenses, a practice that often leads to unwanted intrusions of privacy.

The second objective is to maximize fairness to individuals about whom records are kept. This requires maintaining accurate records and limiting their distribution. To prevent damage from the use of incorrect information, the Commission recommended that organizations have reasonable procedures for assuring the accuracy, timeliness, completeness, and relevance of the information that they keep. Moreover, it recommended that individuals have the right to review and, where necessary, to correct their records. At the request of the individual, the organization would pass the corrections on to past recipients of the incorrect information.

Recognizing the perils stemming from the unlimited distribution of information, the Commission proposed that organizations be required to obtain the authorization of the individual before divulging confidential information to other agencies. It also recommended that organizations obey the principle of limited disclosure, which stipulates that an agency should not pass on entire records but only the authorized information that is relevant to the task at hand.

The third objective is to create legitimate, enforceable expectations of confidentiality. This objective was formulated in part as a reaction against the Supreme Court decision in the *Miller* case, which gave the banks the legal right to distribute their confidential financial information as they wish. The Commission recommended that there be legal restrictions on the ability of organizations to give information to others. It also proposed the creation of legal statutes that would enable individuals to protect themselves against improper or unreasonable demands for disclosure of information by government or private agencies.

Finding the Balance

Movement toward a national policy for protecting privacy has been slow, but this should not be too surprising. Nations, like individuals, embody many conflicting tendencies, and proposals for a national policy must find their way through a maze of competing interests. Furthermore, it is difficult for a comprehensive policy to address all of the underlying tensions in a manner that is politically appealing to a very broad constituency.

In the U.S., there is an ongoing conflict between openness and secrecy. On one hand, our democratic government stands on the open exchange of ideas and information, as the First Amendment explicitly prohibits the government from infringing upon the rights of people to speak openly. The government itself also has a strong interest in having relatively open access to information. For example, open information access enables the government to conduct projects such as Project Match that aim to detect cases of welfare abuse. Similarly, businesses want relatively open access to information in order to make credit checks, employment investigations, and predictions about the market. On the other hand, our society also has extensive secrecy needs. Individuals often want secrecy in order to keep particular kinds of information and experiences private. Many corporations rely upon trade secrets to protect their intellectual property. And the government often wants secrecy in order to protect national security interests.

No one knows exactly where to draw the line in balancing these competing interests for openness and secrecy, and the balance changes over time as public attitudes shift and as society encounters new challenges. Indeed, there are built-in tensions that make for a pendulum effect. For example, the strong emphasis on national security during the 1980s led the federal government to enact stiff controls over scientific information even though it was not classified (Shattuck and Spence, 1988). But too much restriction on the international exchange of scientific information can put us behind other countries in science and technology, which eventually damages our economy and even our national security. When this occurs, the controls will be relaxed.

A similar pendulum effect may occur in regard to individual privacy. In the current political environment, there is much greater pressure to satisfy the information needs of the government and of business than to protect the privacy rights of the citizens. But this situation is not fixed in stone, particularly since nearly half the citizens believe that their privacy is being threatened (OTA, 1986). If large numbers of citizens choose to voice their beliefs and to act in ways that protect their privacy, then this state of affairs will change.

Amidst this welter of competing and shifting interests, it is perhaps for the best that movement toward a national privacy protection policy has been slow. A pluralistic society needs to be patient in order to achieve compromises that preserve and extend the legal and philosophical foundations of the nation. Should patience lapse into apathy, however, the resulting losses of privacy could silently erode our hard won freedom.

Conclusion

The right to privacy is the cornerstone of a free society. Without privacy, individuals lose their freedom to be who they really are and to conduct their lives out of the public eye. Invasions of privacy threaten individual dignity and compromise creativity and mental health. Privacy invasions also carry an exorbitant social cost. If the government watches unusual or deviant groups closely, this will limit the social diversity that is essential in a pluralistic society. When the government obtains and uses too much information on large numbers of citizens, freedom is stripped away, and society drifts toward a Big Brother state in which the government watches and controls the people.

Significant threats to privacy have emerged as society has become populated with large numbers of organizations and government agencies that use computers to collect an ever expanding array of information about citizens. In addition to providing an affordable means of storing vast quantities of information, computers produce a quantum leap in the ability to retrieve information quickly and to distribute it widely via electronic networks. Currently, record matching poses the greatest threat to privacy. In the 1980s, there has been an explosion of record matching, as governments and corporations acquired many thousands of computers and used them to compare and to consolidate the records held by different agencies on particular individuals. Although this practice has succeeded in identifying criminal activities, it has also given the government unprecedented ability to collect detailed information about individual citizens and to do so without any evidence of wrongdoing. Advocates of civil liberties worry that we have created a *de facto* national data base that puts too much power in the hands of the government.

In the past twenty years, new laws have attempted to strike a balance between the individual's right to privacy and organizations' need to collect and to use information. Protecting privacy by law is no easy matter, since, as was true in the realm of security, computer technology and social practices race ahead of the law. At the federal level, there are gaping holes in privacy protection legislation. The most comprehensive law to date, the Privacy Protection Act of 1974, antedated the onslaught of record matching, and it has been seriously damaged by weak enforcement and by administrative encouragement of the widespread exchange of information between federal and state agencies. In the current environment, piecemeal laws will not go far enough to provide the broad protection of privacy that is needed.

What is needed now is a comprehensive framework for guiding the construction of new laws and policies regarding privacy protection. This framework could build upon the report issued in 1977 by the Privacy Protection Study Commission. The acceptance of such a framework, however, requires a delicate compromise between the competing pressures for openness and secrecy. It also requires that individual citizens make strong choices in favor of protecting their privacy. Making these choices will become even more important as we face the formidable new challenges that are sparked by research on artificial intelligence, the subject of the next chapter.

8

Artificial Intelligence

For centuries, people have courted the idea of intelligent machines: automata that could talk, perceive, and think. In Hellenic Egypt, around 200 B.C., inventors made moving statues that danced and shot out flames in clever religious shows designed to invoke awe of the gods (McCorduck, 1979). By the eighteenth century, it was fashionable for noblemen to display life-size automata that, driven by gears and levers, could draw, write and play musical instruments (Peat, 1985). Although intriguing, these attempts fell far short of the ideal of a thinking machine.

In contemporary times, the fascination with the idea of intelligent machines has centered around the field of artificial intelligence (AI), which Marvin Minsky, one of the founders of AI, defined as "the science of making machines do things that would require intelligence if done by men" (1968, p. v). Research in AI has moved the idea of intelligent machines out of the realm of fantasy and into the real world. In 1982, for example, a computerized expert system called PROSPECTOR helped locate a molybdenum deposit in Washington state worth $100 million (Harmon and King, 1985). This event ignited a flurry of interest in AI in the business community, which was quick to recognize the profits to be reaped from developing systems that file income taxes, handle nuclear wastes, and so on. Indeed, profits from using expert systems are expected to reach $800 million by 1990 (Szolovits, 1987).

The reasons for building intelligent machines, however, extend far beyond commercial profit, for personal and national power are also at stake. The project of making intelligent machines offers humans a rare opportunity to act as gods, creating machines in their own image. In addition, intelligent machines have extensive military applications, as witnessed in smart weapons and the Strategic Defense Initiative. Many defense authorities believe that intelligent systems are an increasingly vital component of national power and security.

The effort to build intelligent machines is also a quest in self-exploration. In building intelligent machines, scientists make new discoveries about what is required for intelligence, and these often shed light on human intelligence, about which a great deal remains to be learned (Sternberg, 1985). In fact, many of the most influential theories of human intelligence and mind are now based upon concepts and models that originated in the field of AI. Research in AI provides a drawing board used to sketch the properties of intelligence, thereby increasing our understanding of what it means to be intelligent and of the mechanisms that underlie intelligence.

Viewed in this light, research in AI has far reaching philosophical implications. For example, the existence of intelligent computers would challenge the view that humans are unique in their capacity to think and to reason. If researchers succeeded in building a system that demonstrated the full range of human intelligence, this would increase the plausibility of the view that the human mind, like the computer, is a machine. And if the human mind turns out to be mechanistic, what becomes of our cherished assumptions of free will and responsibility? The profundity of these issues has forced scholars from many different disciplines to take AI research seriously.

Excitement about the idea of intelligent machines, however, should not blind us to the ethical and social issues associated with the AI enterprise (Weizenbaum, 1976; Winograd and Flores, 1986). For example, should intelligent systems be allowed to make life and death decisions? If an AI system makes a costly error, where does the responsibility lie? These questions are particularly pressing in light of recent advances in the development of expert systems.

Expert Systems

When Laura played tennis for the first time in a year, she developed lower back pain that bed rest and aspirin did not help and that went on for three weeks. Wanting a more powerful pain reliever, she went to see her new family physician, Dr. Jones, in the city to which she had just moved. Dr. Jones turned to her personal computer, which connected to a nationwide medical information network, and retrieved Laura's medical history. Having learned that a small tumor had been removed from Laura's breast five years ago, Dr. Jones thought to herself that Laura's problem could be cancer rather than the more obvious alternatives of muscle strain or arthritis. Wanting a second opinion, Dr. Jones called up QMR (Quick Medical Reference), a computerized expert system for diagnosing illnesses. QMR suggested that Laura may be suffering arthritis, muscle strain, or a recurrence of cancer with metastasis to the base of the spine. Glad that QMR's diagnosis agreed with her own, Dr. Jones ordered a bone scan in order to check the possibility of recurrent cancer (Rennels and Shortliffe, 1987).

Scenarios such as this are not entirely futuristic, as expert systems are fast becoming essential tools in fields such as medicine. An expert system is a rule-based system that embodies part of the skill of a human expert in a computer program (Forsyth, 1984). Most expert systems are designed to offer advice about how to perform a particular task such as diagnosing diseases, and most can tell the user how they reached a decision. Typically, they are easy to interact with, allowing users to communicate in relatively normal English. Their knowledge, however, is usually restricted to a highly specialized domain—they do not even come close to displaying the full scope of human intelligence.

The Anatomy of Expert Systems

The core of an expert system consists of a knowledge base that contains rules, usually in an IF–THEN format, as in the following example:

RULE 024

IF: (1) THE THERAPY UNDER CONSIDERATION IS GENTAMYCIN AND
       (2) THE IDENTITY OF THE ORGANISM IS DEFINITELY
       PSEUDOMONAS

THEN: RECORD THE FOLLOWING AS A MORE APPROPRIATE
       THERAPY THAN GENTAMYCIN ALONE: THE COMBINATION OF
       GENTAMYCIN AND CARBENICILLIN

The knowledge base also contains new facts that may be acquired while the expert system is in use. Indeed, the knowledge base contains rules that guide the generation of new facts or hypotheses, making the expert system an active information seeker. This contrasts sharply with a conventional data base, which is a passive repository of information.

The core of the expert system also contains an inference engine, a set of strategies for generating and testing hypotheses concerning the problem at hand. Two commonly used strategies are backward and forward chaining. In backward chaining, the computer generates a hypothesis, often on the basis of its knowledge that a particular event is highly likely in the situation under consideration. Then it attempts to collect data that will either confirm or disprove the hypothesis. In contrast, forward chaining follows the more inductive route of collecting many data and then formulating a hypothesis that explains them. Since the real world often allows only probabilistic statements rather than certainties, expert systems typically make probabilistic hypotheses to deal with uncertainty (Forsyth, 1984).

Designing an effective expert system requires the development of powerful rules and inference strategies. But it also requires the extraction of the appropriate information from human experts, and this has proven to be remarkably difficult. Many experts can execute a task with virtuosity and with little conscious effort or reflection, yet they find it difficult to explain how they have accomplished a task. In order to appreciate this difficulty, consider how hard it is to explain to someone how to ride a bicycle. For most people, bike riding is a very well learned skill that has become so automatic that it is difficult to describe clearly. Typically, it takes many long and painstaking sessions to collect the necessary information from an expert. Nevertheless, a number of successful expert systems have been developed, one of the earliest and best known of which is called MYCIN.

MYCIN

Infectious diseases are a serious problem for patients who have suffered burns or who have undergone surgery. It is important to run the proper tests early because these diseases require immediate treatment and because it can take hours and even days to track down the bacteria responsible for the infection. This need poses problems in smaller hospitals, particularly in rural areas, where there is often a shortage of specialists who can diagnose and treat infectious diseases effectively. In addition, there is evidence that many physicians do not follow safe, rational procedures in diagnosing and treating microbial infections (Shortliffe, 1976).

To remedy this problem, AI researchers and physicians designed MYCIN, an automated consultation system which assists in the diagnosis and treatment of infectious diseases (Shortliffe, 1976). MYCIN enters a dialogue with the attending physician, who supplies information concerning the results of various tests. MYCIN uses the input from the doctor, coupled with its rules, to form hypotheses, each of which is associated with a probability or confidence level. The ability to generate hypotheses through the use of rules and factual information is apparent in MYCIN's rule 047:

IF: (1) THE SITE OF THE CULTURE IS BLOOD, AND
        (2) THE IDENTITY OF THE ORGANISM IS NOT KNOWN WITH
            CERTAINTY, AND
        (3) THE STRAIN OF THE ORGANISM IS GRAMNEG, AND

(4) THE MORPHOLOGY OF THE ORGANISM IS ROD, AND

(5) THE PATIENT HAS BEEN SERIOUSLY BURNED

THEN: THERE IS WEAKLY SUGGESTIVE EVIDENCE (.4) THAT THE
IDENTITY OF THE ORGANISM IS PSEUDOMONAS

MYCIN tests the hypotheses it has formed by requesting new information, and
it uses the results to generate new hypotheses. Eventually, MYCIN reaches a
hypothesis that is consistent with the evidence and that can guide treatment.
Then it gives its diagnosis and treatment recommendations.

The following is a sample of a hypothetical dialogue (From Arbib, 1984):

MYCIN: Enter patient's name.

DOCTOR: Dorothy Thomas

MYCIN: What is the patient's sex?

DOCTOR: Female

MYCIN: How old is the patient?

DOCTOR: 51

MYCIN: Have you obtained positive cultures from a site at which Dorothy
Thomas has an infection?

DOCTOR: Yes.

MYCIN: What is the infection?

DOCTOR: Primary-bacteremia.

Having collected information about the specimen and the tests performed,
MYCIN makes its diagnosis:

MYCIN: The identity of ORGANISM-1 is PSEUDOMONAS
(.357) KLEBSIELLA (.177) ENTEROBACTER (.166)
E. COLI (.137) PROTEUS (.118) SERRATIA (.042)
My therapy recommendations will be based on the following possible
identities of the organism(s) that seem to be significant:
1 The identity of ORGANISM-1 may be PSEUDOMONAS
2 The identity of ORGANISM-1 may be KLEBSIELLA
3 The identity of ORGANISM-1 may be ENTEROBACTER
4 The identity of ORGANISM-1 may be E. COLI
5 The identity of ORGANISM-1 may be PROTEUS
[Because it was so unlikely that SERRATIA was the source of the infection,
MYCIN did not consider it in its therapy recommendations. MYCIN then
continues.]

MYCIN: On a scale of 0 to 4, where higher numbers indicate increasing
severity, how would you rate Dorothy Thomas' degree of sickness?

DOCTOR: 4

MYCIN: Does Dorothy Thomas have a clinically significant allergic reaction to any antimicrobial agent?

DOCTOR: No.

MYCIN: My preferred therapy recommendation is as follows: In order to cover for items 1   2   3   4   5:
Give the following in combination:
1   GENTAMYCIN
Dose: 1.7 mg/kg q8h–IV or IM
Comments: Modify dose in renal failure
2   CARBENICILLIN
Dose: 25 mg/kg q2h–IV
Comments: Modify dose in renal failure

Wanting to doublecheck this recommendation, the physician can ask MYCIN how it decided that ORGANISM–1 is a PSEUDOMONAS. MYCIN would then indicate which rules it followed and display any rules that the physician asked to see. In addition, the physician could ask whether MYCIN ever prescribes the use of carbenicillin alone in the treatment of a pseudomonas infection. MYCIN would then display the various rules pertaining to the use of carbenicillin.   These features of MYCIN allow the physician to reject inappropriate treatment recommendations, making the physician the final arbiter regarding therapy. Because MYCIN will answer questions about its recommendations and about how it reached a decision, it allows the physician to learn more about the treatment of infectious diseases. This is no small advantage in an era in which medical knowledge is advancing at a breakneck pace.

Numerous tests have indicated that MYCIN performs very well in comparison with human physicians.   In one study, MYCIN and five physicians from Stanford University who were experts in the treatment of infectious diseases made independent assessments of ten clinically challenging cases.   Then a team of eight judges who were experts in the treatment of infectious diseases rated the adequacy of the clinical summaries and the prescriptions made by MYCIN and each of the physicians. The judges made their decisions blindly, not knowing whether MYCIN or a human physician had produced a particular clinical record. Surprisingly, the judges rated the performance of MYCIN more highly than that of the human physicians. It is sobering to note, however, that both MYCIN and the human physicians performed far from perfectly. Seventy percent of MYCIN's recommendations were judged as acceptable, compared to only forty-four percent of the physicians' recommendations (Yu et al., 1979).

The success of MYCIN and other early systems has sparked the development of new expert systems, many of which are used in fields outside of medicine. Researchers at the University of Pittsburgh developed CADUCEUS, a system that can diagnose over 500 diseases. CADU-CEUS was a predecessor of QMR, and it contained information about some 4,100 signs, symptoms and patient characteristics (Rennels and Shortliffe, 1987). Similarly, researchers at Stanford University invented a system called DENDRAL that identifies different organic molecules by interpreting mass spectrographic data (Feigenbaum, Buchanan, and Lederberg, 1971). And at MIT, mathematicians developed MACYSMA, a system that carries out a large number of symbolic mathematical operations such as differentiation and integration.

Among the new generation of expert systems are systems that can learn and that can make very complex inferences. For example, the EURISKO system developed at Stanford can use its experience to extend its own body of rules. In addition to having won difficult naval games three years in succession, EURISKO made a breakthrough in the design of very large scale circuits by coming up with a three-dimensional AND/OR gate (Forsyth, 1984). The designers of expert systems believe that additional research on machines that can learn and make decisions will close the gap between human and machine expertise.

The Trouble with Experts

Expert systems are an important source of new wealth since they can be used to extend services, to create new products and to guide automated manufacturing systems. In principle, they could also aid remote and underdeveloped areas where expertise is scarce. They could, for example, be used to improve agriculture and health care in the Third World countries where hunger and disease are rampant. In industrialized nations, expert systems could assist in controlling nuclear power plants and cleaning up dangerous accidents. Used in these humane ways, expert systems would increase the quality of life of millions of people.

This optimistic assessment, however, is shaken by a simple question: Who will benefit from this technology? Because of the high costs involved, only large companies or agencies can develop new expert systems. These companies, however, tend to produce and to distribute systems that will enhance their own operations and profits, and the benefits seldom trickle down to the poor and the hungry. As a result, expert systems will probably be yet another means whereby the rich will become richer. The unequal distribution of this source of new wealth could significantly increase the social inequities that already exist, contributing to the misery of the poor and sowing the seeds of discontent.

Further development and use of expert systems may also aggravate the problem of unemployment. Whereas robotic systems displace large numbers of blue collar workers, expert systems may displace large numbers of white collar workers. The work of many accountants, lawyers, insurance representatives and bankers can probably be done by well-designed expert systems. The long-term result may be soaring unemployment in a social class that historically has been relatively insulated from the displacing effects of technology.

Responsibility

In an understaffed health care clinic in a remote part of Montana, Bill Trivers lay dying of third degree burns and complications produced by the accompanying infectious diseases. Wanting to give Bill the latest in medical treatment for the infectious diseases, the attending physician consults a MYCIN-like expert system. The expert system diagnoses Bill's diseases and recommends the administration of several prescription drugs, which the physician administers. But Bill soon dies. Other physicians who review the case believe that Bill could have been saved had he received proper treatment. Bill's family decides to sue the physicians for malpractice.

This scenario raises a difficult question: who or what is responsible for Bill's death? This type of question is gaining prominence as expert systems become standard tools for medical treatment (Johnson and Snapper, 1985). On one hand, the computer program might bear some causal responsibility since it proposed the treatment that brought about the death. But the computer program simply did what it had been designed to do by human knowledge engineers. Lacking choice, the computer cannot be held responsible legally or morally.

An alternative view is that the attending physician is responsible (Blois, 1980; Newman, 1988). After all, the physician chose to accept the expert system's recommendation. He might therefore be liable for professional malpractice, that is, for the failure to exercise reasonable care (Brannigan, 1985). But this approach puts the physician in a double bind. If he had lacked the extensive knowledge required to treat an infectious disease, he might have felt it necessary to follow the advice of the expert system in order to save the patient. This might constitute reasonable care since, in using the computer, he was following the advice of experts on infectious disease. The alternative would have been to trust his own judgment over the advice of the expert system. But this approach could also have caused his patient to die, and it may not have constituted reasonable care. At issue here is what constitutes reasonable care in regard to the use of an expert system. Because expert systems are relatively new in medical treatment, few legal decisions have been rendered on this issue. Consequently, the physician's responsibility in this arena is uncertain.

Yet another alternative is to hold the supplier of the expert system liable for having marketed a defective product. The standards of professional liability (malpractice) do not hold physicians responsible for damages inflicted as the result of exercising reasonable care. In contrast, standards of product liability hold the supplier of a product strictly liable for injuries caused by defective products, even if the defect could not have been prevented (Brannigan, 1985). The law, however, is not clear about whether a computer program is a product as opposed to a service. Most products are tangible objects, but programs are not. In addition, standards of product liability apply only if the product reaches the consumer in defective condition. A device such as a heart monitor clearly reaches the patient directly. But the physician stands between the expert system and the patient. Since the physician can reject the advice of the expert system, it is not entirely accurate to say that the expert system reaches the patient (Brannigan, 1985). As in the realm of privacy, the development of computers has outpaced the law, which remains fuzzy about whether a program is a product or a service.

The upshot is that it is uncertain as to who is responsible for damages that result from the use of expert systems. Until the law resolves these issues, there will remain a disconcerting amount of unaccountability surrounding the use of expert systems, and this could work much to the disadvantage of consumers.

Credibility

Another risk is that people will assign too much credibility and authority to expert systems. Computers have always been surrounded by a mystique of perfection because they perform such an impressive array of tasks at high speed and without errors, fatigue, or fits of irrationality. Anyone who has been clobbered by a computer in a game can appreciate the sense that the computer is closer to perfection than people are. In addition, part of the folk wisdom about computers is that after a program has been debugged, it can be trusted to get the job done flawlessly and rapidly.

The problem of excessive credibility is evident in how people talk about computers. We have been highly anthropomorphic in our language, and we have tended to attribute more and more human characteristics to computers. Initially, computer users spoke of "data processing." Then they spoke of "information processing," implying that the computer, like people, can interpret raw data. Now members of the artificial intelligentsia speak not of information processing but of "knowledge processing" (Roszak, 1986), which suggests that computers are even more similar to humans in their capabilities.

The term "expert system" escalates this trend significantly by implying that a computer can function as a human expert does. In fact, current computer expertise falls far short of that of humans. Virtually all expert medical systems have a narrow expertise in a specialized domain such as infectious diseases. They simply do not incorporate the broad knowledge required to treat the full scope of human illnesses competently. In addition, a human physician has common sense and will know immediately whether a patient has a knife sticking in his back. But a computer program must engage in extensive questioning to find this out (Newman, 1988). Furthermore, a human physician can evaluate the overall health of a patient, use a warm bedside manner to comfort him, and assess whether his illness stems from chronic psychological stress. And human physicians' responses are not preprogrammed, allowing them to respond to unforeseen problems and to act spontaneously.

These differences between human experts and computerized expert systems should be kept in mind. Computerized experts may well acquire additional capabilities in the future. But until they do, their credibility and authority should be restricted.

Dehumanization

Expert systems also present new risks of dehumanization. Thinking is an essential human activity, a source of much joy, creativity, and pride in accomplishment. Following additional development, expert systems could be assigned much of the thought work of humans. On one hand, this could liberate people from routine thought tasks such as accounting, allowing them to develop their creative talents. On the other hand, however, the widespread use of expert systems could rob many people of desired opportunities to think and to exercise choice, reducing them to monitors of expert systems that do most of the work. This problem is analogous to that encountered by skilled machinists following the introduction of CNC systems. The difference is that expert systems stand to affect a much larger number of workers ranging from accountants to legal analysts to finance managers.

In a society that relied extensively on expert systems, people would probably spend increased amounts of time with the machines that they depend upon. In seeking tax advice or making airline reservations, for example, people may soon find themselves interacting with computers rather than people. Smart computers have already entered the home, controlling the robot that does the cleaning and coordinating energy control, cooking, and security systems (Elmer-DeWitt, 1989). At work, people might also spend more time with computers than with other people, making them feel socially isolated and alienated.

These negative effects, however, are preventable. With careful planning, expert systems can be used in highly humane and productive ways. In science, for example, they could perform much of the routine work and provide useful summaries of literatures that are expanding rapidly, allowing researchers to stay abreast of developments in their fields. They could also improve the delivery of health services in remote areas. Ultimately, it is human experts who will decide how to use automated experts, so people, not machines, must bear the responsibility for humanization or dehumanization.

Problem-Solving and Language

The development of expert systems is an impressive accomplishment, but it does not answer the desire to construct a machine that exhibits general intelligence. Expert systems cannot solve many different kinds of problems, as people can, nor can they carry on an ordinary conversation. In order to meet the challenge of building a truly intelligent system, AI researchers must develop systems that have sophisticated capacities for language and problem solving.

This line of reasoning presupposes that we know what intelligence is and how to assess it accurately. In fact, heated debates continue in psychology over what intelligence is and about how to measure it. Not all of the likely components of intelligence have been studied (Gardner, 1983; Sternberg, 1985). Further, the current generation of IQ tests exhibits a strong culture bias, meaning that intelligent people from one culture could do very poorly on an IQ test not because they are dull but because they are unfamiliar with the culture that many of the questions on the test concern. Dissatisfied with the prospect of unresolved debates and long waits for the verdict of psychological research, Alan Turing, a brilliant British mathematician, took a different tack in deciding whether a machine is intelligent.

Turing's Test

Turing proposed a test that is a variation on a three-person parlor game in which a blindfolded person asks questions of a man and a woman and tries to decide from the responses which one is the woman (or a man). The fun part of the game is to trick the interrogator by having the man respond as if he were a woman and vice versa. To eliminate voice differences, the responses of the man and the woman can be given by a fourth person or in typewritten form.

In the adaptation of this game for computers, a human interrogator sits at a computer terminal, sending questions to and receiving messages from two other rooms. One of these rooms contains a person and the other contains a computer programmed to respond as humans do. The interrogator does not know which room contains a person. His task is to ask any questions he wants in order to determine which one contains the computer. Turing's idea was that if human interrogators were unable to distinguish between the computer's responses and the person's responses, then the computer would have proven itself to be intelligent. The logic is that people are intelligent, and if a computer responded in a manner that was indistinguishable from people, then it too must be intelligent. Turing predicted that computers would pass a modest version of his test by the year 2000, but he died at an early age and never saw his vision realized.

The Turing test is useful because it allows the interrogator to explore the full scope of intelligence by asking cleverly designed questions. He might, for example, request the production of a sonnet or ask about the meaning of "The spirit is willing but the flesh is weak." Or he might ask emotionally loaded questions or pose demanding mathematical problems. Although each researcher might ask his or her own pet questions, the AI community has accepted Turing's test as a standard for assessing intelligence.

Despite this agreement, there is no consensus on how to build a system that passes the Turing test. Some researchers have claimed that it is unrealistic to try to build a system that matches the human capacity for solving problems. They contend that it is more reasonable to develop limited systems that can reason and solve problems in particular realms, postponing the task of building a system that can pass the Turing test. This is an attempt to identify and to understand the individual pieces before assembling the entire puzzle of intelligence. In contrast, other researchers have claimed that it is impossible to understand intelligence by breaking it down into isolated parts because higher intelligence integrates mental abilities and skills fully. As a result, an intelligent system may exhibit properties not apparent in any of its components—the whole is greater than the sum of its parts. These two approaches, which are illustrated in the brief sketch of AI projects that follows, continue to color research on AI.

Much of the early AI research concentrated on games because games of skill are both interesting and conducive to the construction of systems that have reasoning and problem-solving abilities. Games such as backgammon and checkers, for example, require substantial amounts of reasoning, but the reasoning is confined to a relatively limited and manageable domain in which clearly defined rules apply. In fact, several impressive game-playing systems have been constructed. In 1979, a computer at Carnegie-Mellon University defeated the world champion backgammon player in a $5,000 winner-take-all match at Monte Carlo (Berliner, 1980). In checkers, Arthur Samuel developed a system that could learn, adapting its strategy according to its experiences. The system learned so fast that it soon humiliated him in every game (Logsdon, 1985). But the strengths and the limits of machine reasoning are most apparent in the work that has been done on chess.

Chess Players

In order for a computer to play chess, the game board, which contains 64 squares, must first be represented inside the machine. One way of accomplishing this is to create a set of maps, called bit maps, using strings of 64 zeroes and ones (these are the binary digits or bits) which correspond to squares on the board. All of the white pawns could be represented by a string in which all of the bits are set to zero except for those indicating squares occupied by white pawns. Similarly, the black bishops could be represented by a different string in which all of the bits are set to zero except for those indicating squares occupied by black bishops. The entire game board can be represented using 12 different strings or bit maps. These bit maps are highly useful in determining the legal moves that could occur in particular board positions (Frey, 1983).

The next step is to decide which move to make. This is extremely difficult since there are so many possibilities and since the successful player must look ahead several moves or plies. The possibilities can be visualized in the form of a game tree. Figure 8.1 shows a small part of a 4-ply game tree for the opening position in chess, though the tree for an entire game would be much larger. On the average, there are approximately 38 legal moves at each board position, and a 6-ply analysis is needed to achieve a reasonable level of play. The trouble is that whereas a 2-ply analysis generates 1444 different possibilities, a 4-ply analysis generates 2,085,136 possibilities. And a 6-ply analysis generates 3,010,936,389 possibilities (Frey, 1983). This combinatorial explosion of potential moves generates an enormous number of alternatives to be examined.

The tremendous number of possible moves militates against the use of a brute force strategy in which the computer analyzes every possibility. It makes more sense to examine only the strongest moves. This can be accomplished through the use of several heuristics, which are rules of thumb that are helpful in solving a problem but which do not guarantee a solution. One widely used heuristic is to examine all capture moves first, taking advantage of opportunities to remove powerful pieces of the opponent. Other heuristics involve remembering killer moves that result in the loss of one's own pieces and occupying particularly powerful board positions (Frey, 1983). These heuristics do not guarantee a win or even the selection of the best move, yet they are

Figure 8.1. Hypothetical game tree for the opening positions in a game of chess (from Frey, 1983).

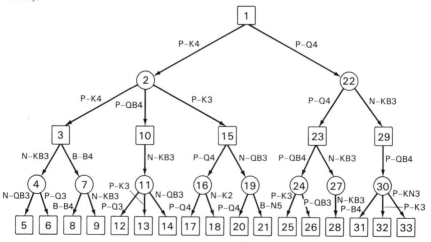

often useful. The idea of using heuristics was borrowed from human chess experts, who routinely apply heuristics in playing.

Having generated a tree of plausible moves, the computer can do a depth-first search in which it starts with the left-most branch and follows it all of the way down before searching the next branch to its endpoint, and so on. Or it can use a breadth-first search in which it first examines all of the possible moves at one ply before examining the ones at deeper plies. Throughout the search, evaluation procedures are applied in order to assess the strength of the various options.

To date, a wide variety of representations, heuristics and search strategies have been tried, and with substantial success. A team at Northwestern University, for example, has developed a system called CHESS 4.6 that can play at the Master's level, allowing it to defeat approximately ninety percent of all rated chess players. Nevertheless, computers have a long way to go before capturing the world title, and few systems can provide a challenging match for a grandmaster, much less a world champion.

The reasons behind the overwhelming human advantage in chess are unclear, but perceptual factors seem to play a very important role (de Groot, 1965). If expert players are shown a game board for five seconds and then look at an empty board and try to reconstruct what they have seen, they recall large numbers of pieces, many more than novices do in the same task. Novices recall the pieces in a random order, but experts recall them in well learned groups such as a castling formation (Chase and Simon, 1973). Unlike novices, experts immediately perceive a game board in terms of standard offensive and defensive patterns. This perceptual skill, which seems to develop following thousands of hours of play, allows them to play numerous matches simultaneously, even with a short time allowed for each move. It also allows them to zero in on the strongest moves, a skill that has been embodied only partially in computers. Until computers develop comparable skills, they will remain limited in their ability to play chess at the highest levels.

The attempts to get a handle on problem-solving through the construction of game playing systems turned out to be problematic in several respects. For one thing, chess programs were too specialized—they played respectable chess but could not solve other kinds of problems. The representations and the processes that made for good chess did not generalize to other areas of problem solving. Chess programs also failed to exhibit the strong linkages between perception and problem-solving that occur when people play chess. Initially, researchers had hoped that they could study problem-solving in relatively simple, well-defined domains uncontaminated by the complexities of perception. With these hopes dashed, many researchers began more holistic research projects, some of which attempted to construct a system that passes the Turing test.

Simulation

A radically different way of building an intelligent computer is to write programs that imitate or simulate what people do. This method is sensible because people behave in an intelligent manner, and some of the processes that underlie human intelligence could perhaps be embodied in a computer program. If a computer were to follow the same steps and processes in solving problems that people do, then it too would behave in an intelligent manner. Further, a computer must imitate people in order to pass the Turing test.

In fact, it is possible to write programs that simulate human thought processes. Consider, for example, a simulation of subtraction as it is done by a typical five-year-old. When a child is asked "What is 8 take away 5?" he holds out five fingers. Then he extends his sixth finger and says "one." Next he extends his seventh finger and says "two." Finally, he extends his eighth finger and says "three—the answer is three." These observations, coupled with data from interviews, make it possible to identify four mental steps involved in the subtraction (Resnick, 1976).

1. Set the counters: Using the fingers as one counter and the voice as another, hold out the number of fingers indicated by the lower number and set the voice counter to zero.

2. Compare the number of fingers held out to the larger number. If they are equal, then say how many times you have incremented the finger counter. If they are not equal, go to step 3.

3. Add 1 to the counters. Hold out one more finger and say how many times you have come to step 3.

Figure 8.2. A flowchart model of addition in children. From THE PROMISE OF COGNITIVE PSYCHOLOGY by Richard E. Mayer. Copyright © 1981 W. H. Freeman and Company. Reprinted with permission.

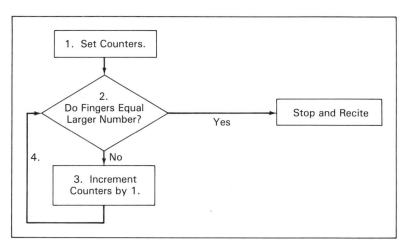

4. Go back to step 2.

These steps may be represented in a flowchart, shown in Figure 8.2. The performance of most children follows one of five simple flowcharts such as the one described above (Resnick, 1976). Having constructed the flowcharts, it is a relatively simple step to write a computer program that successfully imitates the behavior of the five-year-old.

The General Problem Solver

The simulation of the subtraction behavior of five-year-olds is interesting in itself, but the broader goal of simulation research is to write a program that embodies general intelligence. Several attempts have been made along these lines, the most notable of which is the General Problem Solver (GPS). Developed by Allen Newell and Herbert Simon (1972) at Carnegie-Mellon University, the GPS successfully solved a variety of mathematical theorems and puzzles such as the Tower of Hanoi, illustrated in Figure 8.3. The problem is to stack the three disks on post A onto post C, keeping the same order of smallest on the top and largest on the bottom. Only one disk can be moved at a time, and a larger disk may not be placed on a smaller one.

Humans tackle this problem by breaking it down into several smaller ones, creating subgoals. Many people, for example, make their first subgoal the movement of the large disk to post C, which requires that post C be open and that the largest disk have nothing on top of it, leaving it free to be moved. They accomplish this by moving the smallest disk to post C, moving the intermediate disk to post B, moving the smallest disk back from post C to post B, and then moving the largest disk to post C. Having accomplished this subgoal, most people solve the problem easily.

The GPS attacks the problem in a similar manner using a strategy called means-end analysis. The first step is to identify the form of the solution to the problem—the goal state. The next step is to compare the current state with the goal state. If the two coincide, then the problem has been solved. Otherwise, the system identifies the difference and searches for methods of reducing it. It does this by scanning a table that lists various goals and operators that lead

Figure 8.3. The Tower of Hanoi problem (from Wessells, 1982).

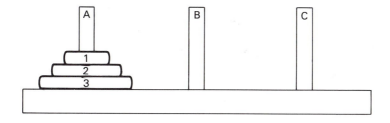

to them. The system tests various operators to determine whether they apply to the problem. If an operator does apply, it yields a result that is closer to the goal state, and the system then attempts to repeat the operation until the goal state has been attained. If the operators do not move the system toward the goal state, then the GPS generates a subgoal that does reduce the difference between the current state and the goal state and to which an operator does apply. In the Tower of Hanoi problem, the GPS generates the subgoal of moving the large disk to post C, and the attainment of this subgoal reduces the difference between the initial state and the goal state. In following this difference reduction strategy to completion, the GPS simulates human performance accurately on this problem and on others (Newell and Simon, 1972).

The successes of the GPS lent credibility to the AI enterprise, and as will be discussed in the following chapter, suggested that programs can in some sense function as minds. The successes of the GPS also suggested a natural linkage between the disciplines of AI and cognitive psychology, which studies human cognitive processes such as memory, perception, and problem solving. AI researchers realized that they could advance their project by simulating the thought processes that cognitive psychologists had discovered. In return, cognitive psychologists could use the computer to model human cognition. The computer provided a useful metaphor of the mind, enabling psychologists to use concepts such as storage, retrieval, and information processing in analyzing cognitive processes. Moreover, programs such as the GPS served as scientific models that explained cognitive phenomena in terms of mental representations and processes. Recognizing the relationships between AI, psychology, and philosophy, a group of researchers developed a new field called cognitive science, an interdisciplinary endeavor that bridges AI, cognitive psychology, and philosophy (Gardner, 1985).

By the same token, the GPS turned out to be limited. Whereas it succeeded in solving numerous logical and mathematical problems, it was unable to solve the full range of problems that people normally solve. It was also limited in its ability to speak and to understand words, an ability that figures prominently in human problem-solving. Eager to overcome this limit, many researchers began to develop models of language processing.

Language Processing

Language occupies a central role in human life. It is our primary vehicle of communication, the medium of much social interaction, and the means through which we express our ideas and feelings. Language both embodies and transmits culture, allowing knowledge, customs, and myths to be passed from one generation to the next. Language may also be a unique capacity of the human mind (Chomsky, 1972), one that exemplifies the powerful capacity to form and use symbols. No AI system will pass the Turing test without having a significant language capability.

Of course, AI researchers are also interested in language for commercial reasons. Consumers would like to talk to their computers in ordinary English, avoiding the task of learning specialized programming languages. A brief overview of two landmark programs demonstrates the advances that have been made in language processing and also illustrate the differences between human and machine language.

One influential language processor is called SHRDLU (pronounced "sherd-lew"). SHRDLU is a simulated robot that can understand questions and execute English commands concerning the artificial block world pictured in Figure 8.4. Sitting at a terminal, a human controller types in questions or commands, and SHRDLU responds in typed English and displays the actions of the robot on the screen. There is no actual robot, nor are any blocks actually moved—all of the action takes place in a microworld on the screen. Nevertheless, the ability of SHRDLU to understand questions and to follow commands is impressive, as shown by the following dialog (adapted from Winograd, 1973) in which SHRDLU's responses are in capital letters.

Figure 8.4. The artificial block world of SHRDLU (from Winograd, 1973).

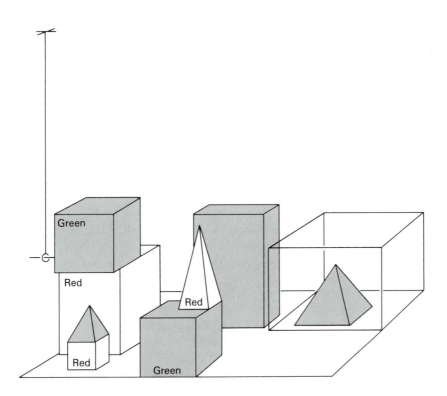

1. Pick up a big red block.

OK. [The system answers "OK" when it executes a command successfully. In order to pick up a big red block, it had to first uncover it by moving the green block on top somewhere else.]

2. Grasp the pyramid.

I DON'T UNDERSTAND WHICH PYRAMID YOU MEAN. [Since there are three pyramids in the scene and "the" indicates that the speaker had a specific object in mind, SHRDLU does nothing.]

3. Can the table pick up blocks?

NO. [SHRDLU contains semantic rules that stipulate that only animate objects can pick something up and that the table is inanimate.]

4. Can a pyramid be supported by a block?

YES. [Finding an actual example in the scene, SHRDLU states that this is possible.]

5. Can a pyramid support a pyramid?

I DON'T KNOW. [Although the question makes sense, there is no example in the scene, so SHRDLU cannot tell.]

6. Stack up two pyramids.

I CAN'T. [The robot tries and fails.]

7. The blue pyramid is mine.

I UNDERSTAND. [This data is added to the data base.]

8. I own blocks which are not red, but I don't own anything which supports a pyramid.

I UNDERSTAND. [SHRDLU creates two new theorems concerning ownership.]

9. Do I own the box?

NO. [The box supports a pyramid.]

10. Do I own anything in the box?

YES, TWO THINGS: THE BLUE BLOCK AND THE BLUE PYRAMID.

11. Does a steeple

SORRY, I DON'T KNOW THE WORD "STEEPLE." [SHRDLU interrupts immediately when it encounters a word it does not know.]

12. A "steeple" is a stack which contains two green cubes and a pyramid.

I UNDERSTAND.

13. Are there any steeples now?

NO. [Having received a definition of "steeple," the system can now recognize steeples.]

14. Build one.

OK. [SHRDLU recognizes that "one" refers back to "steeple." Then it clears off one of the green cubes and stacks two green cubes and the red pyramid to make a steeple.]

In this dialog, SHRDLU responds appropriately to a variety of questions and commands and makes inferences about relations such as ownership. It also says what it does not know, which is more than many people will do, and it adds new words to its vocabulary. These impressive accomplishments give hope to the idea that computers might eventually master language. SHRDLU was intended as a first step in building a system that can understand English, and many regarded it as a step in the right direction.

On the other hand, SHRDLU's language capabilities fall far short of human language. Since it is a machine, SHRDLU has no social context within which it interprets meaning. People are always immersed in a social context, and language use is woven into it. For example, someone who was bored by SHRDLU's prosaic conversation might say "Gee, this is fun." Even if SHRDLU understood the literal meaning of this statement, it would miss the sarcasm. Sarcasm, humor, irony, expressions of love, and many other facets of ordinary language arise out of a social context and of language users' knowledge of their social world. Lacking this social context, SHRDLU and other computerized language processors are inherently limited. Furthermore, SHRDLU is severely limited in its knowledge of the world. It does not know, for example, that the larger an object is, the heavier it tends to be. Nor does it know that if blocks are pushed off the table they will fall. Unlike people, it cannot talk about politics or explore the point of its own existence.

SHRDLU's successors were designed to process natural language, particularly the connected discourse that occurs in everyday stories and conversations. SAM (Script Applier Mechanism) is a program that paraphrases and answers questions about stories concerning episodes such as eating at a restaurant. SAM processes a story by applying a script, which is a data structure that describes the events that typically occur in a standard situation (Schank, 1979). A script that describes eating at a restaurant, for example, includes players such as a customer, a waiter, and a cashier who interact in a relatively stereotyped manner. First the customer goes to the restaurant and is seated at a table. The server brings a menu and subsequently takes the customer's order. Then the server brings the food and the customer eats, perhaps while talking with a friend. Finally, the server brings the check and the customer leaves a tip, pays the cashier, and leaves the restaurant.

In processing a story, SAM encounters words such as "restaurant" that trigger a particular script. SAM then uses the script to form a representation of the causal chain of events that took place in the story. On one occasion, the following story was presented to SAM (Schank, 1979, pp. 202–203).

"A New Jersey man was killed on Friday evening when the car in which he was riding swerved off Route 69 and struck a tree. David Hall,

27, was pronounced dead at the scene by Dr. Dana Blanchard, medical examiner. Frank Miller, 16, of 593 Foxon Road, operator of the vehicle, was taken by Flanagan Ambulance to Yale-New Haven Hospital. He was treated and released. The Branford Fire Department extricated the passenger from the vehicle. No charges were made. Patrolman Robert Onofrio is continuing the investigation."

SAM generated an accurate paraphrase of the story and also answered a series of questions about it.

Q1: Was anyone killed?

SAM: YES, DAVID HALL DIED.

Q2: Was anyone hurt?

SAM: YES, FRANK MILLER WAS SLIGHTLY INJURED.

Q3: Why was Frank Miller hurt?

SAM: BECAUSE THE AUTOMOBILE HIT A TREE.

Q4: Did Frank Miller go to the hospital?

SAM: YES, HE WAS IN YALE-NEW HAVEN.

SAM is interesting because it can use scripts to make inferences about events that were implied but not mentioned explicitly. In order to answer the second question, for example, SAM had to go beyond the stated information that Frank Miller had been treated and released. It did so by using its knowledge that people who sustain minor injuries are often treated and released from a hospital.

Not all stories, however, are based on scripts. Many stories involve the goals and the plans of central characters and their efforts to overcome unexpected problems. PAM (Plan Applier Mechanism) is a program that analyzes these goals and plans, processing nonscripted stories such as the following (Schank, 1979, pp. 207–208).

"John disliked his job as the bank janitor. One day, a thief tried to rob the bank. John jumped on the thief and knocked him out. The bank president made John the bank guard. John enjoyed his new job."

PAM paraphrased this story in this manner:

JOHN DISLIKED BEING A BANK JANITOR. A THIEF TRIED TO ROB THE BANK. JOHN LEARNED THE THIEF HAD ROBBED IT. JOHN WANTED THE THIEF TO NOT HAVE THE BANK'S MONEY. JOHN KNOCKED THE THIEF OUT. THE BANK WAS INDEBTED TO JOHN. THE PRESIDENT MADE JOHN A BANK GUARD. HE LIKED BEING IT.

In making this paraphrase, PAM had to infer that John wanted to keep the thief from getting the bank's money and also that the bank was indebted to John.

SAM and PAM and their recent offspring are significant accomplishments in natural language processing. Yet they lack many of the abilities that humans take for granted. In particular, they lack a fundamental human capacity called linguistic creativity or productivity, the ability to say and to understand an infinite number of sentences (Chomsky, 1972). Although we seldom think about it, we routinely read and speak sentences that we have never seen or heard before. Even in a newspaper in which the articles fit a particular style, it is rare to find two identical sentences. Because of our linguistic creativity, we can make up novel words and sentences in order to talk about novel events. Yet this ability, which is utterly commonplace in humans, remains beyond the scope of computer programs.

Computer programs also have limited conversational skills, which require extensive knowledge about social norms and about speakers' intentions and expectations. Someone who wants to know the time, for example, might ask "Do you know what time it is?" Literally, this question calls for a "Yes" or "No" answer, but a "Yes" response would by itself be seen as a wisecrack or a rebuff. In fact, most people realize that the question "Do you have the time?" is an indirect request, and they respond by giving the correct time. It is difficult, however, to get computers to go beyond the literal interpretation.

Being literal devices, computers have trouble processing figurative statements such as "I've been on an emotional roller coaster lately" or "Boy, that hitter has a hot bat tonight." In general, computers do not handle ambiguity well. This makes it very difficult for them to engage in ordinary conversation, which is filled with figures of speech and laden with potential ambiguity. It is one thing to build a program that can process simple newspaper stories, which tend to be literal and straightforward. But it is another thing entirely to build a program that can interpret figures of speech and unearth hidden meanings.

Despite the rapid advances that have occurred recently in problem solving by computer, no machine yet comes close to passing a full blown Turing test. Computers are exceptional problem-solving tools, but they have a long way to go before achieving the heights of human intelligence.

The Myth and the Machine

Every advanced technology functions as something of a projective medium onto which people transfer their hopes and fears. As this occurs, our fantasies color our perception of reality, and technology becomes enshrouded in myths and futuristic visions. Regardless of whether these myths and visions eventually come true, they influence our behavior now, sometimes in subtle ways.

One of the most dominant myths of contemporary Western culture is the myth of the intelligent computer, the idea that computers can achieve general intelligence and will probably do so soon. This myth, which is evident in films such as *War Games* and in cartoons such as *Transformers*, is part of our general propensity for anthropomorphizing the computer, attributing human characteristics to it. If, for example, the computer prints out an incorrect answer, we may complain that it has made an error, when in fact it is probably the programmer who made the error. Similarly, we may say that the computer has made particular decisions, but the computer in fact operates according to a program written by people. All too often, we treat the computer as though it were an independent agent, when in fact it is a medium through which human agents act. The myth of the intelligent computer tempts us to attribute responsibility to computers, but it is we who must accept responsibility for what computers do.

Belief in intelligent machines is the touchstone of futuristic writers such as Robert Jastrow, founder of NASA's Goddard Institute, who believes that computers will eventually change the conditions of life. He states that "the era of carbon-chemistry life is drawing to a close on the earth and a new era of silicon-based life—indestructible, immortal, infinitely expandable—is beginning. By the turn of the century, ultra-intelligent machines will be working in partnership with our best minds on all the serious problems of the day....Man will also provide for computer reproduction, as he does today. In return, the computer will minister to man's social and economic needs. It will become his salvation in a world of crushing complexity." (Jastrow, 1981, p. 18) Of course, this optimistic assessment may be wide of the mark. Marvin Minsky harbors the more somber prognosis that if we are lucky, superintelligent computers might decide to keep us as harmless pets.

The myth of the intelligent computer stems in part from some inflated claims made by highly prestigious members of the AI community. As early as 1958, Herbert Simon and Allen Newell, two of the pioneers of AI, proclaimed "There are now in the world machines that think, that learn, and that create. Moreover, their ability to do these things is going to increase rapidly until—in the visible future—the range of problems they can handle will be coextensive with the range to which the human mind has been applied." (p. 8)

The readiness with which people accept this myth and the resulting dangers are illustrated by the experience of an MIT computer scientist, Joseph Weizenbaum, with a program called ELIZA.

ELIZA

ELIZA was an early script-based program named after the Eliza of Pygmalion since it could give the appearance of speaking increasingly well. Superficially, ELIZA could mimic the initial interview of a Rogerian psychotherapist, who attempts to create a supportive atmosphere and to draw the client out by reflecting his statements back to him. The following excerpt illustrates the interaction between a person and ELIZA, the responses of which are printed in upper case.

Men are all alike.

IN WHAT WAY

They're always bugging us about something or other.

CAN YOU THINK OF A SPECIFIC EXAMPLE

Well, my boyfriend made me come here.

YOUR BOYFRIEND MADE YOU COME HERE

He says I'm depressed much of the time.

I AM SORRY TO HEAR YOU ARE DEPRESSED

It's true. I am unhappy.

DO YOU THINK COMING HERE WILL HELP YOU NOT TO BE UNHAPPY

I need some help, that much seems certain.

WHAT WOULD IT MEAN TO YOU IF YOU GOT SOME HELP

Perhaps I could learn to get along with my mother.

TELL ME MORE ABOUT YOUR FAMILY

My mother takes care of me.

WHO ELSE IN YOUR FAMILY TAKES CARE OF YOU

My father.

YOUR FATHER

You are like my father in some ways.

WHAT RESEMBLANCE DO YOU SEE

You are not very aggressive but I think you don't want me to notice that.

WHAT MAKE (sic) YOU THINK I AM NOT VERY AGGRESSIVE

You don't argue with me.

WHY DO YOU THINK I DON'T ARGUE WITH YOU

You are afraid of me.

DOES IT PLEASE YOU TO BELIEVE I AM AFRAID OF YOU

My father is afraid of everybody.

WHAT ELSE COMES TO MIND WHEN YOU THINK OF YOUR FATHER

Bullies.

DOES THAT HAVE ANYTHING TO DO WITH THE FACT THAT YOUR
BOYFRIEND MADE YOU COME HERE

(Weizenbaum, 1976, pp. 3–4)

Weizenbaum, knowing that ELIZA could not handle the ambiguities and
the contextual richness of ordinary human conversation, never intended that
ELIZA actually be used to provide psychotherapy. Nevertheless, users of the

program rapidly anthropomorphized it, treating it as a legitimate provider of psychotherapy. Weizenbaum's secretary, having had a few interchanges with ELIZA, asked to be alone with the machine. On another occasion, Weizenbaum announced that he might alter the system so that he could examine all of the conversations people had had with ELIZA. He was promptly accused of wanting to spy on others' most intimate thoughts, indicating that people were talking to the computer as if it were a person. Even more stunning, several practicing psychotherapists considered the possibility of extending the program and actually using it to provide automatic psychotherapy (Weizenbaum, 1976). In fact, some psychologists are using computers as assistants in psychotherapy (Joyce, 1988).

Knowing that Rogerian psychotherapy cannot be reduced to mere technique, Weizenbaum was justifiably shocked by these developments. ELIZA could not even understand ordinary language, let alone respond sensitively to intimate human thoughts and feelings. The deep encounter which ideally occurs in psychotherapy requires the full range of human sensitivity, emotion, and creativity. Research on Rogerian psychotherapy has consistently demonstrated the importance of the therapist's empathy (Truax and Mitchell, 1971). Providing none of this, ELIZA is at best a parody of genuine psychotherapy. Of course, ELIZA may be useful because it gives people a means of getting things off their chest, but this is a very small part of psychotherapy.

The case of ELIZA also illustrates the dangers of treating computers as people. Human psychotherapists shoulder a tremendous burden of responsibility, for a wrong move on their part could lead to emotional disaster or even suicide. In some cases, it is inappropriate to use a method such as the Rogerian method of reflection. If, for example, the client were paranoid and believed that he was constantly being plotted against, the method of reflection might amplify the paranoia and push him over the cliff. Using their experience, insight, and moral judgment, human psychotherapists can make responsible judgements about whether and how to use a particular therapy. ELIZA, however, cannot—it can only apply technique in the mechanical, unfeeling, and amoral way of a machine.

The myth of the truly intelligent computer tempts us to assign computers a privileged position within society. After all, if computers are as intelligent as people and are less prone to error, it may make sense to allow them to make life and death decisions and to turn our most difficult tasks over to them. The case of ELIZA, however, serves as a poignant reminder of the dangers of the myth and of the readiness with which people accept it.

This is not to say that the myth will never become reality. It might be possible someday to build computers that are fundamentally different from the ones now available and that demonstrate intelligence on the same order as humans. Already, efforts are well underway in the U.S. and Japan to build computers that are parallel processors (Fox and Messina, 1987). Most current computers are serial processors that do one thing at a time, which makes for relatively slow speeds. In parallel processing systems, the work is distributed among many processors that work simultaneously, much as the members of a carpentry crew work simultaneously in building a house. It is widely expected that parallel processing will dramatically increase the speed of computing and enable computers to perform tasks that are beyond their current capacity. For now, however, computers remain limited. For this reason, we should be cautious in turning over decisions to computers and think carefully about what kinds of decisions computers ought to be allowed to make.

The Limits of Making Decisions by Computers

Computers are rule-governed machines that execute faithfully the commands included in computer programs. All of the decisions that are made by computer are made through the application of rules. ELIZA, for example, followed the rule of looking for particular keywords such as "mother" and using stock sentence frames such as "Tell me more about your _____"

It is commonplace for people to make decisions using rules, particularly in areas that are conducive to quantification. In order to decide how much tax to pay, for example, citizens use the rules stipulated by the IRS, together with information about their income, to calculate the amount owed. Similarly, organizations such as insurance agencies use rules to decide which risk category a potential customer belongs in. These rules provide clear, standardized criteria for making decisions, and they enable individuals and organizations to make large numbers of decisions swiftly and effectively.

It would be a mistake, however, to suppose that all decisions can or should be made by following rules. For example, what rules should be used in deciding whether to permit someone to have an abortion? And what rules should decide whether to pull the plug on someone who is brain dead but whose body can be maintained artificially? These are ethical issues, and their resolution must be based upon a careful analysis of values. Because Western society has not yet reached a consensus on which values should carry the greatest weight in these cases, there are no widely accepted rules for making these decisions. It would be foolish, perhaps dangerous, to pretend otherwise. Until the underlying issues concerning values have been clarified, these decisions cannot legitimately be made by computer or by any rule-governed procedure.

In addition, there are many areas in which people make decisions without following rules. Decisions about whom to marry or where to live, for example, are often based upon feelings, which current computers simply do not have. Although it is possible to make these kinds of decisions using rules, this would be to put reason over feeling in matters of the heart. But reason alone cannot tell us what is right in matters of feeling, just as feeling alone cannot tell us what is correct in the solution of a mathematical problem. To turn over all decisions to computers is to elevate reason to an unacceptably high plane, relegating feelings to a secondary status. It would be both unethical and dehumanizing to make all decisions using computers (Weizenbaum, 1976).

There are also serious practical limits on making decisions by computer. As discussed above, the rules that underlie problem-solving and language are poorly understood. Even the rules that underlie a seemingly simple ability such as common sense remain obscure. For example, it is obvious to any reasonably intelligent person that a string can be used to pull an object but not to push it. This is obvious to people because they have extensive knowledge of the world, of the hardness of various objects, and of the requirements for motion. Computers, however, lack this knowledge, and research in AI has not succeeded in building ordinary common sense into the machine. As a result, it is simply impossible at present to use computers to make all of the decisions that people can make.

The problem of making accurate specifications, which was discussed previously (see pages 120-122), also places serious practical limits on making decisions by computers. Because we lack perfect ability to foresee what will happen in the future, we are correspondingly limited in our ability to specify exactly what a computer program ought to be able to do. Consider, for example, a hypothetical program intended to guide a robot, the primary function of which is to watch over children. Naturally, the robot is programmed to save human lives, even at the risk of its own destruction. While it is standing on the bank of a river holding the hand of a three-year-old girl, a plane crashes into the river, and several wounded survivors surface fifteen meters from shore, calling desperately for help. Horrified by the loud noise and the chaos, the little girl immediately begins crying and clutches the robot tightly.

Should the robot swim out to save the injured survivors, who will probably die otherwise? But if it does so, will it risk the life of the child, who is clearly upset and who would drown if she followed her caretaker into the water? In this situation, many adults would probably try to calm the child, explain what they were about to do, and then attempt to swim out to the survivors. Yet it is impossible to foresee how the child would react, and if the child's life were threatened by the adult entering the water, many caretakers would not go. Because we cannot foresee everything about this situation in advance, it is impossible to specify exactly how a computer ought to respond to it. The limits on human foresight limit the ability of computers to deal effectively and responsibly with real world crises, which are peppered with surprise and ambiguity.

What Role Computers?

These limits on feeling, common sense and foreseeability should make us reluctant to turn over all decisions to computers. In particular, people should remain in the decision-making loop whenever a decision ought to be based in part on emotion or on common sense. Furthermore, humans should remain in the loop when there are high degrees of uncertainty about whether a program will work effectively. Because many decisions that people make every day do involve emotion, common sense, and high degrees of uncertainty, it should be the exception rather than the rule that complex decisions, particularly life-and-death decisions, are made without direct human involvement.

Direct human involvement in decision making is also important in avoiding excessive dependency. If people become too dependent upon the computer, their own decision-making capacities will be blunted, and they will probably become increasingly inclined to turn more decisions over to the computer. This situation could make us too vulnerable to acts of God, to power shortages, or to hostile events such as terrorist attacks on computers. If the plug were somehow pulled, a highly computerized society would fall to its knees, making it very difficult to deliver fundamental human services. This problem can be reduced by keeping open and active noncomputerized channels for making decisions.

Direct human involvement in decision making is also important for moral reasons. In particular, we could become morally lazy or underdeveloped by turning over too many decisions to computers. We become moral beings by making choices and by accepting responsibility for them. By allowing machines to make many of our choices, we accept less individual responsibility and lose the opportunity to become moral agents. In addition, if people were stripped of their opportunities to make choices, they would feel disempowered and helpless. This feeling is already one of the towering psychological problems of this era, and it would be inappropriate to amplify it.

As computers become more sophisticated, we will no doubt rely extensively on computers for purposes of making decisions. Turning decisions over to computers is appropriate in many cases, particularly those that require high speed and that conform to prespecified rules. But in the final analysis, computers should supplement, not replace, human decision making.

Conclusion

The quest to build intelligent machines is an ancient one, and it is alive and well in the clothing of artificial intelligence. Although the initial promises made by prominent AI researchers have not been fulfilled, there are many computer programs today that perform tasks that are said to require intelligence when performed by people. Significant advances have occurred in expert systems, which embody highly specialized forms of information and limited inferential powers. But expert systems fall far short of human intelligence. They exhibit neither the common sense nor the broad knowledge that human experts do, and they are not designed to achieve the full scope of reasoning and thinking skills that people exhibit. More sophisticated programs have been developed to play chess, to solve problems, and to use ordinary human language. But these programs, too, fall far short of human capabilities. In general, computer programs have trouble handling ambiguity and dealing with metaphors and figures of speech. Unlike people, they lack emotions and they do not exist in the social, moral context that people do.

Initially, research in AI had a monastic quality, and there were few real world applications of AI systems. Now, however, computers are being used routinely to give expert advice and to make complex decisions in fields such as business and medicine. This raises difficult questions about who or what is responsible for errors that occur, for example, for malpractice in medical cases. Because computers are outpacing the law and standards of medical practice, there is a shortage of clear policies regarding what constitutes reasonable care in cases involving expert systems. The development of increasingly intelligent machines will only amplify the current uncertainty.

American faith in technology, coupled with popular images of super-intelligent computers, creates a powerful tendency to build more capable machines and to turn important decisions over to them. Civilization has yet to come to grips with the questions of whether we ought to turn over key decisions to computers, what kinds of decisions computers should be allowed to make, and what role people should play in decision making. In answering these questions, we should be aware of the limits of computers—they lack emotions and a social context, and the full scope of human intelligence remains a distant hope for the most powerful computer today. In addition, there are many moral decisions that cannot be made according to rules of the sort that guide computers. Ultimately, it is people, not computers, who act as moral agents. For this reason, we should keep people in the decision making loop.

Minds and Selves

On CompuServe, one of the largest public computer networks, "Talkin' Lady" was a celebrity with whom hundreds of people wanted to talk (van Gelder, 1985). Her real name was Joan Sue Greene, a physically disabled neuropsychologist in her late twenties living in New York. As everyone knew, she had been traveling in a car with her drunken boyfriend when their car crashed, killing him and leaving her severely disfigured, mute, and confined to a wheelchair.

After the accident, she had lost her will to live. But a former professor gave her a computer and a year's subscription to CompuServe so that she could "meet" and talk with other people. And she did. On line, she had a bright and brassy personality that contrasted sharply with the limpness of her physical being. She routinely gave support to other disabled individuals, inspiring them to reach beyond their physical limits. She developed many deep friendships with other women, and, being bisexual, became romantically involved with some, engaging in private "sextalk" via electronic mail. But because of her shattered face, which could not be repaired by plastic surgery, she was profoundly embarrassed to actually meet her computer friends. Although no one actually saw her, she became an eminent presence on the network.

It came as a tremendous shock to Joan's friends and fans when they learned that Joan was not disabled. Nor was she a woman. In fact, Joan was really a prominent New York psychiatrist who had cultivated a female identity using the computer networks. He had stumbled into his female role by accident when a woman mistook him for a female psychiatrist and opened up to him in a way that he had never experienced before with a female client. Wanting to experience the full intimacy that women share, he took on his "Joan" identity consciously and even crafted a detailed biography and adopted a separate electronic mail box for her. In real life, he was a quiet, shy workaholic. But on line, he was wild, flashy, and daring. Through the computer, he had created a new identity.

Some of Joan's friends described this startling case of gender fraud as "mind rape," and several of them considered the possibility of pressing legal charges. Others argued that what really mattered was not his physically-defined gender but his soul, which clearly had a strong female component. Van Gelder (1985), who reported this case, pointed out that Joan may have been the person that the male psychiatrist wanted to be.

Whatever interpretation is correct, this case illustrates that the computer has become a medium of personal expression, a tool for carving out one's identity and answering the crucial question "Who am I?" The computer has also become a model that people use to analyze and construct their identity. Indeed, many psychologists and philosophers believe that the human mind is like a computer in that it encodes, stores, retrieves, and processes information. This computer metaphor of mind implies that people are machines, and it questions our cherished assumption that we alone have free will. If the computer metaphor turns out to be correct, then we must admit that everything we do has natural causes. This view, which challenges our claim that we are morally responsible beings, will be examined in the first part of this chapter.

Aside from the unusual case of Joan that was described above, computers have become a medium through which many people discover their personal identity (Turkle, 1984). The computer provides a microcosm within which people can try out different cognitive styles and methods of problem-solving, discovering which ones they prefer. As people develop their own unique styles of computing, their computational environments become extensions of themselves, much as the way we dress is an extension of our personality. In this sense, the computer is a medium of self-expression as well as of self-discovery.

Of course, the discovery and expression of one's personal identity occurs not in a vacuum but in a social context. As William James (1890), a prominent philosopher and psychologist, pointed out, one's self is defined not only by one's inner experiences and values but also by social relations such as with family and friends. For increasing numbers of people, the computer is the center of social communities that shape and support particular individual personalities, styles, and values. This is apparent in computer clubs filled with avid hobbyists who spend most of their free hours writing programs, playing computer games, or devouring popular literature on computing. But it is most apparent in the communities of hackers, the virtuoso programmers who regard computing as a way of life (Levy, 1984; Turkle, 1984). For many technically oriented individuals, the hacker community provides a support system within which they can find and express themselves.

This centering of life around computers, however, raises some nagging personal and social concerns. Will computers become a retreat from the uncertainty and the lack of control that are inherent in the social world? Will they become instruments of alienation or of personal empowerment? Because computers have penetrated the broader culture only recently, it is too early to answer these questions definitively. Yet they are questions that we must struggle with if we are to make our own informed choices about how to use computers.

Mind as Machine

The tension between science and religion runs very deep within Western society. Each promulgates a different view of what people are and of what our place in the universe is. Traditionally, Christian religion taught that we are unique beings who were created in the image of God and who, unlike other creatures on earth, have an eternal soul. Through reason and the exercise of moral choices, we can attain the very Kingdom of Heaven. Needless to say, this idea gave humans a special status in the cosmos.

Science, on the other hand, has dealt serious blows to this exalted view of humans. Copernicus, stating that the earth is one of numerous planets that revolves around the sun, rejected the traditional view that the earth and its people are the center of the universe. Similarly, Darwin shocked Church authorities by showing that humans had evolved from nonhumans, thereby removing humanity from the pedestal of divine creation. In Darwin's time, however, it was widely believed that people are rational beings who guide their actions through conscious choices. Not until the late nineteenth century did Freud undermine this view by showing that people are often driven by unconscious motives rather than by conscious deliberation. According to scientific wisdom, then, humans have no special place in the cosmos and are subject to the same laws of physics, biology, and psychology that apply throughout Nature.

This tension between the religious and the scientific views of humankind continues today. Attempting to resolve the tension, many people follow the path of Rene Descartes, the seventeenth century mathematician who divided the human being into two substances, mind and matter. According to this mind-body dualism, mind or soul is immaterial—it lacks extension in time and space, and it cannot be touched or seen. Being immaterial, the mind does not obey the laws of the natural universe but is guided by free will. Our bodies, by contrast, consist of matter and are governed by natural processes.

This resort to dualism is manifest in our everyday language. For example, the popular press usually describes the ability of an Indian guru to walk across a bed of burning coals without injury in terms of mind over matter. Similarly, many religious leaders continue to speak of a spirit as separate from our physical embodiment. Indeed, as recently as 1986, Pope John Paul II affirmed the belief of the Catholic Church in the existence of angels.

This dualism is particularly important to religious leaders because it supports their beliefs about human freedom and morality. The dualistic outlook assumes that people have free minds that can exercise free choice. In turn, free choice is a prerequisite for moral action. After all, we must accept moral responsibility for a crime that we chose to commit. But we would not be held responsible for robbing a bank if someone forced us to do so at gunpoint. By protecting free will, the doctrine of dualism preserves the traditional view of the person as a moral agent.

The idea that people are complex machines threatens our belief in free will. No matter how sophisticated they are, machines obey natural law and do not exercise free choice. Historically, numerous theorists have proposed that people are in fact machines. In 1748, for example, La Mettrie published a book entitled *Man a Machine* in which he concluded that "...man is a machine, and that in the whole universe there is but a single substance differently modified...." (p. 148) La Mettrie's analysis, however, was not entirely convincing since most of the evidence he cited concerned the workings of the body. The possibility remained that the body is a machine but that the mind is not. A stronger case that people are machines would establish that the human mind is a complex mechanism. Using the computer as a model of mind, psychologists and philosophers have recently attempted to make just this case.

The Computer Metaphor

During the first fifty or so years of this century, psychology was in its behavioristic phase in which it either deemphasized the mind or rejected mind as an acceptable subject for scientific inquiry. The behaviorists focused primarily upon observable stimuli and responses, analyzing, for example, whether children would speak more clearly if they had received a reward for achieving correct enunciation. Behaviorists treated the person as a black box that receives inputs and responds with particular outputs. Behaviorists said little about what might be going on inside people who are solving problems or reading books.

By the 1950s, the limits of behaviorism had become painfully obvious. Most behaviorist theories had little to say about complex cognitive activities such as reading and problem solving. Equally disturbing, behaviorist theory had no place for symbols and rules, though it had long been recognized that many higher thought processes involve the manipulation of symbols. In speaking, for example, people use words, which are symbols that stand for things and events in the world. By the late 1950s, linguists such as Chomsky (1957) had shown that people make words into sentences by using their knowledge of linguistic rules. What researchers needed, then, was an alternative model that incorporated symbols and rules and that was sufficiently complex that it could be used to conceptualize the mind.

The computer seemed to provide just the model that was needed. In exactly the period during which behaviorism was faltering, early research in AI demonstrated that computers have some ability to solve difficult problems and even to simulate human thought. During that same period, computer scientists recognized that computers are not just powerful calculators but are general purpose symbol manipulators. In principle, computers can process virtually any linguistic or visual input that can be specified precisely. Further, computers are rule-governed systems, so computer models can accommodate rules as well as symbols. Since both the computer and the mind appeared to be symbol-manipulating systems that operate according to rules, psychologists picked up on the idea of using the computer as a theoretical tool, a metaphor for the conceptualization of mind. Before long, psychology had abandoned behaviorism, and the cognitive revolution was on (Gardner, 1985; Lachman, Lachman and Butterfield, 1979; Wessells, 1982, 1986).

The computer also gave psychologists a rich vocabulary to be used in analyzing mental processes. For example, computer scientists spoke of computers as systems that encode, store, retrieve, and manipulate information. Inside a computer, an English word such as "Print" is represented or encoded symbolically as a string of zeroes and ones. When a print command has been issued, the corresponding string is stored in the memory of the computer, and a subsequent command can retrieve it from its memory location, allowing it to be executed.

The human mind can also be viewed as a sophisticated information-processing system that operates in a manner analogous to the computer. For example, if someone gave us directions about how to drive to the city hall, we might encode the verbal information into a visual image, a mental map that, together with verbal self-instructions such as "turn left at the third light," helps us to find our way. At the appropriate choice points, we could retrieve this information from memory and read off the map in our mind's eye. Like computers, people too can be viewed as systems that encode, store, and retrieve information.

Knowledge Transformed

The computer metaphor has enabled cognitive scientists to understand complex mental processes that had eluded behaviorist theory. For example, computational theories shed light on processes such as making inferences, whereas behaviorist theories had not.

To illustrate, one early computer model, the hierarchical network model, attempted to explain how people understand simple sentences such as "A fish is an animal" and make inferences about whether, for example, a canary has skin (Collins and Quillian, 1969). The model assumed that human knowledge consists of concepts and relations, which can be represented graphically as nodes and pointers in a memory network. Figure 9.1 shows a tiny portion of the memory network of most adults, although a much larger network would be needed to describe all of a person's knowledge. In this hierarchical network, the categories at the top (e.g., *animal*) subsume the ones below (e.g., *bird* and *canary*). Further, a property such as *has wings* is stored only once in the network and at the highest level possible. Since all birds have wings, the property *have wings* is stored at the level of the *bird* node rather than at each node below it. By eliminating redundancy, this maximizes the economy of storage, an important concern in constructing a computer model.

The model makes predictions about and explains how people answer questions such as "Does a canary have skin?" Most of us must make inferences in answering this question since we have never actually seen canary skin. The model proposes that people respond to this type of question by accessing the *canary* and the *skin* nodes in the memory network. Then they search the paths from each of these concepts, looking for an intersection. If they find one, then they can answer "Yes," but otherwise they answer "No." This process of accessing memory nodes and searching the memory network occurs rapidly and unconsciously. Since the intersection search takes time, however, there

Figure 9.1. A computational model of the human memory network (after Collins and Quillian, 1969)

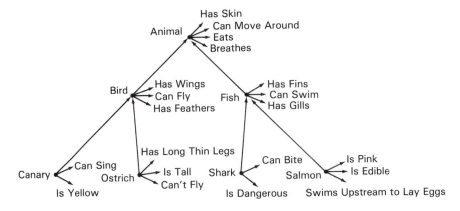

are measurable differences in how long it takes to answer different questions. In particular, the greater the distance that has to be searched in the network, the longer it should take to answer a question. Because the *skin* node is farther from the *canary* node than is the *feathers* node, it should take longer to answer "Does a canary have skin?" than "Does a canary have feathers?" In fact, this prediction and several others have been confirmed.

The fate of the hierarchical network model, which has subsequently had to be revised, is less important than its implications for theorizing. In addition to illuminating the process of inference making, it demonstrated that human knowledge can be conceptualized usefully in terms of computational data structures. It also gave psychologists a new way of evaluating whether their theories could really do what they claimed to. By embodying the model in a computer program, theorists could actually test whether the model could respond to the variety of questions it was intended to. If the model were incomplete or illogical in some regard, this would become apparent in the response of the computer to a particular question. Encouraged by the promise of this type of model, which forged strong links between cogitive psychology and artificial intelligence, cognitive theorists developed computer models of how people use their knowledge to understand language, to solve problems, to perceive figures, and so on (Anderson, 1985; Stillings, et al., 1987). In cognitive psychology, then, human knowledge is depicted as computational data structures.

Serial Processing

Numerous research projects have suggested the existence of deeper similarities between human cognition and the operation of computers. For example, the von Neumann computer is a serial processor that does only one thing at a time, and the same seems to be true of people in some circumstances.

In one experiment (Sternberg, 1966), people heard a list of two to six single numbers. Then they heard a test digit, which occasionally matched one of numbers in the list. Having heard the list followed by the test digit, their task was to press either a "Yes" or a "No" button as quickly as possible in order to indicate whether the test digit had occurred in the list. If, for example, the list had been 49207 and the test digit had been 2, the correct response would have been a press of the "Yes" button. In performing this task, the subjects had to hold the list in memory and scan through it to determine whether the test digit matched an item in the list. The placement of test digit varied over trials, encouraging the subjects to scan the entire list. The interesting result was that the longer the list was, the longer it took the subjects to scan their memories and to make their "Yes" or "No" responses.

In this instance, people seemed to be scanning their memories serially, operating much as computers do. This outcome, coupled with the results of early studies in which computers simulated human thought (see pp. 186-188), strengthened the idea that there are fundamental similarities between mental processes and the operations of computers.

Mind as Computation

The similarities between the operations of minds and computers has led to the radical proposal that both minds and computers are information-processing systems. This idea, which is called the computational theory of mind, holds that the mind is not merely like a computer. Rather, the mind *is* a computer.

Initially, the computational theory seems blatantly incorrect. After all, computers are lifeless objects made of silicon and metal, whereas minds are rooted in living human bodies. But a what makes a computer a computer is not its physical composition. In fact, a computer can be made out of practically any material available. Even stones and pieces of paper can be used to make a computer, albeit a very slow one (Weizenbaum, 1976). What all computers have in common is not their physical makeup but their ability to represent information through the use of symbols and to process this information through the use of well-specified rules. In this sense, a computer is a physical symbol system—a system that is made of physical materials and that uses symbols to represent and to process information.

The computational theory asserts that the mind too is a physical symbol system (Newell, 1981). The mind is rooted in a physical medium, the brain, and it uses symbols to represent and to process information. In speaking, for example, we represent objects and events using spoken words as symbols, which we manipulate in order to talk about the things around us. This theory recognizes that minds and computers are made out of very different materials. But it holds that the material differences are far less important than the fact that both computers and minds are physical symbol systems, systems that are made of physical components and that process symbolic information in similar ways. In other words, minds and computers are similar with respect to their functions even though they have very different structures or, using computer terminology, hardware (Fodor, 1968).

The most compelling similarities between minds and computers are to be found at the level of representations and programs. For example, both the computer and the nervous system employ binary representation. At the machine level, everything that happens inside a computer can be represented in terms of zeroes and ones. Similarly, activity within the nervous system can be represented in terms of zeroes and ones, for neurons fire in an all-or-none manner, though gradual activity occurs, too. Further, programs guide activities in both computers and mental processes. In a computer system, it is the program that guides the representation and the processing of information. The mind can also be thought of as an immensely complex program that contains rules that determine how people represent and process information. This view is strengthened by the success of simulation models of cognition, which depict human thought processes as rules and steps in a computational program. In fact, most proponents of the computational theory view the mind as a program (Haugeland, 1985; Putnam, 1967; Pylyshyn, 1984).

Mind and Matter

The computational theory is philosophically appealing because it provides a new way of conceptualizing what mind is and of avoiding the pitfalls associated with traditional philosophies of mind. Overall, Westerners have followed Descartes, conceptualizing the mind as an immaterial substance that coexists and interacts with the physical body. This view, however, has always been plagued by its inability to explain how mind and body influence each other (Churchland, 1984). How, for example, can an immaterial mind which is not even part of the physical universe cause the body to move? And why does ingesting large amounts of alcohol into the body blur the mind and even induce unconsciousness? By treating the mind as a separate substance from the body, dualism wraps the mind in mystery and locks it out of the house of science.

Dissatisfied with the unscientific approach of dualism, many scientists and philosophers proposed the physicalist theory, which asserts that states of the mind are really states of the brain and that mind is therefore a physical entity. The hopes of this theory ride on the observations of contemporary neuroscience. For example, neurosurgeons have observed that the electrical stimulation of the surface of the brain evokes strong images and vivid memories (Penfield and Roberts, 1959). Further, damage to particular parts of the brain can produce lapses of hunger, losses of memory, or deficits in vision (Carlson, 1984). Encouraged by these and other data, many neuroscientists believe that thought consists of neural activity within the brain. This equation of mind and brain escapes the problem of dualism by postulating that mind and body are made of the same substance and are governed by the laws of the physical universe.

Although this unitary view is more compatible than dualism with the scientific outlook, it introduces problems as vexing as those it had intended to solve. In particular, it attempts to reduce sensations and perceptions, the stuff of our conscious mental life, to neural activity, a very tenuous step. For example, when we see a patch of red, extensive neural activity occurs in the parts of the brain that subsume vision. But where amidst the neural activity is the sensation of redness? No matter how far one goes in examining the neural circuitry that is active when we see red, one does not at any point find redness in the circuit itself. Similarly, activity in particular centers of the brain may accompany the sensation of pain, but the neural activity itself is not the pain. In short, conscious sensations do not reduce easily to neural events.

One way out of this conundrum is to propose that sensations such as redness and pain are emergent qualities that grow out of neural activity (Eccles, 1982). Although this possibility cannot be ruled out, it is every bit as puzzling as to how redness emerges from neural activity as to how Descartes' immaterial mind influenced the physical body (Churchland, 1984). In addition, this emergentist view does not sit well with several *Gedanken* experiments or thought experiments that have been proposed (Hofstadter and Dennett, 1981). Imagine, for example, that a quadriplegic man's scalp had been fitted with electrodes, which transmit his brain waves to a distant robot, which then acts according to the man's thoughts. In a sense, this person's mind is in two places at once. This violates the physicalist theory, which equates mind and brain. Since physical things like brains cannot be at two different places simultaneously, how could a presumably physical mind be at two different places at once?

Beyond Dualism and Physicalism

In contrast, the computational theory avoids the problems of dualism and physicalism. Unlike dualism, it regards the mind is a physical system that is subject to the laws of the natural world. In addition, it escapes the problems encountered by physicalism because it does not reduce mental events to particular physical events. An analogy involving computers illustrates this point. When a word processor performs an operation such as deleting a word, it does so in the physical context of the computer on which it is running. One might think that the deletion operation could be equated with the particular physical events that are occurring inside the machine and the instruction is executed. The trouble, however, is that programs are portable—a program that runs on an IBM microcomputer may also run on a Tandy microcomputer. The deletion operation can be performed on both systems, yet different physical events are occurring in each.

Consequently, the deletion operation does not reduce to a particular set of physical events. In other words, an operation such as deletion is instantiated or embodied in the physical medium of the computer, but it is not identical with one particular set of physical events. The same can be said of the mind, viewed as a program. Although a mental operation such as subtraction is instantiated in a particular medium, the brain, this operation cannot be reduced to a particular set of neural events. As discussed above, it is at least conceivable that the same mental operation could be instantiated in different physical media. The achievement of this theory is that it keeps mind on a physical footing without reducing mind to matter.

At the same time, the computational theory is highly congenial to the AI enterprise. If the human mind is a program, then it may be possible to write a computer program that does everything of which the human mind is capable. Further, if a computer is executing a program that simulates a facet of the human mind, then it must in some sense be thinking. This view does not merely open the door to the possibility of machines having minds—it provides a welcoming reception as well. What is most radical about this idea, however, is that it remakes the human mind and its vast repertoire of knowledge entirely in the image of the computer.

The Limits of Computation

As discussed earlier, the computational theory of mind poses grave challenges to our cherished ideas about human freedom and morality. With so much at stake, it would be unwise to accept the computational theory without also examining its limits, some of which concern issues of feeling.

Feelings are responsible for much of the richness of human cognition. Feelings are not mere affective accompaniments of abstract ideas but are integral parts of the ideas themselves, giving them qualitative texture and sensory embodiment. For example, the ideas of "love" and "pain" have strong affective components. In order to understand what "pain" or "love" means, we must be capable of actually feeling pain or love (Weizenbaum, 1976). Similarly, it is doubtful that we could understand a great symphony without experiencing the deep emotions it evokes. These emotions are an integral part of one's cognitive appreciation of the symphony, giving it sensory texture and personal meaning.

The trouble with the computational view is that it forges a wide chasm between ideas and feelings. By reducing all human knowledge to symbols and rules, it suggests that human cognition exists apart from emotionality. It portrays cognition in terms of events that occur within a memory network, representing concepts such as love and pain as nodes. But the actual feelings of love and pain cannot be incorporated into such a network, which is a strictly symbolic medium. This view is dehumanizing because it cleaves the total self into separate cognitive and emotional realms, relegating emotions to a secondary cognitive status.

The computational view also fails to capture some aspects of human skill. In learning to drive a car, to play tennis, or to nurse patients, people progress through several stages on their way to becoming experts (Dreyfus and Dreyfus, 1986). During the early stages, an aspiring driver learns facts such as "Wet roads are slippery" and rules such as "Look both ways before turning" and "If the car skids, turn in the direction of the skid." Typically, the novice concentrates so hard on following all of the rules he knows that he has little capacity to carry on a conversation while driving.

In contrast, expert drivers seem not to be conscious of rules and facts while driving. They seem to drive effortlessly, feeling as if they are on automatic pilot, with their bodies doing the driving while their minds are elsewhere. Indeed, many drivers have had the experience on a long trip of lapsing into a daydream, only to come to later, wondering where they are. The remarkable thing is that expert drivers may suffer no impairment of driving performance even while daydreaming. Similarly, expert chess players perform intuitively, sensing the strongest moves almost immediately, with little conscious effort. Experts do reflect, but when they do, they seem to be evaluating their intuitions rather than engaging in the calculative reasoning in which computers specialize. Knowing exactly what to do and how to do it, experts seem to transcend rule-following and calculative rationality (Dreyfus and Dreyfus, 1986).

This line of thought suggests that the use of rules is only one form of human cognition, though not necessarily the most important one. The computational view errs by elevating one aspect of cognition, the rule-governed aspect, to a position of dominance which it does not deserve. It is true that people are rational and that they often use rules in thinking. But they also use mental imagery, intuition, and other modes of thought that do not conform readily to the computational perspective (Dreyfus and Dreyfus, 1986; Gardner, 1983; Weizenbaum, 1976).

To some extent, it may be possible to circumvent these problems without abandoning computational models of mind. For example, these problems do not apply forcefully to the connectionist models of mind that are becoming prominent in AI research (Graubard, 1988; Grossberg, 1988; Waltz and Feldman, 1988). Connectionist models are based on the observation that in the human brain, processing is distributed among millions of neurons that are richly interconnected and that process information simultaneously. By itself, no neuron exhibits higher intelligence—the capacity to solve problems and to perceive problems arises out of neural activity in densely connected neural networks in which many neurons process information in parallel.

Connectionist models conceive of the mind as a system in which there is extensive parallel, distributed processing of information by elements that are richly interconnected (Cowan and Sharp, 1988). In contrast to rule-based models, the system does not process information by using internal symbols and rules. Rather, incoming information is processed by a network of elements in which the weighting or influence of particular elements changes according to experience. A pattern such as the letter "A" is not encoded as an abstract symbol but as a particular pattern of processing within a network of elements that do such things as respond selectively to angled lines or horizontal lines. Likewise, understanding a sentence stems from particular patterns of activation in a processing network, not from the manipulation of abstract symbols according to rules.

In addition to circumventing some of the problems associated with rule-based systems, connectionist models offer the possibility of uniting research in AI and the brain sciences, showing how intelligent behavior may emerge out of neural networks. At present, however, there is heated debate about how successful connectionist models are and will be (Pinker and Mehler,

1988). Even if they turn out to be highly successful models of mind, they will still encounter the problem of meaning and culture.

Meaning and Culture

The human mind has a great propensity for finding and making meaning. We understand countless sentences, we question the meaning of works of art, and we ponder the meaning of life itself. The ability to find meaning, to understand things, is an important capacity of the human mind. But it may not be a capacity of computational devices which follow rules aimlessly or which process information in the absence of a social context.

A simple thought experiment, called the Chinese room experiment, illustrates this point (Searle, 1981). Imagine that you are locked inside of a large room, which contains huge volumes of rules and cards showing Chinese letters. In front of you is a story written in Chinese, which you do not understand at all. To you, the story seems like so many meaningless squiggles. From one window, you receive cards containing questions about the story, again written in Chinese. Of course, you have no knowledge of how to answer the questions or even that there are questions. You do, however, have the rules, which state in English what to do with the different cards. A rule might, for example, tell you that when you see one particular squiggle, it is to be followed by another particular squiggle, leading you to choose the appropriate Chinese character. Although the process is painfully slow, you continue following the rules, matching up the appropriate Chinese characters with each question. Then you output the Chinese characters that answer the questions correctly.

Aside from your slow responses to the questions, which could be speeded up with the aid of a staff, it might appear to someone outside the room that you understand the meaning of the story and the questions. In fact, however, you comprehended neither but simply obeyed a set of rules mindlessly. John Searle, a linguist and a philosopher, has argued that this is exactly what computers do. For all their ability to do the work of minds, computers remain distinctly unlike minds because they cannot grasp meaning.

Searle's critics have replied that meaning cannot be found at the level of individual rules or processors but at the level of the entire system. This reply, however, treats meaning as an emergent property. But it remains as mysterious as ever as to how meaning can emerge out of a physical system, which was part of the problem that plagued the physicalist theory discussed above. In a sense, the computational view simply moves the mystery to a different level of analysis without solving it. At best, the computational theory is incomplete. At worst, it may be downright wrong.

The reason why computational models, connectionist or otherwise, have problems with meaning, and with emotion for that matter, is that computers have no social context. From birth, we are raised in a social context in which we learn how to respond emotionally to various events and what it means when someone says "I love you" or "I am depressed today." Human culture is laden with values and meanings, and we learn these, often without even knowing it, through the process of socialization. Lacking a culture and existing outside of the human socialization process, computers cannot apprehend the meanings that pervade human life.

The human mind may well turn out to be a complex machine. But even if that is true, it will turn out to have unique biological and cultural properties that set it apart from the world of computers. Because of the limits discussed above, we should avoid the temptation to remake ourselves in the image of the computer. It is too early to sacrifice our assumptions about human freedom and morality on the silicon altar.

Becoming a Person in the Age of Computers

People and things have a long and intimate relationship. We define ourselves in part by the things we own, and we form such strong personal attachments with cars and clothes that we often tend to keep them long past their day. And so it is with regard to computers. Programmers frequently comment that their programs are an extension of themselves, windows to their minds. Many people who use computers to write or to design things comment that their computers feel less like tools than like familiar companions without which they feel lonely and incomplete. Particularly since the advent of the personal computer, computers have for many people become an important extension of self.

Things are also an important medium for self-development. By reading books, we gain new ideas that color our outlook on life and our view of ourselves. By working on cars, some people discover they have unusual mechanical ability, thereby enhancing their self-esteem and even shaping their identity as automobile mechanics. Through their activities with things, people take on identities as engineers, carpenters, artists, and so on.

Computers, too, are an important medium through which self-development occurs, allowing people to express themselves and to explore their abilities. Relative to other objects, however, computers deserve special attention. Unlike cars and televisions, computers raise deep philosophical issues concerning mind and freedom. In addition, many people are spending large amounts of time with computers. This stems in part from the relative novelty of computers and from the advent of personal computers, which brought computers into millions of homes and schools. Being highly interactive, computers are much more captivating than passive media such as television. The tremendous holding power of computers is evident after school, when throngs of children crowd around their favorite microcomputers to play games or to write programs. In light of this captivation by the machine, it is important to ask how this increased interaction with computers affects self-development.

Evocative Objects

The rapid infusion of computer toys and cartoons such as *Transformers* into our culture is regarded by some computer skeptics as a sign of a retreat into the shallow world of things, one that puts us out of touch with ourselves and with other people. But the situation is much more complex. An intriguing study by Sherry Turkle (1984), for example, discovered that children use their interactions with computers to explore with each other such basic psychological questions as what is alive or dead.

On one occasion, she observed Robert, a seven-year-old, play tic-tac-toe with a computer toy called Merlin. Merlin typically played a perfect game but was programmed to occasionally make a mistake at random, allowing a child to win. Robert, having watched a friend, Craig, beat Merlin, tried his hand. Unfortunately, Merlin played to perfection, and the game ended in a draw, whereupon Robert accused Merlin of being a "cheating machine." Saying "And if you cheat you're alive," Robert angrily tossed Merlin to the ground. Then he exclaimed "Cheater, I hope your brains break." (p. 29) On seeing this, two of Robert's friends tried to explain that Merlin really did not know if it was cheating or even winning. But Robert replied that Merlin does know if he loses since he makes different noises.

For adults, Merlin is a simple child's toy. But for children, Merlin is what Turkle called an evocative object, an object that stimulates reflection about philosophical and psychological issues such as whether something is alive, whether it is smart, or whether it has an intention to cheat. By exploring these issues in the context of a machine, the children learn about the differences between people and machines and about what it means to be a person. In this sense, their interactions with Merlin are part of their voyage of self-discovery.

Developing a Personal Style

An important part of finding oneself is the development of a personal style, a way of doing things that is well suited to an individual's own talents and needs. Computers provide a medium that allows people to develop distinctive styles at an early age. In Turkle's (1984) work with children, she repeatedly encountered two distinct styles, called hard and soft mastery.

Jeff, a fourth-grader, exhibited a flair for hard mastery, a style in which the programmer uses hard logic to exercise premeditated control over the computer. In developing his own space shuttle program, he begins by making a detailed plan. Next he divides the overall plan into parts such as making a rocket appear on the screen. He then writes and debugs the program for each part. In this top-down approach, which is characteristic of the manner in which most engineers and computer scientists work, the planning precedes the writing of the program, and there is little spontaneity or room for deviations. Hard masters such as Jeff tend to be very precise, and they emphasize control, leaving nothing to chance (Turkle, 1984).

In contrast, soft masters take a more fluid, spontaneous approach to programming. Kevin, who exhibits the style of soft mastery, also made a space scene, but he followed an entirely different approach from Jeff's. Kevin proceeds without a precise plan, putting up different objects on the screen, observing them as an artist might observe his canvas, and making modifications as he goes along. For Jeff, the most important thing was to get the entire system working properly. Kevin, however, pays much more attention to aesthetics, carefully sculpting each object on the screen. He programs intuitively, letting the program take shape as he goes along, much as an artist might do. More attuned to art than to control and planning, Kevin works in a highly interactive mode. Nevertheless, Kevin is a very successful programmer for his age. The style of soft mastery can be as successful as that of hard mastery, at least on relatively small projects.

Mastery, whether soft or hard, is an important source of self-esteem. Peers and teachers give attention and even special privileges to people who are highly skilled users of computers. As pointed out by Erik Erikson (1963), a prominent psychoanalyst, children need to develop mastery in order to feel good about themselves. Without self-esteem, they will be unable to accept themselves and to establish a personal identity that they feel is worthwhile.

On the other hand, mastery can be carried too far. Some children who become master computer users become preoccupied, even obsessed, with the machine. Turkle (1984), for example, observed a child named Henry whose isolation and personal difficulties were reinforced by mastery of the computer. Small, unathletic, and not very popular, Henry used his skill in computing as the base for his self-esteem and as a way of achieving social recognition. His computing activities were carefully calculated to keep him in a position of superiority, which he tried to protect by keeping good computing ideas to himself. His mind was filled with fantasies about making things intended to help him win out over his competitors. When asked about his thoughts or feelings, he tended to change the subject to building things or taking them apart. He was noticeably tense and awkward on most social occasions, and he appeared to relax only at the computer, which he could control completely. His was a lonely world of machines and of machine fantasies.

The computer per se did not cause Henry's problems. But it certainly reinforced preexisting patterns of tension and of social isolation. Henry's case is a poignant reminder that mastery alone is not enough, particularly if it comes at the expense of one's humanity.

Finding Personal Identity

In the West, adolescence is a time of intensive self-reflection, a time during which individuals struggle on a deep and personal level with the question "Who am I?" In their quest for personal identity, adolescents often experience a sense of heightened self-awareness, and nearly everything associated with oneself assumes symbolic importance. Clothing, for example, often becomes a badge indicating one's social and political orientation. A bedroom ceases to be merely a comfortable place to live—it becomes a personalized space, a reflection of one's values and personal style. All of the things that adolescents own and carry with them become expressions of self-identity.

The computer, too, has become a stage upon which personal identity is expressed and even shaped. In one case, Bruce, a fifteen-year-old, used computers to develop and to extend his sense of being special (Turkle, 1984). Bruce deplored the suburban neighborhood in which he grew up since everyone there was too much alike. His family was different, largely because his father was an intellectual, a college professor, who had nightly movie parties for rather large groups of students. While other homes in the neighborhood were very orderly and conventional, his home, which was filled through the night with students drinking, playing guitars, and sitting around, was quite chaotic. For Bruce, this disorder symbolized the difference between his family and the rest of the neighborhood.

Bruce made disorderliness part of his identity since it allowed him to feel special or set apart from others. By choosing disorder over order, he rebelled against the established norms of behavior and the tendency of many people to do things in highly similar, conformist manner. He cultivated disorder in everything he did, including his computing. For example, Bruce refused to use standard tools for editing programs that would have made it easy to incorporate new material into the body of a program. If he discovered a mistake in the middle of a program, he retyped the entire program in order to avoid using a standardized tool. Things that were standardized were conformist and were therefore to be avoided. Bruce used the computer as an expression of his individuality, externalizing himself on the machine much as a painter might do on a canvas.

For others, the computer is more than a medium for self-expression. It is a tool for the discovery and the shaping of personal identity (Turkle, 1984). Deborah, a sixth-grader who was overweight, had been withdrawn and had lacked confidence and self-control. When others called her "Fatso," she burst into a rage or pouted alone. The computer provided a safe world, free of ostracism, in which she was the master of her own constructed world. Having experienced substantial success in programming, she understood that rules could be used to construct and to change microworlds on the computer. Soon, this became a metaphor for her own development, a way of achieving the self-control she desperately sought. As she put it, "You program yourself how to be...Like today I will not do this thing. Don't eat candy for lunch. If you're angry, hold it in and scream after school...." (Turkle, 1984, p. 145) Deborah's experiences with computers enabled her to establish her identity as one who has control over herself.

With the recent popularization of artificial intelligence, the computational view of mind has diffused out of academic quarters and into the public arena, where it now influences the identity of increasing numbers of people. Mark, for example, is a junior at MIT who majors in computer science and spends many hours playing Dungeons and Dragons (Turkle, 1984). He views the brain as a computer that has several processors, each of which can give rise to its own impressions. He believes that conscious thought is only a helpless observer, a mere by product of the causal events, which occur between neurons. Depicting himself as a machine, Mark rules out free will and rejects the idea of the self as a moral entity. Aside from its questionable validity, this view illustrates the manner in which some people, even nonacademicians, use the computer to forge their self-identity.

Unfortunately, the computer can become a trap, an obstacle to further development, for some adolescents. Joe, for example, dropped out of Stanford University in order to concentrate fully on computers. Viewing computers as a psychological fix, he loves to take on the challenge of writing a seemingly impossible program and then pursuing the project with feverish intensity, neglecting eating and other activities (Turkle, 1984). When passion turns into obsession, one becomes locked into a unidimensional existence that precludes development outside of a narrowly circumscribed corridor.

Of course, the computer alone did not cause Joe's obsession. But its interactive nature, combined with the powerful social pressures for computing, makes the computer a highly seductive tool for many individuals. Nowhere is this more apparent than in the culture of hackers.

The Hacker Culture

Personal identity and group affiliation go hand in hand. For one thing, personal identity is defined in a group context. We define ourselves partly in terms of who our friends are and which groups we actively participate in. We actively identify with particular groups, taking on their values and obeying their unwritten norms of behavior. The group with which one identifies becomes an extension of the self that allows personal development in a communal context of shared values and social meanings.

At the same time, groups play an important role in discovering and shaping a personal identity. An adolescent, for example, might try out his identity as a "jock" by playing many sports, associating with athletes, and dressing like other athletes. If the athletes accepted and supported him and if he were comfortable in this identity, he might cultivate it and center his life around athletic affairs. If, on the other hand, he had been rejected, or had found that he had little in common with athletes, he might try out other identities such as those of the scholar or the punk rocker. This process of exploring individual identity in the context of different groups continues throughout life.

Adolescence can be a time of painful loneliness and social isolation. This is particularly true for people who are either not physically attractive or who take a strong interest in arcane subjects that are beyond the grasp of most students. People who love to work on computers, for example, are often castigated as "nerds," and they are treated as part of the "out" group. Many of these people develop an acute sense of being different and of being socially isolated. Although they see themselves as loners, they too need the support and nurturance of a group. They find it in the culture of the hackers that originated at MIT and that has since spread to computer centers across the nation.

Hackers are virtuoso programmers who make computers a way of life. They view programming not as a means to a conventionally defined end but rather as a creative blend of art, science, and play to be pursued with great passion and unyielding devotion. Through programming, hackers often experience a sense of union with the computer. Alex, who usually spends fifteen hours a day on the computer, says about programming that "I have basically assimilated the process to the point that the computer is like an extension of my mind. Maybe of my body...." (Turkle, 1984, p. 212). By working on their own programs and on others', hackers experience a deeply satisfying and meaningful engagement having the intensity that most people associate with sexual activity.

Being radical individualists, hackers usually have unconventional lifestyles, working in a computer center all night and sleeping during the day. It is not uncommon for hackers to work thirty hours straight, denying themselves sleep and pushing themselves to the limits of physical endurance in an effort to complete a self-selected project (Levy, 1984; Turkle, 1984). As Weizenbaum (1976, p. 116) described them, "Their rumpled clothes, their unwashed and unshaven faces, and their uncombed hair all testify that they are oblivious to their bodies and to the world in which they move. They exist, at least when so engaged, only through and for the computers."

Most people who work on computers regard them as tools, as means to an end such as money and career advancement. In contrast, hackers spurn money and traditional views of success. They regard computing as an end in itself, an activity having great aesthetic quality. Whereas the average programmer is often interested in simply getting a system to work, the hacker is interested in designing the most simple, elegant system. A system that works but that lacks elegance is regarded as a kluge, a technically crude and impoverished system that is undeserving of the attention of the serious programmer. Anyone who writes kluges or who tolerates them is called a loser, something no self-respecting hacker wants to be. For hackers, the emphasis is on winning, that is, on writing and using programs that are elegant and aesthetically pleasing.

Within the hacker community, there is acceptance, support and a lifestyle all to its own. Typically, this lifestyle involves staying up all night, eating at the same 24-hour restaurants, and working with terrific zeal on technical yet aesthetically appealing computer programs. There are always interesting projects to work on and other interesting hackers to associate with, creating a sense of community within which hackers can develop their personal identities.

The Hacker Ethic

The hacker community has a strong and distinctive code of ethics in which freedom and elegance are the primary values (Levy, 1984). Hackers believe that every system, from computer systems to traffic control systems, stands in need of improvement. They want total access to computer systems in order to take them apart, see how they work, and make the changes they feel are needed. They also want to remove all barriers to free access, including standard devices such as passwords that limit who can access a particular system or file. They also dislike bureaucracy, which often embodies a flawed, inelegant system and which generates its own rules that limit hackers' freedom.

This hacker ethic is embodied in the exploits of the original hacker community that evolved at the AI laboratory of MIT (Levy, 1984; Turkle, 1984). MIT used an operating system called the Compatible Time-Sharing System which was compatible with systems outside of the Institute, an obvious practical advantage. But the hackers disliked it because it required the use of passwords and because it gained its practical advantage at the expense of computational power. Loving the machine for itself, hackers disliked this compromise and the inaccessibility that was built into the system. Consequently, they decided to build a new operating system.

In industry, it often takes programming teams months or even years of highly organized work to develop a new operating system. The MIT hackers abandoned the standard model in which programmers worked under the authority of a manager, who dictated the time schedule, the specifications of the system, and the work to be done by different programmers. Instead, they worked in an anarchistic mode in which there was no hierarchy of command and in which the individuals achieved power by exercising control over the machine, not over other people.

What the MIT hackers lacked in organization, they made up for with nearly superhuman dedication and virtuosity. Working sixteen to eighteen hours a day, seven days a week, they developed a new system in record time and at a fraction of the usual cost (Turkle, 1984). The new system, which they playfully named the Incompatible Time-sharing System (ITS), did not use passwords, and it gave hackers maximum access to the files of any user. This allowed hackers to examine the files of other people and to correct any bugs in their programs. It also allowed easy access to the programs of master hackers, giving them new ideas for their own projects and fostering the sharing of software. The openness of the system also made it easy to play hacker games such as making a bug appear on the screen of another hacker and having it eat up his code, leaving a trail of phosphorus crumbs behind (Levy, 1984). Mastering these games became something of a rite of passage among the hackers.

The hacker ethic, however, conflicts with the values of the institutional cultures that support computer centers, even at MIT, a mecca of innovative computing. On one occasion, an MIT hacker discovered a way of improving a widely used campus computer by changing its hardware (Levy, 1984). He knew that it would have taken months to have the change formally approved, and, like most hackers, he disliked going through channels of authority in order to make a change that improved the machine. Together with a group that became known as the Midnight Computer Wiring Society, he made the change clandestinely, ensured that the machine worked following the change, and then covered his tracks by reassembling the system. But on the following day, the system failed to run a weather simulation program that usually worked well. The user complained to the Director, and an investigation and reprimands followed soon thereafter. This incident highlights the fact that the hacker ethic leaves little room for traditional values such as respect for authority and for adherence to institutionally defined operating procedures.

The hacker ethic also conflicts with values such as security and privacy. As discussed in Chapters Six and Seven, many individuals and organizations wish to keep their files private. Hackers, however, view privacy as an impediment to the broader goal of improving the system. Consequently, they deliberately try to break into protected systems, not to damage them but to express their dislike of limited access and to show that the system needs improvement. But this activity is illegal since federal laws now prohibit unauthorized entry into federal computers. Furthermore, it is not clear why open access to information should be the highest value, particularly since there are thieves and criminals who would take advantage of truly open access to computers.

The hacker ethic, with its overarching emphasis on elegance and freedom of access, makes the hacker culture an attractive haven for talented people who may otherwise be misfits. The trouble is that the ethic makes for clashes between the hacker culture and the dominant culture, which can result in significant amounts of personal stress. In addition, the hacker ethic reinforces radical individualism and actively undermines compromise and accommodation to the complexity and the inelegance of human social affairs. Consequently, hacking carries a rather high personal price.

The Hazards of Hacking

Because hackers view computing as a passion and an art form, they push themselves to the limits of physical and psychological endurance. The risk is that they will go beyond their limits, a phenomenon they call "sport death." As stated by Anthony, a twenty-year-old MIT student, "Computer hacking is kind of masochistic...The essence of sport death is to see how far you can push things, to see how much you can get away with. I generally wait until I have to put in my maximum effort and then just totally burn out." (Turkle, 1984, p. 210). This tendency to push oneself to the limits is found in many different professions and activities. But that does not make it more condonable. No matter how burnout occurs, it is not in the best interests of personal development.

Hacking can also be an escape from the complexities and uncertainties associated with interpersonal relationships. As one hacker put it, "hacking is easy and safe and secure. I used to get into relationships that usually led to me getting burned in some way" (Turkle, 1984, p. 217). Hackers need interaction, but they overrely on interaction with the machine, which is entirely predictable and controllable. Most hackers are men, and they often feel insecure around women, not only because of their social ineptitude and disinterest but also because of the perceived unpredictability and uncontrollability of women. Romance is dangerous because it might not work out, and it might not even be clear why. In contrast, computer programs are intelligible, and they can be worked out. Computers are safe, but people are risky.

Social interaction occurs within the hacker culture, but it is quite limited in comparison to that which occurs within the broader culture. Almost all of the interaction centers around the machine, and there is little time for sex, movies, parties, and other typical adolescent activities. The hacker culture is also highly individualistic, and even when many hackers are working on a project, they tend to be working alone. Solitariness is built into the hacker culture, making hacking a rather monastic existence. Because the hacker culture is oriented toward ideas and conceptual elegance, this solitariness is pursued in the cold world of the machine, leaving little room for feelings and for the sensual world of sex, of Nature, and of art.

The combination of sport death, solitariness, and avoidance of intimacy makes hacking a risky enterprise, something which many hackers admit. This is not to say that hacking is entirely a bad thing. After all, hackers demonstrate a remarkable degree of creativity, and Western society nurtures individual freedom and diversity by allowing the development of subcultures such as that of the hackers. The hacker culture is an important avenue for the personal development of the few, but it will remain distant from the social reality that most computer users inhabit.

Disability and Development

In Western culture, achieving independence is an important step toward becoming a person. Most of us achieved a high degree of physical independence in early childhood after we learned to walk, to feed and dress ourselves, and so on. Toward late adolescence, a time at which society recognizes the individual as a legal entity, most people achieve a significant degree of psychological and financial independence, often moving out on their own.

The course of personal development is not so straightforward, however, for individuals who are physically disabled, a group that society has often neglected in the past. Jim Brooks, for example, was born with spastic athetoid cerebral palsy. Unable to control the movements of most of his body, he could not communicate with other people, who assumed that he was retarded. His parents, however, realized that he was not retarded since he learned to communicate by typing on a typewriter the only way he could manage—with his big toe. Today Jim can still control only his right foot, which he uses to control a joystick. In turn, the joystick guides a computer, enabling him to call up words from its memory and to construct sentences on a computer screen. When Jim has completed a sentence, he uses a computer synthesized voice to speak it. And people listen when he speaks since he has a brilliant scientific mind (Hales, 1987).

Similarly, Maxene Pentecost is a quadriplegic who is unable to type using a standard keyboard. But she can type by pointing a light pen attached to her head at a special keyboard, Once a sentence has been written, it can be read aloud by means of a voice synthesizer (Shapiro, 1988).

These cases and many other indicate that computers are opening new avenues of personal development for the physically disabled. Traditionally, these people were relegated to a position of psychological dependence, robbing them of the opportunity to develop their full potential. Using computers in their homes, many disabled individuals have taken on interesting jobs and become more connected to the world outside. The economic benefits alone are significant, since approximately 36 million Americans suffer some form of disability (Bowe, 1987). But the benefits of improved communication and increased dignity cannot be measured in terms of dollars.

Unfortunately, not all disabled individuals have equal access to computers. The costs of designing and building custom keyboards and computers are very high, and many disabled people cannot pay them. For example, Bob Magee is a retired Air Force photographer who suffers from amyotrophic lateral sclerosis and who is unable to control his body. His wife communicates with him by pointing to a letter that is part of the alphabet printed in large block print, and he blinks his eyes or jerks his head if the letter is the one he wants to use. Spelling out even a few words can be profoundly frustrating, and these episodes often end with Bob and his wife crying. What is even more frustrating is that the technology that Bob needs in order to communicate already exists and is in fact used by Stephen Hawking, the eminent British physicist. Bob, however, cannot afford the expensive synthesizer that Hawking uses (Shapiro, 1988).

Cases such as this one challenge us to think carefully about our values. If we allow large inequities in computer use to exist, we deny people equal opportunity to actualize their full potential. On the other hand, correcting the inequities in access to computers is an expensive project, and we must ask whether it is more important to remove this inequity or the inequities in housing and health care that are prevalent in American society. In the final analysis, it is the fate of people, not of computers, to struggle with such difficult choices.

Conclusion

The computer has become a central medium through which we explore such ancient questions as "Who am I?" and "Are people machines?" In cognitive science, theorists have argued that minds and computers belong to the same species—both are physical systems that encode, store, retrieve, and manipulate symbols. This idea remakes people in the image of computers, and it challenges our cherished assumptions that we have free will and can be held morally responsible for our choices.

It would be inappropriate, however, to accept the computer model of mind. Lacking human bodies, computers cannot experience the feelings that are an integral part of our mental life. In addition, not all mental skills fit the mode of calculative rationality that is the hallmark of computers. Perhaps the main limit on computers, however, is that they are not social beings who create shared meanings and who are socialized to live in a human culture. For this reason, the realm of human meaning lies outside the reach of computers.

The computer is also a significant tool for personal development. For children, it is an evocative object that provokes questions about what is alive or what can cheat. For the disabled, it is the source of increased independence, communication, and job opportunities. For hackers, however, the computer is a way of life and a means of overcoming social isolation. Although hacking offers many intrinsic rewards, it carries significant risks as well. It is all too easy to become more attached to the machine than to other people and to use the computer as a retreat from the ambiguity of life. The goal of computing should not be to retreat from human life but to enrich it. One of the keys to enrichment is education, to which we turn next.

10

Education

Karen Ruef, who works for Shearson Lehman Hutton in New York, is in charge of hiring people for clerical jobs. There is no shortage of applicants, but she is frustrated by their lack of basic skills. Many can neither divide nor take fractions, and they cannot file because they do not know the alphabet. And she states that "They don't have the verbal communications skills to survive in a service environment, where a lot of the work is done over the phone" (Kurtz, 1989). Karen's situation is not uncommon. Despite the four percent unemployment rate in New York, many jobs are open, but there are not enough minimally educated workers to fill them.

This situation gives a hint of the profound crisis in American education. Nationwide, we have a twenty percent rate of illiteracy (Kozol, 1985), widespread ignorance and disdain of science and technology, and very high dropout rates in urban areas, particularly among minority groups such as blacks and Hispanics. In addition, recent polls indicate that Americans seem to have very little knowledge of the world. For example, as many as half the American public believes that the Soviet Union was allied with Hitler during World War II, and most people cannot answer simple questions about geography, such as "Which country is adjacent to the southern border of the U.S.? Many analysts fear that education is failing in its mission of preparing Americans to become informed citizens.

Hoping to deal with this crisis, educators have sought improved means of teaching, particularly means of ensuring that students master the fundamental skills. Enter the computer. Twenty-five years ago, a handful of educators had the vision of using computers in the service of teaching and learning. Today, that vision has come much closer to reality as computers have become essential tools at all levels of education. From elementary to secondary schools, students use computers to write, to learn geography, to explore simulated environments, and to create their own microworlds. College students use them to create art and music, to control experiments in the natural sciences, to search for information needed for research projects, and to learn basic concepts in areas as diverse as foreign languages and mathematics. In short, computers have become integrated into the curriculum.

The flood of computers into the schools has been so swift that by 1986, there was one computer for every 38 students nationwide, with states such as Connecticut offering one computer for every 16 students (Reinhold, 1986). Some 300,000 microcomputers were in use on college campuses in the U.S. by 1985 (Gilbert and Green, 1986). By the mid-1980s, computers had become big ticket items. For example, colleges and universities spend approximately $100 billion annually on computing (Heerman, 1988). Public primary and secondary schools also spend large sums on computers. In the 1985-86 school year, state departments of education in the U.S. spent approximately $550 million for computer hardware and $130 million for software (Bozeman and House, 1988). As the costs of computers plummet and as educational software becomes increasingly available, the trend toward high spending on computers will probably continue.

This extraordinary upsurge in computing owes in part to concerns over our national competitiveness. Rightly or wrongly, many school districts, states, and nations believe that success in computing is the key to economic vitality. In 1983, for example, a national report entitled *A Nation at Risk* called for higher levels of scientific and technological literacy, and it identified computers as one of the five new basics. It stated that as a nation, we are falling behind our competitors such as Japan, and it listed competency in using computers as a fundamental skill that all students should have.

This alarm has been echoed in more recent studies such as the 1988 report entitled *Computer Competence: The First National Assessment.* It documented the appallingly low levels of knowledge that high school students have about computers. For example, only 46 percent of eleventh graders successfully identified the correct answer to this question:

What is the main role of a computer program?

a. To put data into the computer.

b. To give the computer a memory.

c. To tell the computer what to do.

d. To let the computer know if it is doing a good job.

The report stated that "America's prominence in the world economy rests to a large extent upon its technological competitiveness. We are no longer so much a nation rich in industry as a nation rich in information. Our future industrial strength depends on how effectively we can use computer-based technologies, such as robotics and computer-aided design" (Martinez and Mead, 1988, p. 7).

At the regional and local levels, too, schools fear that without computers, they will inevitably drift into a second-rate status. Indeed, computers have become badges of educational prestige and currency that no school that has high aspirations can afford to do without.

The rising tide of educational computing and the accompanying rhetoric raise urgent questions regarding the national educational agenda. For example, computers are expensive investments, ones that create continuing needs for teacher training, software development, and hardware upgrading. How much of our public educational funds should be spent on computers rather than on other priority items such as new school facilities and higher salaries that attract the most capable teachers? In order to answer this question, we need to reflect upon about our educational priorities and examine carefully the benefits and the limits of computer-assisted instruction and of educational computing.

Educational computing also raises difficult issues regarding our societal priorities and the kind of nation we want to be. For example, who benefits from computers? At first glance, it may seem that students everywhere could benefit from the use of computers. But not everyone has computers. Moreover, some schools have teachers who are poorly trained to teach students to use computers, and schools vary widely in the quality and the quantity of their computing resources. There is an ever present danger of enlarging the educational gap that already exists between whites and blacks, whites and Hispanics, or males and females. Careful analyses of equity and gender issues ought to inform our choices about how to use computers in education.

Computers in the Curriculum

Education is fundamentally a human enterprise, one that seeks to develop the full potential of each individual. Most teachers agree that the ideal educational environment allows extensive one-on-one interaction between teacher and student. But this is a remote ideal in our educational system, which, after all, is a system of mass public education. In a typical classroom, a teacher works with a group of approximately twenty-five students, using lectures and group activities as the primary modes of teaching. Although most teachers work very hard to provide as much individual attention as possible, they admit readily that the system allows them to spend too little time with each student. This makes it difficult to form a significant relationship with each individual, to analyze the learning needs and style of each student, and to construct an educational program that is tailored to the ability and the needs of each person. Working in groups, many weaker students attempt to withdraw or hide, which only worsens their situation. And brighter students often feel they are held back by being forced to work at a slower pace than they are capable of.

Computers alone cannot solve this problem, but they can reduce its severity. By using computers as teachers, it is possible to create individualized learning environments in which each student learns at his or her own pace. Instruction via computer also makes it possible to give students the extensive practice that is required to master basic concepts and skills. This does not mean that computers can or should be substituted for teachers. At best, computers should play a supplementary role, preparing students and freeing teachers' time for significant classroom interactions. As Thomas Dwyer put it, "computers in education are revolutionary because they make possible great teaching in a system dedicated to mass education" (1980, p. 113). This idea of computer as teacher is the driving force behind computer-assisted instruction, which has enjoyed substantial success in the schools (Kulik, Kulik, and Bangert-Drowns, 1985).

Computer-Assisted Instruction (CAI)

Jim, a sophomore at a small liberal arts college, is struggling to learn Russian. He has never been particularly good at learning language but he wanted to study Russian since he plans to visit the Soviet Union in his senior year. Feeling bewildered by the different alphabet and the multitude of verb forms, he asks his instructor what he can do to master the fundamentals of Russian verbs. His instructor gives him a software package that provides drill and practice on Russian verbs. First the program presents a Russian verb and asks Jim to pick the correct translation from a list of alternatives displayed on the screen. When he picks the correct answer, the computer displays the message "That's correct" and advances him to the next question.

As long as he gives correct answers, Jim moves ahead, receiving harder questions. The harder questions require him to generate the proper translation rather than choose the correct response from a list of items. But if he picks the wrong answer, the computer displays the message "No, that's incorrect. Try again." If Jim picks the wrong answer on the second try, the computer explains why his responses were wrong and displays the correct response. As Jim moves through the program, his score is tallied, and when his score drops below a particular point, the program "branches," guiding him into an elementary tutorial that explains the basic verb forms and gives him the information needed to answer correctly the questions in the main part of the drill program. When he reaches the end of the program, the computer asks whether he would like to take a brief quiz to assess his level of knowledge. Jim finds that this type of practice helps him to master the material, and he likes being able to practice and make mistakes in private. He also likes having the quiz option, which provides valuable feedback about where he stands and about how he can expect to do on tests.

This type of drill-and-practice program is one of the most widely used forms of computer-assisted instruction (CAI), which may be defined broadly as the use of computers as teaching machines. Drill-and-practice programs are used in nearly every academic discipline today. They have long been used in mathematics to sharpen basic skills in applying mathematical operations (Suppes, 1980). Historians use drill-and-practice programs to help students to remember key historical events and to learn basic geography. And music teachers use them to help students learn to identify major composers and musical works.

Drill-and-practice CAI has proven to be effective in teaching elementary skills and also basic concepts and vocabulary in various disciplines. Many students enjoy the opportunity to move at their own pace and to receive immediate feedback on how well they are doing. Instructors like having a means of presenting concepts and principles in a step-by-step manner and of giving students the repeated practice required for mastery. Instructors also welcome the opportunity to turn over some of the repetitive drill work to an infinitely patient machine, which frees up their time for more important activities such as one-on-one conversation with students. In addition, teachers like keeping track of students' progress automatically, which allows them to decide what students need to do in order to advance further.

Used in a supplementary role, drill-and-practice can ensure the mastery of fundamental skills and concepts. But it is a relatively passive method that does not challenge the student to be critical and creative. It cannot teach the higher level skills of thinking and communication that education seeks to nurture. Furthermore, it underutilizes the capacities of the computer, and this has led some teachers to develop more powerful methods of CAI (Bork, 1985).

One such method involves linking computers with media such as video in order to create tutorials that resemble real dialogues. For example, Sarah is a freshman who plans to do a double major in business and French, and she wants to brush up on her skills of elementary French conversation before her next French class. She goes to the language laboratory, where she signs onto a personal computer that is connected to a video tape player. On the computer monitor appears a man who says

"Good morning, how are you?" in French. Sarah types in her response, a rather mechanical "I'm fine, thanks" in English. But the man on the screen responds "Please respond in French." Sarah retypes her answer in French, leading the man on the screen to say "Thank you" in French.

Next the man asks whether Sarah has studied French for long. In French, Sarah replies that she has studied for two years but that her French is not very good. The man replies "I understand. If you need help at any time, simply type 'Help' and I will try to give you some advice. Could we have a simple conversation about eating in a restaurant?" Sarah responds "Yes," and their talk turns to the subject of eating. After thirty minutes, Sarah sees that some of her French is coming back. Before the session, she had had some misgivings about "talking" with a computer since she loves human conversation. Yet she realizes that she is now better prepared to carry on a conversation with people, and she feels more confident about entering class and talking with her teacher.

This type of activity is becoming increasingly common in colleges and universities. It will probably become even more common as the prices of the technology fall and as the forms of media evolve. Like drill-and-practice, however, it should be used in a supplementary role. A steady diet of conversation with a computer would be a thin substitute for the richness of human conversation. And the point of this kind of activity is not to get people talking with computers but to prepare them for communicating more effectively with people.

Simulation

An even more powerful type of CAI is simulation, which is fast becoming a staple in colleges and medical schools throughout the country. At Stanford University, medical students study anatomy using the Electric Cadaver, which simulates the human body in an electronic world that blends computers and thousands of high quality pictures. By moving the cursor on a computer screen, students can inspect knee joints, travel up the spine, or examine facial nerves. They can also learn about the function of each body part by, for example, paralyzing a particular facial nerve and seeing instantly the resulting facial droop (Rogers, 1988). Simulation is also used in teaching in the humanities. An English professor at Stanford, for example, has developed a computer simulation of *Hamlet* that allows students to manipulate actors, props, and scenery on a computer screen. By exploring various arrangements on this simulated stage, students can gain a sense of how all of the parts interact to form the whole production (Turner, 1986).

The great potential benefit of computer simulation is that it enables students to experience things that are so dangerous or rare that they usually cannot be experienced naturally. Earthquakes and volcanic eruptions, for example, cannot be created in the laboratory, and violent chemical reactions are too dangerous to expose students to directly. Through computer simulation, however, students can acquire experience with these and other natural phenomena. By providing captivating graphics to illustrate mathematical concepts, historical episodes, or unseeable events in the world of microparticle physics, simulations can bring difficult and abstract ideas to life and motivate students to learn.

Whereas some traditional teaching methods such as lecturing allow students to lapse into passive learning by rote, simulations can encourage active learning by asking them to change variables and to determine the effects of the changes. Sociology students, for example, can learn about the effects of sampling size by experimenting in a simulated environment. First the students are shown a particular population such as an urban population that is broken down according to age, gender, ethnicity, and income level. Then they construct random samples of the population, trying sample sizes of, say, 50, 100, 250, and 1,000 people. By comparing the characteristics of each sample to those of the overall population, they learn that the larger the sample size is, the more closely the characteristics of the sample match the characteristics of the population. Teaching this principle via simulation challenges students to make correct inferences and to actively apply the principle instead of memorizing it.

Simulations, however, are no substitute for first hand experience. Simulations are always built upon models of reality, and these models often simplify or downplay the complexity and "noisyness" of real world phenomena. If students have experience with only simulated rather than real phenomena, they could acquire an oversimplified picture of the world, and they may be ill-equipped to deal with the unpredictability and uncertainty that pervades the real world. At best, simulation is a supplement that should be combined with exposure to the real world.

Another limit is that most computer simulations encourage students to explore an already constructed environment, but they do not challenge students to be creative. Of course, this criticism applies to traditional methods of teaching, such as the lecture method. Nevertheless, it has stimulated interest in more active methods of discovery learning.

LOGO and Discovery Learning

Outside the Hennigan Elementary School in Boston are the standard signs of a decaying urban combat zone—rusting frames of stripped cars, corroding buildings covered with graffiti, and heavily locked doors. Inside, however, is a different story. Inner city children spend much of the day working with 252 personal computers donated by IBM and a software package called LOGO (Bass, 1987).

The brainchild of Seymour Papert, an MIT mathematician, LOGO places an electronic "turtle" (usually in the shape of a triangle) on the computer screen. By issuing simple commands, the children write programs that move the turtle around the screen. If commanded to, the turtle lays down a line as it goes, enabling the children to draw and to create Turtle graphics. For example, a child could use the following program to draw a square.

```
TO SQUARE
FORWARD 100
RIGHT 90
FORWARD 100
RIGHT 90
FORWARD 100
RIGHT 90
FORWARD 100
END
```

Using LOGO, the children created intriguing graphics ranging from flowers to complex spiral arrangements and maps of the solar systems.

But it is not graphics per se that Papert is interested in. He sees drawing with LOGO as a means of learning mathematical concepts and of bringing to life abstract principles that ordinarily seem unrelated to children's experience (Papert, 1980a; 1980b). For example, in drawing a circle using LOGO, children typically order the turtle to go forward two steps, turn right twelve degrees, and repeat this sequence 30 times. In drawing the circle, children must deal with interesting geometric concepts such as angles and degrees. They learn that a circle consists of 360 degrees (12 x 30), and that no matter how long the lines drawn in each step are, the turtle must turn a total of 360 degrees in order to complete a closed figure that looks like a circle (Bass, 1987). Similarly, children who use the program listed above learn that a square includes 90-degree angles and four equal sides.

It was Papert's intent to break away from standard educational practices, which often have students doing prearranged exercises or passively listening to the teacher. What he wanted was a flexible tool that children could use to construct their own microworlds, electronic environments that mirror their own cognitive development and complexity. Working without the constant direction of others, children would be free to create their own environments and to explore them. The premise behind LOGO is that children are naturally curious, and, following some initial instruction, will use LOGO and that in the process, they will learn to solve problems and discover interesting principles of geometry and programming.

In the 1980s, LOGO was used extensively, particularly in elementary schools, and most teachers have been impressed by how eager children are to learn to draw using LOGO. Critics, however, point out that although the LOGO environment is conceptually rich, it is perceptually impoverished since it does not immerse children in the real world of sounds, touches, smells, and sights beyond the realm of the computer (Davy, 1984). Moreover, the experience of creating turtle graphics pales by comparison with the experience of painting—the computer does not provide the full texture, smells, and qualitative associations evoked by the experience of working with real paints (Cuffaro, 1984). Because children do find LOGO captivating, critics fear that turtle graphics, like television, will lead children to spend an excessive amount of time in front of the screen, living in an increasingly electronic reality.

There are also concerns about having children learn programming, particularly at an early age. Because programming involves logical, step-by-step analysis, it emphasizes one mode of thought which involves following rationally defined rules (see pp. 211-214). But this mode of thought is not inherently superior to other modes, which involve intuition, emotion, and automatically executed skills (Dreyfus and Dreyfus, 1984, 1986; Sloan, 1984; Weizenbaum, 1976). If children become too engaged by LOGO, they may spend less time developing other modes of thinking and judgment, leading them to rely excessively on calculative rationality.

Whether these criticisms hit their mark, however, depends largely on the manner in which teachers actually use LOGO. If, for example, teachers use it to teach mathematical concepts that are necessary and that the children would not learn readily through other methods, then these criticisms do not apply. But they do apply to classrooms in which LOGO is the primary teaching tool and in which children spend more hours in front of the computer than in interacting with the natural environment and their teachers and peers. In itself, LOGO is neither good nor bad for education. It becomes so only through the wise or unwise choices that teachers make about how to use it.

Learning Tools

The computer is a remarkably powerful learning tool that enables improvements in areas such as writing, research, and statistical analysis. For example, Aaron was a kindergartener for whom writing by hand was still so slow and arduous a process that it strained his patience to write more than two sentences by hand. But like most bright and capable five-year-olds, he had a lot that he wanted to write about. Using Apple computers and printers, Aaron learned quickly to type in phonetic spelling practically any word that he could say. By the end of two months in the program, which included only two hours per week on the computer, he was writing paragraphs and entire pages on his favorite topics such as soccer and his Mom. In the process, he learned to love expressing himself, and he also made significant improvements in his ability to read. In fact, this program is called Writing to Read because it not only encourages writing but also nurtures reading skills. The program has been so successful that the elementary school that Aaron attends exposes all kindergarteners and first graders to it.

In higher education, too, word processors have become basic tools that students use to become better writers. Many students entering college believe incorrectly that their first drafts should be close to the final product and that writing is done in a sequence of three steps: planning, writing, and revising. Writing instructors, however, are quick to point out that writing involves more than spewing out what one already knows in a linear manner. Rather, writing is a constructive process in which one learns to think by writing out the ideas and rearranging them in a nearly continuous manner, creating new forms and meanings (Dougherty, 1985). Furthermore, many college students treat revision as an afterthought, when in fact frequent and ongoing revision is the backbone of the writing process.

Word processing makes it much easier for students to approach writing as a constructive process and to make frequent revisions. Revision on paper can create scratchy messes and many confusing lines pointing in different directions. Unless one actually cuts and pastes the paper, it is difficult to see the piece in its revised form. Using word processors, however, students can correct errors easily and restructure entire documents in minutes. Word processors per se do not make students better writers, but they do enable them to make frequent corrections as they write, making revision a central part of the writing process, and to approach writing as an act of construction (Schwartz, 1985).

Of course, word processing only hints at the power of computers as learning tools. The linkage of computers with storage media such as videodisks has opened the door to interactive, multimedia learning environments. At a high school in San Francisco, for example, students read John Steinbeck's *The Grapes of Wrath* and then move to a computer-controlled videodisc player, which stores huge numbers of photographs, frames of moving pictures, magazine articles, and radio programs. By using this system to listen to Roosevelt's fireside chats, to listen to Woody Guthrie's songs, and to browse through magazines from the 1930s, they learn more about life in America during the Depression era about which Steinbeck wrote. This type of learning environment is called hypermedia since it blends computers, photography, video, and sound (Rogers, 1988). Hypermedia is growing in popularity because it provides a rich mix of visual, auditory, and textual information and also because the prices of the technology are dropping rapidly.

The compact disk (CD) is one of the key technologies in the spread of hypermedia. Readable by a tiny laser beam, a CD can store an hour of Beethoven, thousands of detailed pictures, or the amount of information that can be stored on a thousand floppy disks. A single disk can store many books, or the equivalent of 250,000 pages of information (Lunzer, 1989).

For example, by using a system called Ibicus, which connects a CD player to a computer, students can search in a matter of minutes for a particular word in all of the classical Greek texts. Using CDs that contain precise, digitized versions of thousands of classical paintings, art students can examine and compare how various artists have painted hands, feet, or any other item. Libraries have been quick to see the potential of CDs linked to computers. Five years ago, most college libraries allowed faculty and students to do computer searches of electronic data bases. Although these searches saved time, they usually provided titles and abstracts, not the complete text of articles. Now, however, libraries are beginning to use CDs and computers to search for articles on a particular topic and to retrieve the entire document for the user (DeLoughry, 1989). This type of system that links computers with CDs hold enormous potential as a research tool.

In the social and natural sciences, computers are already significant research tools that enable students to conduct complex projects and to interpret large amounts of data. Traditionally, undergraduate students in fields such as sociology and psychology often had to avoid questions that required analyzing large amounts of data using paper and pencil or a manual calculator. But computers have enabled them to not only pursue these questions but also to conduct much more sophisticated analyses of the data than had been possible before (Heise and Simmons, 1985). In addition, many instructors have found it advantageous to use computers to teach topics such as statistics. By turning over the number crunching to the computers, students have more time to think about the method they are using and about what the data mean. This approach also allows students to try out different statistical tests, exploring the effects of violating particular assumptions and weighing the strengths and weaknesses of different tests.

In all of these cases, however, the computer is an enabling tool, but its use does not guarantee that learning will occur. Students can write poorly or do the wrong statistical analyses via computer, just as they can by hand. Students still need careful instruction, guidance, and feedback from a knowledgeable teacher. Computers may eventually be able to meet some of these needs. For example, some researchers are developing artificial intelligence methods to produce intelligent tutoring systems that analyze students' problem-solving activities and give them guidance and feedback (Anderson, Boyle, and Reiser, 1985; Brown, 1985; Corbett, 1988). It is too early, however, to see how far these efforts will go.

Computer Literacy

Throughout the 1970s, there was an increasing awareness of the importance of computers, but the costs were too high and the public pressures too sparse to produce a sustained movement to teach students to use computers. That changed quickly following the introduction of personal computers and the development of powerful software. Parents and teachers who used packages such as *1-2-3* became increasingly concerned that the citizens of the future needed to understand computers and know how to use them effectively. Teachers also came to believe that workers who feared computers or who did not know how to use them would be severely disadvantaged. As one school superintendent stated, "We don't want to send 'new' people out into a new world with old attitudes. We want to safeguard our students against 'psychological obsolescence'" (Green, 1985, p. 101).

Before long, educators across the nation were talking about a new literacy—computer literacy. The term "literacy" was intended to convey the idea that everyone needed certain minimal levels of skill and understanding, just as they do with regard to traditional literacy in English. Most educators defined "computer literacy" in terms of the ability to use computers as tools and to understand what computers can and cannot do. The computer literacy movement spawned a large number of courses having titles such as "The Information Age" and "The Computer as a Tool" (Helms, 1985).

Right from the start, advocates of computer literacy have disagreed about what all students should learn in regard to computing (Barger, 1983). Initially, some people argued that students needed to know how to program computers (Luehrmann, 1980). The idea was that in learning to program, students would learn how computers work and prepare themselves to solve problems by writing their own programs. This position, however, lost its appeal as quality commercial software arrived on the heels of the personal computer boom. Many educators pointed out that it is no more necessary for computer users to be able to program computers than it is for automobile drivers to be able to do the mechanical work on their cars.

Attention soon shifted from programming to using commercially available software packages to solve problems. By the mid-1980s, students no longer learned the BASIC language that had been the mainstay of the early courses in computer literacy. Instead, they learned to use commercially available software packages such as *Word Perfect* and *1-2-3*, doing exercises in word processing, electronic spreadsheets, and data base management. In addition, many courses surveyed the applications of computers in areas such as business, education, and government, occasionally raising topics such as privacy, crime, and security.

Even in this second wave of computer literacy courses, however, there were many different and sometimes conflicting definitions of computer literacy (Neibauer, 1985; Van Dyke, 1987). Whereas some definitions emphasized the importance of understanding what computers are and how they work, others emphasized the ability to actually use computers in their chosen field (Barger, 1983). Furthermore, many teachers in liberal arts colleges, which attempt to develop students' ethical awareness, said that computer literacy consists of not only being able to use computers effectively but also of being aware of the social and ethical issues that arise in using computers.

By the late 1980s, talk about computer literacy had faded into the background. For one thing, educators had tired of investing so much energy in defining what computer literacy is or ought to be. Defining what every student should know about computers turned out to be nearly as difficult as defining the canon, the common core of great books, in the humanities. Many educators wanted to get on with what they saw as the more fundamental tasks of acquiring computers in the disciplines and helping students to solve interesting intellectual problems. In addition, on many campuses, faculty members were dissatisfied with the low levels of knowledge and skill that students acquired in computer literacy courses (Neibauer, 1985).

Still others felt that setting up separate courses on computer literacy was an error since becoming computer literate was a lifelong endeavor, whereas many students treated the courses as an end rather than a beginning. To avoid or overcome this problem, many colleges and universities set up programs designed to integrate computing into the entire curriculum (Carlson, 1985; Pritchard and Spicer, 1983). This integrative strategy has proven to be more effective for most institutions, and it has fostered the development of many computer-intensive campuses.

The Electronic Campus

Mark, a psychology major at a liberal arts college, is doing his senior thesis on the effects of racial stereotypes. Wanting to begin his project by reviewing the literature on the subject, he sits down at the personal computer in his room and calls up the campus library. Perusing the electronic catalog, he finds four books that look like they might provide a good overview of the subject, and the system tells him that all of the books are on the shelves currently. He immediately makes plans to visit the library that afternoon to check out the books. But he also notices that the holdings do not include what his thesis advisor had said was the classic work on the subject. He decides to call his advisor to ask whether she has a copy of the book and would be willing to let him borrow it for several days. But as he picks up the phone, he remembers that she is in class, so he decides instead to send his request via electronic mail, which she checks frequently. He switches his computer into the electronic mail mode, sends his request to his advisor, and heads over to the dining hall for lunch.

When he returns an hour later, he is happy to find a return message from his faculty advisor, who said that he can stop by her office before 3:30 to pick up the book. She also recommended that he do an electronic search of the periodical literature using the library's access to DIALOG, an electronic data base that contains hundreds of references on the subject.

He exits electronic mail and dials up the library system again. Then he enters DIALOG and, using a list of keywords provided by his advisor, requests a list of references and abstracts. By mid-afternoon, he has obtained the main books that he needs and has identified forty-five key articles, some of which he will order electronically from the reference librarian. He feels satisfied that his literature search is off to a good start.

Although this scenario has some futuristic elements, it is consistent with projects that are already underway. Perhaps the most ambitious project to date is Project Athena at the Massachusetts Institute of Technology (MIT). Sponsored by corporations such as IBM and DEC, Project Athena is a $50 million effort to create new educational software in virtually all academic departments and to fully integrate computers into the curriculum. The hardware for the project consists of advanced workstations that provide interactive graphics of very high quality and that interface with a variety of peripheral devices such as keyboards, video recorders, and sound generators (Balkovich, Lerman, and Permelee, 1985). All of the workstations will be tied into a campus network that links up the computers from all the various departments.

Around the nation, the idea of the computerized library is fast becoming a reality. Most libraries are either converting or planning to convert to computerized catalogs that allow users to search electronically for books and other materials and to determine with a few keystrokes whether the items they want are actually available. In addition, institutions that are at the forefront of educational computing are developing ways of helping users to make better use of library services. Carnegie Mellon University, for example, has announced plans to develop a prototype library called "Mercury." It will feature an AI system called "reference assistant" that will help users to find the data bases and reference tools they need (Turner, 1988).

This movement toward the electronic campus, however, extends beyond institutions such as Carnegie Mellon. Increasing numbers of colleges and universities such as Dartmouth College in New Hampshire and Wesleyan College in Georgia are placing computers in the room of every student, on the assumption that computers are essential tools for learning and intellectual productivity. Many institutions are also providing faculty members with computers and free training sessions. Administrative offices, too, have swelled with computers, as officers such as presidents, deans, and treasurers have become aware of the usefulness of spread sheets, data bases, and decision support systems (Green, 1988; Powell, 1988).

The proliferation of computers across the campus has created strong pressure to tie the units together into a unified network. When colleges first entered the computing arena, each department tended to develop its own computing resources and to act as an independent entity. As a result, different offices on campus could not access the information they needed from other offices. In fact, the different offices often used computers and

software that were not compatible. The result was a separatist environment in which one office, for example, that of the academic dean, could
not access the records of the admissions office to get the enrollment data
needed to make budget projections. Moreover, faculty members in one
department could not send electronic mail to other departments, and
students could not communicate via computer with the faculty.

Now, however, tools are available for overcoming compatibility problems and creating campus-wide networks (Charp and Hines, 1988). As a
result, many campuses are keeping their distributed computing facilities—the
microcomputer laboratories and the departmental computers—but are linking
them together into a large network. This distributed network arrangement
gives departments and individuals control over their own computers, and it
also gives them access to information from all over the campus. By means of
such a network, faculty can access the library from their offices, and administrators can retrieve information from various offices directly, without having
to make telephone calls or await written reports.

Computer networks also enable institutions to overcome barriers of
distance and time. For example, U.S. colleges often have study-abroad programs in other countries, but communications with students and faculty in
those countries has traditionally been slow and difficult. Using computers,
however, it is possible to link students and faculty abroad with the home
institution. Furthermore, it is possible to link different institutions together
into networks. For example, BITNET links colleges and universities both
nationally and internationally, allowing faculty to exchange ideas via electronic mail in a fraction of the time that would be required by traditional mail.
Services such as BITNET open the possibility of moving toward a world
academic community in which the intercultural exchange of ideas becomes
woven into the daily fabric of education.

Promise and Reality

Despite the many advantages and the potential of using computers, there
remains a disturbing sense that computers have not always lived up to the
promises made about them. This stems in part from the lack of a coherent
rationale for using computers. In fact, there has been a tremendous amount of
public excitement and media hype surrounding computers, which has probably
led some schools to purchase computers before they knew exactly how they
would use them. Parents, worried that their children might fall behind, have
pressed schools to acquire computers and to do something with them. In
addition, pressure has come from computer manufacturers, who have been
quick to market their products as state-of-the-art learning tools that good
schools cannot afford to do without. Computer enthusiasts within the schools
have also sounded the call for acquiring more computers. Furthermore, as

schools have nervously watched their competitors acquire computers, they have felt compelled to acquire them, if only for the sake of not falling behind. In a very short period of time, computers have become badges of prestige.

Needless to say, any tool that is introduced without a clear and compelling educational rationale will probably not fulfill its potential. The point of buying computers and other educational tools is not to acquire more advanced technology but to do a better job of educating students. In order to use computers appropriately and effectively in a school, careful attention must be given to the school's mission and to the ways in which computers may help to fulfill it.

Careful attention must also be given to the issue of teacher training. If teachers are not trained properly in the use of computers, they may elect not to use them. Or they may use them in inappropriate ways. For example, a recent Carnegie report entitled "From Drill Sergeant to Intellectual Assistant: Computers in the Schools" pointed out that the dominant use of computers in American classrooms remains the relatively passive method of drill and practice. Marc Tucker, who did much of the research behind the report, points out that this is in keeping with the traditional American emphasis on passive methods of learning. It is unrealistic to think that teachers will put computers to more innovative uses without additional training and incentives.

One of the main obstacles to effective uses of computers has been the shortage of educational software of high quality (Gilbert and Green, 1986). Commercially produced software is often low in quality and poorly suited to the needs of the instructor. Moreover, it is unrealistic to expect individual teachers or schools to prepare their own software. Producing good educational software is so demanding that it typically takes from 100 to 400 hours of authoring time to develop a one-hour instructional program. Typically, it is produced not by an individual but by a team consisting of a project manager, a subject matter expert, a programmer, and an instructional designer, someone who is trained in adapting different concepts to different educational media. For this reason, EDUCOM, a national consortium of people interested in educational computing, has launched a software initiative aimed at helping teachers develop and distribute better educational software.

High costs have also made it difficult to maximize the educational benefits of computers. Few schools can afford to buy and to make widespread use of hypermedia and the kinds of technologies involved in Project Athena. The most advanced computer systems, the ones that actually have the potential for transforming the curriculum, remain beyond the reach of all but a handful of elite institutions. Furthermore, schools often err by assuming that they can purchase computers on a one-time basis. In fact, colleges must budget money for maintenance, new software, training sessions for staff, and technical assistants who can help faculty to use computers effectively. These are ongoing costs that must be included in the annual budget. Moreover, the acquisition and use of computers often stimulates the demand for more computers. The growing demand for computers, coupled with continuous development of better hardware, creates such a heavy financial burden that one frustrated college president defined a computer as a black hole into which one sinks endless amounts of money.

What contributes most to the gap between the promise and the reality of educational computing, however, is the existence of unrealistic expectations about computers (Fleit, 1987). American educators have often turned to technology for a quick fix for our educational woes. Some time ago, television was hailed as the technology that would turn our educational system around, creating an educational bandwagon that many schools climbed onto. These unrealistic expectations were never fulfilled.

Today inflated expectations and excessively lofty rhetoric pervade discussions about using computers in the schools (Robins and Webster, 1985). To be sure, computers can improve access to information, motivate some students to learn, and provide environments for individualized learning, at least for relatively simple skills. There is very little hard evidence, however, that the use of computers has significantly enhanced students' ability to produce penetrating new insights or to come up with profound ideas such as "God is dead," "Life is a pilgrimage," or "The Tao that can be named is not the true Tao" (Roszak, 1986). In making informed choices about using computers in education, it is essential to steer a middle course between believing all of the claims made about computers and becoming so skeptical as to overlook the very real benefits that computers offer.

Values, Equity, and Gender

Education in the U.S. labors under the myth that education is value-free since public education attempts to avoid bias in teaching and is careful not to push a particular political agenda. Although American education has steered away from extreme political biases, no educational enterprise can be truly value-free. The fact that we decide to teach subjects such as science and mathematics rather than other subjects reflects our values. When we teach courses on literature and history, what we choose to include reflects our values and our cultural perspective, our beliefs about what is important, what counts as art, and why the world is the way that it is.

When computers entered the schools, they entered an educational system that is permeated by our values and cultural perspective. The fact that we have embraced the computer so mightily indicates the strong value attached to technology. As computers are used in the schools, some values are emphasized while others are not, and which ones are emphasized is not always a conscious decision. Yet we must try to make these values conscious since awareness is necessary for making informed choices.

One of the key questions that educators must ask about computers is whose values are being served? In other words, who benefits from the use of computers in education? Does everyone benefit equally, or do some groups reap larger benefits than others? These questions are particularly important in regard to minority groups, who will constitute one-third of the U.S. population by the year 2000. Although our educational system is one that seeks to provide equal opportunity, the fact is that these groups are educationally disadvantaged.

In fact, there is growing sentiment among teachers that our educational system is failing minority peoples. For example, black and Hispanic sophomores in high school drop out at rates of seventeen percent and nineteen percent, respectively, while white sophomores drop out at a rate of thirteen percent. Further, the percentage of black and Hispanic high school graduates entering college declined from 1975 to 1985, even though their Scholastic Aptitude Test (SAT) scores increased. During the same period, the number of black students earning M.A. degrees dropped by 32 percent, and the number receiving Ph.D.s dropped five percent (Educational Testing Service, 1988). These figures challenge us to think carefully about how computers are affecting minority groups, reflecting on whether minorities and whites have truly equal opportunity. Women, too, have encountered significant educational disadvantages, particularly in areas such as the sciences and mathematics. In computer science and throughout the natural sciences, fewer than five percent of the people who earn their Ph.D. each year are women. At an early age, girls learn that science is for boys and that other subjects such as English are for girls. The establishment of gender stereotypes early on can lead women to limit their aspirations in areas such as science and mathematics. Through exclusion, they are robbed of opportunities that are readily available to men, and the national pool of talent is arbitrarily restricted. If we are not careful, computers may inadvertently be used to perpetuate these stereotypes and disadvantages.

The Hidden Curriculum

Our schools reflect the tensions and conflicting values that exist in our highly pluralistic society. On one hand, education seeks to socialize students and to prepare them for lives as productive workers. From this perspective, education is an integral part of the national economic project, and it serves to inculcate the values, knowledge, and modes of behavior that are required in order to mold a productive workforce. Operating in this vein, education socializes people and prepares them to accept well defined social norms and roles. In short, it preserves the social order.

On the other hand, education seeks to liberate minds and souls from political shackles and the shallows of mindless conformity. From this perspective, the aim of education is to challenge students to think critically, even if this leads to the construction of radical views of the social order. In order to resist pressures that could constrain this transformative thinking, institutions have usually attempted to insulate themselves, creating an environment in which the life of the mind takes precedence over economics.

There is a delicate balance between these perspectives in our schools, although communities and institutions vary widely in which side they lean towards. Whenever schools adopt new technologies or new curricula, there can be corresponding shifts in the influence of these perspectives. If, for example, a school adopts a new history curriculum that emphasizes the importance of learning about many different cultures, including non-Western ones, that change shifts the balance away from teaching and reinforcing the existing social order.

Many educators fear that computers have indeed upset the balance since they have been used to push a "hidden curriculum" that is ideological in nature and that is seldom stated explicitly (Barakett and Prochner, 1987; Broughton, 1985; Magrass and Upchurch, 1988; Sloan, 1984). The ideology is that of the dominant class in the U.S., and it embodies the values of work, free enterprise, and the preservation of the existing social order. This suggests that the real function of computers in education is to prepare students to assume their places as subordinate workers in the corporate order.

From this standpoint, when students learn via drill-and-practice CAI, they are not only learning a particular subject but are also learning to obey commands and to endure repetitive work, which is what most workers must do. Even when students are learning via computer in a more interactive, simulation mode, it is still clear that the students are not the experts and that they must rely on the authority of the people who designed the simulation. Although the students can explore the simulated environment on their own, the boundaries of the environment have been set by someone else. The students are expected to accept the authority of the program and to allow those in power to direct their learning and to construct their social reality.

Proponents of the "hidden curriculum" position have tended to overstate their case. Nevertheless, they have challenged us to look beneath the rhetoric about computers to see the underlying values and assumptions that guide the use of computers in education. They also remind us that education in general and computers in particular are often used to preserve the existing economic order. It may be true that computers are vital for economic success. But not all groups are benefitting equally from computers, either in education or in the workplace.

Race, Ethnicity, and Computer Competence

Jackson, a black seventh-grader, is looking forward to working on computers, something he has tried once or twice but has never learned much about, in part because his parents do not have a computer at home. When he enters his school's new computer laboratory before his first class, he notices that several of the white kids in the class are already working and seem to know what they are doing, while the black and Hispanic kids are talking instead. Feeling less sure of himself now than before he had entered, he takes his seat as the teacher enters the room. During the class, he watches as the white students answer many of the questions asked by the teacher, who then begins to pay increasing attention to the white students. Jackson still feels determined to learn, but he sees that even at the starting line, he is already behind.

This type of scenario has been played out at countless schools, and the results are not entirely surprising. In 1988, the Educational Testing Service (ETS) published the first comprehensive study of computer competence among third, seventh, and eleventh graders from schools across the nation. It reported that at all three grade levels, white students showed higher levels of knowledge about computers and their applications than did black or Hispanic students. Moreover, the advantage of whites increased over grade levels. These results provide compelling evidence that minority groups are not receiving the same educational benefits as whites with regard to learning about computers.

The ETS study also identified some of the possible causes for the knowledge gap between whites, blacks and Hispanics (Martinez and Mead, 1988). For one thing, there were large differences in how much each group had been exposed to computers. Among the eleventh graders, approximately twenty percent of the black and Hispanic students had never used a computer, whereas thirteen percent of the white students had never used a computer. Further, among the eleventh graders who were studying computers, there were significantly more white students than there were black and Hispanic students. In addition, a higher percentage of whites had computers at home than did black or Hispanic students. This factor alone can make for large differences in competence since the students who had computers at home said they learned more about computers at home than at school.

Black and Hispanic students also suffer from a lack of effective role models. Approximately ninety percent of the computer lab coordinators are white, but only four percent are black, and less than three percent are Hispanic (Martinez and Mead, 1988). This state of affairs deprives minority group members of role models to be emulated. It also sends a tacit message that advanced levels of computer competence and entry into the world of computing is mainly for whites.

Other studies have reported that white attendance at computer camps and summer classes far outstrips that of blacks and Hispanics (Miura and Hess, 1984). And the poorer schools, many of which are in urban ghettos, have many fewer computers than do wealthier schools of comparable size (Anderson, Welch, and Harris, 1984). Overall, then, black and Hispanic children are not receiving equal learning opportunities in regard to computers.

This inequity is part of a larger package of educational inequities suffered by minority groups. But it is a key one. Those who lack equal levels of computer competence may be excluded from many positions later in life. Since the computer has become an important learning tool, those who have lower levels of computer competence will be disadvantaged in learning via computer. Unfortunately, black and Hispanic students are not alone in suffering these educational inequities.

The Gender Gap

In elementary schools, both girls and boys are enthusiastic about learning to use computers, particularly languages such as LOGO (Alvarado, 1984; Underwood and Underwood, 1987). This enthusiasm leads to effective learning for both boys and girls, who demonstrate equal levels of computer competence in the third grade. But this situation changes as the years pass. By the seventh grade, the computer competence of boys outstrips that of girls, and this male advantage appears at the eleventh grade as well (ETS, 1988).

This male advantage in computing stems in part from preferential access to computing resources. Even among third-graders, boys are more likely to have computers at home than are girls. By the eleventh grade, boys are forty percent more likely to have a computer at home than are girls (ETS, 1988). This is significant because children who have a computer at home show higher levels of computer competence than those who do not. Moreover, equal percentages of boys and girls say they are studying computers in the third grade, but by the eleventh grade, the percentage of students who are studying computers is higher for boys than for girls (ETS, 1988). And males are three times more likely than females to enroll in summer computer camps (Miura and Hess, 1984). This pattern occurs despite the fact that among high school students, approximately eighty percent of girls and boys say that knowing about computers is important for their future (Lockheed and Frakt, 1984).

This preferential access for males is not achieved by physically denying females computers or locking them out of computer camps and centers. Rather, it is achieved through a subtle process of socialization that teaches males and females to adopt particular gender-typed roles (Barakett and Prochner, 1987; Hawkins, 1985; Hess and Miura, 1985). In American culture, boys are supposed to like things like science, math, and computers, whereas girls are expected to have weaker interests in those areas. By the seventh grade, students say that boys like using computers more than girls do (ETS, 1988). Furthermore, gender segregation often occurs in situations in which males and females have equal physical access to computers. One study reported that among 400 high school students enrolled in a required introduction to computer science, nearly half of the males but none of the females used the computer center outside of class time (Lockheed and Frakt, 1984). Whether this results from peer pressure, biased role models, or the students' adoption of gender stereotypes, the tacit message is the same: computers are for men.

This message is powerfully communicated by the software used in many schools. Many software packages emphasize action, loud noise, competition, and aggressiveness. Typically, the symbols and objects used in the programs are those favored by boys. A drill-and-practice program for mathematics, for example, shows cars racing across the screen as students' scores are displayed. And one of the more popular versions of LOGO provides balls, cars, rockets, boxes, and airplanes as the main objects to be manipulated on the screen. Of course, these are the favorite objects of males, and it is rare to find girls' favorite objects included (Fisher, 1984).

Gender biases also permeate the content and the methods used to teach many computer science courses. For example, there is a strong emphasis on math in the most widely used books on programming in the BASIC language, which is taught in many high schools. Because "math phobia" is more common among girls than boys, girls are less likely to sign up for these courses, and if they do, they will probably feel or actually be disadvantaged (Fisher, 1984). In addition, computer programming is usually taught with an emphasis on logic, top-down structure, and rules. This approach is compatible with the "hard mastery" approach that males often take in writing programs, but it is far less compatible with the programming style that many women employ.

Anne, for example, is a student who enjoys using LOGO to create colorful scenes of birds in the sky. Like a painter, she takes an interactive approach to her programming, moving objects around on the screen and trying out different combinations of color and position. She loves the graphic aspects of her activity and shows little interest in generating the most powerful or elegant program. Yet she is one of the best programmers in her class in terms of what she can actually get the computer to do (Turkle, 1984).

Students such as Anne can be limited by too strong an emphasis on formal logic and rules. And she is not alone. Women tend to be less rule oriented in their thinking than men, and they often value intuition and subjective interaction with their material over formal logic and objectivity (Belenky, Clinchy, Goldberger and Tarule, 1986; Gilligan, 1982; Keller, 1985). These women's ways of knowing and thinking are both powerful and rich in the insights and perspectives that they offer. But in many computer science courses, they are valued less highly than the traditional male mode of thought, which emphasizes rules and logic and which is usually modeled daily by the male teacher. This not only puts women at a disadvantage but also robs men of the opportunity to learn to use different modes of thinking in using computers.

There are many steps that teachers can take to overcome these problems (Lockheed and Frakt, 1984). For example, they can select software that is oriented toward both males and females and eliminate packages that have obvious gender biases. In teaching programming, they can encourage and model a diversity of approaches and generate class discussion about their strengths and weaknesses in working on different problems. They can also change their computer center so that it is no longer viewed as "male turf," perhaps by adding art and by arranging special out-of-class projects for women. Of course, these actions will not remedy the larger set of gender biases that pervade the educational system. Nevertheless, they are an important first step.

Technique, Ethics, and Curriculum

As we move toward the twenty-first century, we need to think about what students are learning in regard to computers and about how this learning fits with the broader mission of education. So far, the dominant orientation in the schools has been that computers are helpful tools that students should know how to use effectively. In nearly all courses in which computers are used, the emphasis is on problem solving and technique.

Technique, however, is not the essence of education. Broadly conceived, the mission of education is to prepare students for lives as well-informed, humane citizens. If citizens are ignorant of the misuses of computers, they will be vulnerable to them. And if they are unaware of the values that guide the prevalent uses of computers, they will march unknowingly in the service of the status quo and the values of those in seats of power, even if doing so erodes their freedom and democratic way of life. For these reasons, those who teach students to use computers should try to raise students' awareness of the ethical and value-laden issues that attend the use of computers. Indeed, inquiry into issues such as those raised in this book should become an integral part of the curriculum. Some of the teaching materials that are needed in this effort are already available (Bear, 1986).

The emphasis on technique also pervades the computer science curriculum in higher education. This is particularly worrisome since that curriculum shapes the thinking of the next generation of teachers and computer professionals (DeLoughry, 1988; Miller, 1988). As stated by Deborah Johnson, an educator who is at the forefront of the movement to integrate ethics and computer education, "students don't know much about the ethical questions, and they don't know much about their profession at all" (DeLoughry, 1988, p. A15). This situation owes partly to the feeling of many computer scientists that they are not well trained to teach about ethical issues. Although this is a legitimate concern, it is also a restatement of the problem—the lack of teaching about these issues only perpetuates the problem and cements avoidance of the issues into the profession.

Miller (1988) has proposed an interesting model for integrating teaching about ethical issues into the computer science curriculum without displacing the technical material that constitutes its core. He recommended presenting case studies to increase awareness of the issues associated with various aspects of programming and professional activity. For example, good programming style requires checking the input data to make sure it is correct. This topic provides excellent opportunities to discuss issues associated with the National Crime Information Center, which, as discussed earlier (see pages 157-159), has very high error rates. This case study approach has the advantages of stimulating discussion and awareness. Since it is intended to increase awareness but not to give the kind of detailed ethical analysis that a philosopher would give, it does not require that the instructor have a Ph.D. in ethics. Nor does it require cutting out large amounts of technical material. In this area, too, useful instructional materials are already available (Bear, 1986; Johnson, 1985; Johnson and Snapper, 1985; Parker, 1981).

In the long run, however, awareness is not enough. Each of us must also be willing to act on our convictions, to take our own stand on the social and ethical issues that attend the computer revolution. If this book has helped to empower even a few students to move along this path, it will have served its purpose.

Conclusion

Seeking a remedy for the current crisis in education and wanting to prepare students for living in an era of technology, schools and colleges have embraced the computer. Computers offer students powerful intellectual tools for searching and analyzing information, for writing, and for problem solving. Computers are also significant teaching instruments and are being connected to video players and other media, opening up exciting possibilities for multimedia learning and simulation experiences. Through the use of languages such as LOGO, computers provide a means of discovery learning in which students make and explore their own microworlds. Because of their great potential and flexibility, computers are being integrated into the curriculum and are being used to create networked campuses having a computer in the room of every student.

There is a significant gap, however, in the promises that have been made about computers and the reality of their use in the schools. Excessive emphasis has been placed on the relatively passive method of drill-and-practice. Too often, schools have rushed to acquire computers but have neither developed effective plans for integrating them into the classroom nor trained their teachers adequately in how to use them. Furthermore, the computer literacy movement intended to make computers accessible to everyone. But in fact, white males have benefitted more from the use of computers than have members of disadvantaged groups such as blacks and Hispanics. In general, it is white males who have enjoyed the greatest access to computers and who have achieved the highest levels of computer competence. Although females have strong interest in computing, they are disadvantaged by a socialization process and a teaching system that treats the realm of computing primarily as the province of men.

The relentless quest for more computers in the schools has come dangerously close to an attempt to provide a technical fix for education. Yet computers are not the panacea for the problems of our educational system. For this reason, we must think carefully about what opportunities we pass up when we choose to spend huge sums on computers.

Our lives will continue to be linked closely to computers. As we enter the next century, which will undoubtedly spawn computers that dwarf the power of current ones, students will need to be able to use computers effectively. But a well prepared citizenry must have more than technique. Citizens will also need to be aware of the possible misuses of computers, of the values behind various applications of computers, and of the changes in themselves and society that stem from the use of computers. It will always be easier to use technology than to use it wisely.

Bibliography

ADLER, PAUL S., "Managing Flexible Automation," *California Management Review*, *30*, no. 3 (Spring, 1988), 34–56.

ALVARADO, ANTHONY J., "Computer Education for ALL Students," *The Computing Teacher*, *11*, no. 8 (April, 1984), 14–15.

ANDERSON, JOHN R., *Cognitive Psychology and Its Implications*, 2nd ed. New York: Freeman, 1985.

ANDERSON, JOHN R.; BOYLE, C. FRANKLIN; and REISER, BRIAN J., "Intelligent Tutoring Systems," *Science*, *228*, April 26, 1985, 456–462.

ANDERSON, RONALD E.; WELCH, WAYNE W.; and HARRIS, LINDA J., "Inequities in Opportunities for Computer Literacy," *The Computing Teacher*, *11*, no. 8 (April, 1984), 10–12.

ARBIB, MICHAEL A., *Computers and the Cybernetic Society*, 2nd ed. New York: Academic Press, 1984.

ARKIN, WILLIAM M., et al., "Nuclear Weapons," in *SIPRI Yearbook 1988: World Armaments and Disarmament*. New York: Oxford University Press, 1988, 23–64.

ATHANASIOU, TOM, "Encryption: Technology, Privacy, and National Security," *Technology Review*, August/September, 1986, 57–66.

ATTEWELL, PAUL, and RULE, JAMES, "Computing and Organizations: What We Know and What We Don't Know," *Communications of the ACM*, *27*, no. 12 (December, 1984), 1184–1192.

BALKOVICH, EDWARD; LERMAN, STEVEN; and PARMELEE, RICHARD P., "Computing in Higher Education: The Athena Experience," *Communications of the ACM, 28*, no. 11 (November, 1985), 1214–1224.

BARAKETT, JOYCE, and PROCHER, LARRY, "The Effects of Computer Use on Early Childhood Socialization," *Computers & Society, 16*, no. 4 (Winter/Spring, 1987), 19–27.

BARGER, ROBERT NEWTON, "Computer Literacy: Toward a Clearer Definition," *T. H. E. Journal*, October, 1983, 108–112.

BARNABY, FRANK, *The Automated Battlefield*. New York: Free Press, 1986.

BARNABY, FRANK, ed., *The Gaia Peace Atlas: Survival into the Third Millennium*. New York: Doubleday, 1988.

BARRY, JOHN, and MORGANTHAU, TOM, "The Defense Dilemma," *Newsweek*, January 23, 1989, 12–18.

BASS, ALISON B., "Computers in the Classroom," *Technology Review*, April, 1987, 52–64.

BEAR, GEORGE G. *Computers in Your Life: Face the Social Issues*. Portland: J. Weston Walch, 1986.

BECK, MELINDA; MEYER, MICHAEL; LEWIS, SHAWN D.; and HAGER, MARY, "Smart Cars, Smart Streets," *Newsweek*, December 5, 1988, 86–87.

BECKER, STEPHEN A., "Legal Protection for Computer Hardware and Software," *Byte, 6*, no. 5 (May, 1981), 140–146.

BELENKY, MARY FIELD; CLINCHY, BLYTHE MCVICKER; GOLDBERGER, NANCY RULE; and TARULE, JILL MATTUCK, *Women's Ways of Knowing: The Development of Self, Voice and Mind*. New York: Basic Books, 1986.

BELL, DANIEL, *The Coming of Post-Industrial Society: A Venture in Social Forecasting*. New York: Basic Books, 1973.

BELL, DANIEL, "The Social Framework of the Information Society," in *The Microelectronics Revolution: The Complete Guide to the New Technology and Its Impact on Society*, ed. Tom Forester. Cambridge: MIT Press, 1980, 500–549.

BERLINER, HANS, "Computer Backgammon," *Scientific American, 242*, no. 6 (June, 1980), 64–72.

BERNSTEIN, JEREMY, *The Analytical Engine: Computers—Past, Present and Future*. New York: Random House, 1978.

BERRY, JOHN M., "The Legacy of Reagonomics," *The Washington Post National Weekly Edition*, December 19–25, 1988, 6–7.

BESSANT, JOHN, "Information Technology and the North-South Divide," in *New Information Technology*, ed. Alan Burns. New York: Wiley, 1984, 170–186.

BETTS, MITCH, "Federal DP Crooks Profiled," *Computerworld*, July 1, 1985, 2.

BLAIR, BRUCE G., *Strategies of Command and Control: Redefining the Nuclear Threat*. Washington, D.C.: Brookings, 1985.

BLOIS, MARSDEN S., "Clinical Judgement and Computers," *New England Journal of Medicine, 303*, no. 4 (April, 1980), 192–197.

BLOOMBECKER, BUCK, "New Federal Law Bolsters Computer Security Efforts, *Computerworld*, October 27, 1986, 53–62.

BLOOMBECKER, BUCK, "Of Systems, Solidarity, and Struggle," *Datamation*, November 1, 1987, 47–55.

BLOOMBECKER, BUCK, "Careful Now—It's Catching," *Computers & Society, 18*, no. 4 (October, 1988), 17–18.

BLOOMBECKER, JAY, ed., *The Computer Crime Law Reporter*. Los Angeles: California State University, 1984.

BLOUSTEIN, EDWARD J., "Privacy as an Aspect of Human Dignity: An answer to Dean Prosser," in *Philosophical Dimensions of Privacy: An Anthology*, ed. Ferdinand D. Schoeman. Cambridge: Cambridge University Press, 1984, 157–202.

BORK, ALFRED, *Personal Computers for Education*. New York: Harper & Row, 1985.

BORNING, ALAN, "Computer System Reliability and Nuclear War," *Communications of the ACM, 30*, no. 2 (February, 1987), 112–131.

BOTELHO, ANTONIO JOSE J., "Brazil's Independent Computer Strategy," *Technology Review*, May/June, 1987, 37–45.

BOULEZ, PIERRE, and GERZSO, ANDREW, "Computers in Music," *Scientific American, 258*, no. 4 (April, 1988), 44–50.

BOWE, FRANK, "Making Computers Accessible to Disabled People." *Technology Review, 90*, no. 1 (Jan., 1987), 52–73.

BOZEMAN, WILLIAM C., and HOUSE, JESS E., "Microcomputers in Education: The Second Decade," *T. H. E. Journal*, February, 1988, 82–86.

BRACKEN, PAUL J., *The Command and Control of Nuclear Forces*. New Haven: Yale University Press, 1983.

BRAMER, MAX, "Intelligent Knowledge Based Systems," in *New Information Technology*, ed. Alan Burns. New York: Wiley, 1984, 148–158.

BRANNIGAN, VINCENT M, "Liability for Personal Injury Causes by Defective Medical Computer Programs," in *Ethical Issues in the Use of Computers*," ed. Deborah G. Johnson and John W. Snapper. Belmont, CA: Wadsworth, 1985, 58–66.

BRANSCOMB, ANNE W., "Who Owns Creativity: Property Rights in the Information Age," *Technology Review*, May/June, 1988, 38–45.

BRAVERMAN, HARRY, *Labor and Monopoly Capital: The Degradation of Work in the Twentieth Century*. New York: Monthly Review Press, 1974.

BROAD, WILLIAM J., "The Chaos Factor," *Science 83, 4*, no. 1 (January/February), 41–49.

BROD, CRAIG, *Technostress: The Human Cost of the Computer Revolution*. Reading, MA: Addison-Wesley, 1984.

BROUGHTON, JOHN N., "The Surrender of Control: Computer Literacy as Political Socialization of the Child," in *The Computer in Education: A Critical Perspective*, ed. Douglas Sloan. Columbia University: Teachers College Press, 1984, 102–122.

BROWN, JOHN SEELY, "Process Versus Product: A Perspective on Tools for Communal and Informal Electronic Learning," in *Children and Microcomputers*, ed. M. Chen and W. Paisley. Beverly Hills: Sage Publications, 1985, 248–266.

BROWN, WARREN, "Next Computers May Be Getting Commuters Out of Traffic Jams," *The Washington Post National Weekly Edition*, January 2–8, 1989, 21.

BUCHANAN, D. A., and BODDY, D. "Advanced Technology and the Quality of Working Life: The Effects of Computerized Controls on Biscuit Making Operators," *Journal of Occupational Psychology, 56*, no. 1 (January, 1983), 109–119.

BUCKLEY, JERRY, "'We Learned That Them May be Us'," *U.S. News & World Report*, May 9, 1988, 48–50.

BUDIANSKY, STEPHEN, "Beating Japan With Cooperation," *U.S. News & World Report*, September 22, 1986, 65.

BUNN, MATTHEW, "Pentagon Modifies SDI Plans, Cutting Costs for 'Phase I'," *Arms Control Today, 18*, no. 9 (November, 1988), 26–27.

BURGESS, JOHN, "Computers, Intruders and Trouble-Shooters," *The Washington Post National Weekly Edition*, November 21–27, 1988, 6–7.

BURNHAM, DAVID, *The Rise of the Computer State: The Threat to Our Freedoms, Our Ethics and Our Democratic Process*. New York: Random House, 1980.

BURNHAM, DAVID, "FBI Says 12,000 Reports on Suspects Are Issued Each Day," *New York Times*, August 25, 1985.

BYLINSKY, GENE, "America's Best-Managed Factories," *Fortune*, May 28, 1984, 16–24.

BYRNE, JOHN A., "Jobs, Jobs, Jobs Galore," *Business Week*, April 18, 1988, 26–28.

CALDICOTT, HELEN, *Missile Envy: The Arms Race and Nuclear War*. New York: Bantam, 1984.

CAMPBELL, BERNARD G., *Humankind Emerging*, 3rd ed. Boston: Little, Brown & Co., 1982.

CARLSON, NEIL R., *Physiology of Behavior*, 3rd ed., New York: Allyn and Bacon, 1984.

CARLSON, WILLIAM L., "Integrating Computing into the Liberal Arts: A Case History," *T. H.E. Journal*, September, 1985, 95–100.

CARLYLE, RALPH EMMETT, and MOAD, JEFF, "IBM and the Control of Information," *Datamation*, January 1, 1988, 34–44.

Carnegie Corporation of New York, "From Drill Sergeant to Intellectual Assistant: Computers in the Schools," *Carnegie Quarterly, 30*, no. 3 & 4 (Summer/Fall, 1985), 1–7.

CARNESALE, ALBERT, et al., *Living With Nuclear Weapons*. New York: Bantam, 1983.

CARTER, ASHTON B., "Assessing Command System Vulnerability," in *Managing Nuclear Operations*, ed. Ashton B. Carter, John D. Steinbruner, and Charles A. Zraket. Washington, D. C.: The Brookings Institution, 1987, 555–610.

CARTER, ASHTON B.; STEINBRUNER, JOHN D.; AND ZRAKET, CHARLES A., eds., *Managing Nuclear Operations*. Washington, D. C.: The Brookings Institution, 1987.

CASTRO, JANICE, "Big vs. Small," *Time*, September 5, 1988, 48–50.

CETRON, MARVIN J.; ROCHA, WANDA; AND LUCKINS, REBECCA, "Into the 21st Century: Long-term Trends Affecting the United States," *The Futurist*, July–August, 1988, 29–40.

CHANDLER, DAVID L., "The Spy Who Stayed Too Long," *The Boston Globe*, November 14, 1988, 29–31.

CHAPMAN, GARY, "Airland Battle Doctrine and the Strategic Computing Initiative," *The CPSR Newsletter, 3*, no. 4 (Fall, 1985), 1–7.

CHAPMAN, GARY, "The New Generation of High-Technology Weapons," in *Computers in Battle: Will They Work?*, ed. David Bellin and Gary Chapman. New York: Harcourt Brace Jovanovich, 1987, 61–100.

CHARP, SYLVIA and HINES, DUFFY, "A Primer on Campus Networks," in *Making Computers Work for Administrators*, ed. Kenneth C. Green and Steven W. Gilbert. San Francisco: Jossey-Bass, 1988, pp. 71–78.

CHASE, W. G., and SIMON, H. A. "The Mind's Eye in Chess," in *Visual Information Processing*, ed. W. G. Chase. New York: Academic Press, 1973.

CHOMSKY, N., *Syntactic Structures*. The Hague: Mouton, 1957.

CHOMSKY, N., *Language and Mind*. New York: Harcourt Brace Jovanovich, 1972.

CHRISTOPHER, ROBERT C., *The Japanese Mind: The Goliath Explained*. New York: Simon & Schuster, 1983.

CHURCH, GEORGE J., "Panic Grips the Globe," *Time*, November 2, 1987, 22–33.

CHURCH, GEORGE J., "High-Tech Horror," *Time*, July 18, 1988, 14–17.

CHURCHLAND, PAUL M., *Matter and Consciousness: A Contemporary Introduction to the Philosophy of Mind*. Cambridge: MIT Press, 1984.

CLARKE, ROGER A., "Just Another Piece of Plastic for Your Wallet: The 'Australian Card' Scheme," *Computers & Society*, *18*, no. 1 (January, 1988), 7–21.

CLARKE, ROGER A., "Information Technology and Dataveillance," *Communications of the ACM*, *31*, no. 5 (May, 1988), 498–512.

CLARKE, ROGER, "The Australia Card: Postscript," *Computers and Society*, *18*, no. 3 (July, 1988), 10–14.

COLLINS, A. M., and QUILLIAN, M. R., "Retrieval Time from Semantic Memory," *Journal of Verbal Learning and Verbal Behavior*, *8*, 1969, 240–247.

CONRAD, THOMAS, "Computing Apartheid," *The CPSR Newsletter*, *4*, no. 2 (Spring, 1986), 5–7.

COOLEY, MIKE, *Architect or Bee? The Human/Technology Relationship*. Boston: South End Press, 1980.

CORBETT, ALBERT, "An Intelligent Tutoring System," *T. H. E. Journal*, *16*, no. 1 (August, 1988), 61–64.

COWAN, JACK D.; and SHARP, DAVID H., "Neural Nets and Artificial Intelligence," in *The Artificial Intelligence Debate: False Starts, Real Foundations*, ed. Stephen R. Graubard. Cambridge: MIT Press, 1988, 85–124.

COWART, ROBERT, and AMIRREZVANI, ANITA, "Using VDTs in the Workplace," *PC Week*, January 21, 1986, 57–60.

CUFFARO, HARRIET K., "Microcomputer in Education: Why is Earlier Better?," in *The Computer in Education: A Critical Perspective*, ed. Douglas Sloan. Columbia University: Teachers College Press, 1984, 21–30.

DAHL, MARY KAREN, "The National Crime Information Center: A Case Study in National Databases," *The CPSR Newsletter*, *6*, no. 1 (Winter, 1988), 2–15.

DALLMEYER, DORINDA G., "National Security and the Semiconductor Industry," *Technology Review*, November/December, 1987, 47–55.

DAVISON, GERALD C., and NEALE, JOHN M., *Abnormal Psychology*, 3rd ed. New York: Wiley, 1982.

DAVY, JOHN, "Mindstorms in the Lamplight," in *The Computer in Education: A Critical Perspective*, ed. Douglas Sloan. Columbia University: Teachers College Press, 1984, 11–20.

DEITEL, HARVEY M., and DEITEL, BARBARA, *Computers and Data Processing*. New York: Academic Press, 1985.

DEGROOT, A. D., *Thought and Choice in Chess*. New York: Basic Books, 1965.

DELOUGHRY, THOMAS J., "A Compact-Disk System with Texts of Articles to be Sold to Libraries by Microfilm Company," *The Chronicle of Higher Education*, January 18, 1989, A13–A17.

DELOUGHRY, THOMAS J., "Failure of Colleges to Teach Computer Ethics is Called Oversight with Potentially Catastrophic Consequences," *The Chronicle of Higher Education*, February 24, 1988, A15–A18.

DEMATTEO, BOB, *Terminal Shock: The Health Hazards of Video Display Terminals*. Toronto: NC Press, 1985.

DENNING, PETER J., "The Science of Computing: Computer Viruses," *American Scientist*, 1988, *76*, no. 4 (May-June), 236–238.

DERTOUZOS, MICHAEL L., "The Multiprocessor Revolution: Harnessing Computers Together," *Technology Review*, February/March, 1987, 44–57.

DICKSON, DAVID, "Eureka!," *Technology Review*, August/September, 1988, 27–33.

DIFFIE, WHITFIELD, and HELLMAN, MARTIN E., "Exhaustive Cryptanalysis of the NBS Data Encryption Standard," *Computer*, June, 1977, 74–84.

DIZARD, WILSON P., JR., *The Coming Information Age: An Overview of Technology, Economics, and Politics*. New York: Longman, 1982.

DIZARD, WILSON P., JR., "Mikhail Gorbachev's Computer Challenge," *The Washington Quarterly*, Spring, 1986, 157–163.

DOUGHERTY, B. N., *Composing Choices for Writers: A Cross-Disciplinary Rhetoric*. New York: McGraw-Hill, 1985.

DOWNING, HAZEL, "Word Processors and the Oppression of Women," in *The Microelectronics Revolution: The Complete Guide to the New Technology and Its Impact on Society*, ed. Tom Forester. Cambridge: MIT Press, 1980, 275–287.

DRAPER, ROGER, "The Golden Arm," *The New York Review*, October 24, 1985, 46–52.

DRELL, SIDNEY D., and PANOFSKY, WOLFGANG K. H., "The Case Against Strategic Defense: Technical and Strategic Realities," *Issues in Science and Technology*, *1*, no. 1 (Fall, 1984), 45–65.

DREYFUS, HUBERT L., and DREYFUS, STUART E., "Putting Computers in Their Proper Place: Analysis versus Intuition in the Classroom," in *The Computer in Education: A Critical Perspective*, ed. Douglas Sloan. New York: Teachers College Press, 1984, 40–63.

DREYFUS, HUBERT L., and DREYFUS, STUART E., *Mind over Machine: The Power of Human Intuition and Expertise in the Era of the Computer*. New York: Free Press, 1986.

DWYER, THOMAS, "Some Thoughts on Computers and Greatness in Teaching," in *The Computer in the School: Tutor, Tool, Tutee*, ed. Robert Taylor. Columbia University: Teachers College Press, 1980, 113–118.

EARLEY, PETE, "Your Government is Watching You," *The Washington Post National Weekly Edition*, May 19, 1986, 6–7.

EARLY, STEVE, and WILSON, RAND, "Do Unions Have a Future in High Technology?" *Technology Review*, October, 1986, 57–80.

ECCLES, SIR JOHN, "The Human Brain and the Human Person," in *Mind and Brain: The Many-Faceted Problems*, ed. Sir John Eccles. Washington, D.C.: Paragon, 1982, 81–98.

EDUCATIONAL TESTING SERVICE, "Minority Students in Higher Education," *Focus 22*, 1988.

EISENSCHER, MICHAEL, "A Serpent in the High-Tech Garden of Eden," *Science for the People*, *17*, nos. 1 & 2 (March/April, 1985), 46–47.

ELLUL, JACQUES, *The Technological Society*, trans. John Wilkinson. New York: Alfred A. Knopf, 1964.

ELMER-DeWITT, PHILIP, "Can a System Keep a Secret?" *Time*, April 7, 1987, 68–69.

ELMER-DeWITT, PHILIP, "Invasion of the Data Snatchers," *Time*, September 26, 1988, 62–67.

ELMER-DeWITT, PHILIP, "The Kid Puts Us Out of Action," *Time*, November 14, 1988, 76.

ELMER-DeWITT, PHILIP, "When the Dead are Revived," *Time*, March 14, 1988, 80–81.

ELMER-DeWITT, PHILIP, "Into the Wild Blue (Digital) Yonder," *Time*, August 1, 1988, 62–63.

ELMER-DeWITT, PHILIP, "Battle for the Future," *Time*, January 16, 1989, 42–43.

ELMER-DeWITT, PHILIP, "Boosting Your Home's IQ," *Time*, January 23, 1989, 70–71.

EPSTEIN, KEITH C., "Hacking: 2 State Bulletin Boards Aid Computer Break-ins," *Richmond Times-Dispatch*, August 4, 1985, 1–8.

ERIKSON, E. H., *Childhood and Society*, 2nd ed. New York: Norton, 1963.

ERISMAN, ALBERT M., and NEVES, KENNETH W., "Advanced Computing for Manufacturing," *Scientific American*, *257*, March 1987, no. 2, 63–72.

EVANS, CHRISTOPHER. *The Micro Millennium*. New York: Viking Press, 1980.

FAUNCE, WILLIAM A., *Problems of an Industrial Society*. New York: McGraw-Hill, 1981.

FEDER, BARNABY J., "Getting Machines to Communicate," *The New York Times*, May 27, 1987, D7.

FEIGENBAUM, E. A.; BUCHANAN, B. G.; and LEDERBERG, J. "On Generality and Problem Solving: A Case Study Using the DENDRAL Program," *Machine Intelligence*, 1971, *6*. Edinburgh: Edinburgh University Press.

FEIGENBAUM, EDWARD A., and McCORDUCK, PAMELA, *The Fifth Generation: Artificial Intelligence and Japan's Computer Challenge to the World*. Reading, MA: Addison-Wesley, 1983.

FERGUSON, CHARLES H., "Chips: The US versus Japan," in *The Information Technology Revolution*, ed. Tom Forester. Cambridge: MIT Press, 1985, 45–55.

FIELDS, CHERYL M., "Need to Retrain People in Changing Fields Confronts Colleges With Creative Challenge," *The Chronicle of Higher Education*, September 17, 1986, 37–39.

FISHER, GLENN, "Access to Computers," *The Computing Teacher, 11*, no. 8 (April, 1984), 24–27.

FLEIT, LINDA H., "Overselling Technology: Suppose You Gave a Computer Revolution and Nobody Came?" *The Chronicle of Higher Education*, April 22, 1987, 96.

FLETCHER, JAMES C., "The Technologies for Ballistic Missile Defense," *Issues in Science and Technology, 1*, no. 1 (Fall, 1984), 15–29.

FLORMAN, SAMUEL C., *The Existential Pleasures of Engineering.* New York: St. Martin's, 1974.

FODOR, J., *Psychological Explanation.* New York: Random House, 1968.

FORD, DANIEL, *The Button: The Pentagon's Command and Control System—Does It Work?* New York: Simon and Schuster, 1985.

FORESTER, TOM, *High-Tech Society: The Story of the Information Technology Revolution.* Cambridge: MIT Press, 1987.

FORSYTH, RICHARD, "The Architecture of Expert Systems," in *Expert Systems: Principles and Case Studies*, ed. Richard Forsyth. New York: Chapman and Hall, 1984, 9–17.

FOULKES, FRED K., and HIRSCH, JEFFREY L., "Robots at Work," in *The Information Technology Revolution*, ed. Tom Forester. Cambridge: MIT Press, 1985, 468–479.

FOX, GEOFFREY C., and MESSINA, PAUL C., "Advanced Computer Architectures," *Scientific American, 257*, no. 4 (October, 1987), 66–77.

FRANCIS, ROBERT, "Apple-Microsoft Suit Raises Issue of Vague Copyright Laws," *Datamation*, May 15, 1988, 22–23.

FREEDMAN, LAWRENCE, *The Evolution of Nuclear Strategy.* New York: St. Martin's, 1981.

FREEDMAN, W., *The Right of Privacy in the Computer Age.* New York: Quorum, 1987.

FREY, PETER W., "An Introduction to Computer Chess," in *Chess Skill in Man and Machine*, 2nd ed., ed. Peter W. Frey. New York: Springer-Verlag, 1983, 54–81.

FRIED, CHARLES, "Privacy [A Moral Analysis]," in *Philosophical Dimensions of Privacy: An Anthology*, ed. Ferdinand D. Schoeman. Cambridge: Cambridge University Press, 1984, 203–222.

FUENTES, ANNETTE, and EHRENREICH, BARBARA, *Women in the Global Factory.* Boston: South End Press, 1983.

GALBREATH, JOHN KENNETH, "Technology, Planning and Organization," in *Values and the Future*, ed. Kurt Baier and Nicholas Rescher. New York: Free Press, 1969, 355–364.

GALKIN, A., "The New Technology and the Problem of Unemployment," in *Technological Change and Workers' Movements: Explorations in the World Economy*, vol. 4, ed. Melvyn Dobofsky. Beverly Hills: Sage, 1985, 35–44.

GARCIA, GUY D., "Sounding the Alarm," *Time*, January 9, 1989, 32–33.

GARDNER, H., *Frames of Mind: The Theory of Multiple Intelligences.* New York: Basic Books, 1983.

GARDNER, H., *The Mind's New Science: A History of the Cognitive Revolution.* New York: Basic Books, 1985.

GARSSON, ROBERT M., "Easy Money," *Datamation*, March, 1984, 32.

GAVISON, RUTH, "Privacy and the Limits of Law," in *Philosophical Dimensions of Privacy: An Anthology*, ed. Ferdinand D. Schoeman. Cambridge: Cambridge University Press, 1984, 346–402.

GEISER, KEN, "The Chips are Falling: Health Hazards in the Microelectronics Industry," *Science for the People*, *17*, nos. 1 & 2 (March/April, 1985), 8–50.

GELFOND, SUSAN M., "The Computer Age Dawns in the Corner Office," *Business Week*, June 27, 1988, 84–85.

GERSTEIN, ROBERT S., "Intimacy and Privacy," in *Philosophical Dimensions of Privacy: An Anthology*, ed. Ferdinand D. Schoeman. Cambridge: Cambridge University Press, 1984, 265–271.

GILBERT, STEVEN W., and GREEN, KENNETH C., "New Computing in Higher Education," *Change*, May/June, 1986, 33–50.

GILLIGAN, CAROL, *In a Different Voice: Psychological Theory and Women's Development*. Cambridge: Harvard University, 1982.

GIULIANO, VINCENT E., "The Mechanization of Office Work," in *The Information Revolution*, ed. Tom Forester. Cambridge: MIT Press, 1985, 298–311.

GORMAN, CHRISTINE, "The Literacy Gap," *Time*, December 19, 1988, 56–57.

GRAHAM, DANIEL O., *High Frontier: There is a Defense Against Nuclear War*. New York: Tom Doherty Associates, 1983.

GRAUBARD, STEPHEN R., ed., *The Artificial Intelligence Debate: False Starts, Real Foundations*. Cambridge: MIT Press, 1988.

GREEN, KENNETH C., "The New Administrative Computing," in *Making Computers Work for Administrators*, ed. Kenneth C. Green and Steven W. Gilbert. San Francisco: Jossey-Bass, 1988, 5–12.

GREEN, MICHAEL W., "Computing Courses Guard Students Against Psychological Obsolescence," *T. H. E. Journal*, September, 1985, 101–103.

GREENBERG, DANIEL, "High-tech America's Myopic Mind-Set," *U.S. News & World Report*, September 22, 1986, 64–65.

GREENWALD, DAVID S., and ZEITLIN, STEVEN J,. *No Reason to Talk About It: Families Confront the Nuclear Taboo*. New York: Norton, 1987.

GROSSBERG, STEPHEN, ed., *Neural Networks and Natural Intelligence*. Cambridge: MIT Press, 1988.

GULLO, KAREN, and SCHATZ, WILLIE, "The Supercomputer Breaks Through," *Datamation*, May 1, 1988, 50–63.

HALES, GERALD W., "The Disabled," in *Information Technology and People*, ed. Frank Blackler and David Oborne. Leicester: The British Psychological Society, 1987, 149–166.

HARMON, PAUL and KING, DAVID, *Expert Systems: Artificial Intelligence in Business*. New York: Wiley, 1985.

HARWOOD, RICHARD, "Espionage: Cloak-and-Computer Stories," *The Washington Post National Weekly Edition*, December 23, 1985, 6–7.

HAUGELAND, JOHN, *Artificial Intelligence: The Very Idea*. Cambridge: MIT Press, 1985.

HAWKEN, PAUL, *The Next Economy*. New York: Holt, Rinehart and Winston, 1983.

HAWKINS, J., "Computers and Girls: Rethinking the Issues," *Sex Roles, 13*, April, 1985, 165–180.

HEERMAN, BARRY, *Teaching and Learning with Computers: A Guide for College Faculty and Administrators*. San Francisco: Jossey-Bass, 1988.

HEIDEGGER, MARTIN, *Discourse on Thinking*, trans. John M. Anderson and E. Hans Freund. New York: Harper & Row, 1966.

HEISE, DAVID R., and SIMMONS, ROBERTA G., "Some Computer-Based Developments in Sociology," *Science, 228*, April, 1985, 428–433.

HELM, LESLIE, "How the Leader in Networking Practices What It Preaches," *Business Week*, May 16, 1988, 96.

HELMS, SUSAN, "The Computer as a Tool: Basis for a University-Wide Computer Literacy Course," *T. H. E. Journal*, September, 1985, 104–106.

HESS, R. D., and MIURA, I. T., "Gender Differences in Enrollment in Computer Camps and Classes," *Sex Roles, 13*, April, 1985, 193–203.

HILTS, PHILIP J., and MOORE, MOLLY, "The 'Shield of the Fleet' May Have a Few Holes in It," *The Washington Post National Weekly Edition*, July 11–17, 1988, 8.

HOFFMAN, KURT, and RUSH, HOWARD, "From Needles and Pins to Microelectronics—The Impact of Technical Change in the Garment Industry," in *Technology and International Affairs*, ed. Joseph S. Szyliowicz. Lund, Sweden: Praeger, 1983, 71–102.

HOFSTADTER, DOUGLAS R., and DENNETT, Daniel C., eds, *The Mind's I: Fantasies and Reflections on Self and Soul*. New York: Basic Books, 1981.

HOHN, HUBERT, "The Art of a New Machine or Confessions of a Computer Artist," *Technology Review*, November/December, 1988, 65–73.

HOWARD, PATRICK, and HAMMER, PATRICIA, "Strategy Implementation: Passing the Systems Test," *Datamation*, February 15, 1988, 67–72.

HOWARD, ROBERT, *Brave New Workplace*. New York: Viking, 1985.

HOWE, CHARLES L., "Circling the Wagons," *Datamation*, May 15, 1986, 42–50.

HUNT, T. L., "Impact of Automation and Robotics on Jobs." Paper presented at the Conference on State Strategies for Economic Revitalization in the North east and Midwest, Council of State Governments, Boston, MA, May 6, 1983.

IRVING, R. H.; HIGGINS, C. A.; and SAFAYENI, F. R., "Computerized Monitoring Systems: Use and Abuse," *Communications of the ACM, 29*, no. 8 (August, 1986), 794–801.

JACKY, JONATHAN, "The 'Star Wars' Defense Won't Compute," *The Atlantic*, June, 1985, 18–30.

JACKY, JONATHAN, "The Strategic Computing Program," in *Computers in Battle: Will They Work?*, ed. David Bellin and Gary Chapman. New York: Harcourt Brace Jovanovich, 1987, 171–208.

JAMES, W., *The Principles of Psychology*. New York: Holt, Rinehart, and Winston, 1890.

JASTROW, ROBERT, *The Enchanted Loom*. New York: The Reader's Library, 1981.

JENKIN, PATRICK, "Employment: The Quantity of Work," in *The Information Technology Revolution*, ed. Tom Forester. Cambridge: MIT Press, 378–380.

JERISON, HENRY J., "The Evolution of Consciousness," in *Mind and Brain: The Many-Faceted Problems*, ed. Sir John Eccles. Washington, D.C.: Paragon, 1982, 13–28.

JOHNSON, DEBORAH G., *Computer Ethics*. Englewood Cliffs, N. J.: Prentice-Hall, 1985.

JOHNSON, DEBORAH G., and SNAPPER, JOHN W., ed., *Ethical Issues in the Use of Computers*. Belmont, CA: Wadsworth, 1985.

JOYCE, CHRISTOPHER, "This Machine Wants to Help You," *Psychology Today*, 22, no. 2 (February, 1988), 44–50.

KARASEK, R. A., JR., "Job Demands, Job Decision Latitude, and Mental Strain: Implications of Job Redesign," *Administrative Science Quarterly*, 24, no. 2 (March, 1979), 285–308.

KATZ, HARRY C., and SABEL, CHARLES F., "The Future of Automaking: What Role for Unions?" *Technology Review*, October, 1985, 64–79.

KELLER, E. F., *Reflections on Gender and Science*. New Haven, CT: Yale University Press, 1985.

KIDDER, TRACY, *The Soul of a New Machine*. Boston: Little, Brown, 1981.

KIESLER, SARA; SIEGEL, JANE; and MCGUIRE, TIMOTHY W., "Social Psychological Aspects of Computer-Mediated Communication," *American Psychologist*, 39, no. 10 (October, 1984), 1123–1134.

KING, JOHN LESLIE, and KRAEMER, KENNETH L., *The Dynamics of Computing*. New York: Columbia University Press, 1985.

KING, KENNETH M., "Overreaction to External Attacks on Computer Systems Could be More Harmful Than the Viruses Themselves," *The Chronicle of Higher Education*, November 23, 1988.

KOEPP, STEPHEN, "The Boss that Never Blinks," *Time*, July 28, 1986, 46–47.

KOZOL, JONATHAN, *Illiterate America*. New York: New American Library, 1985.

KRAEMER, KENNETH L.; DUTTON, WILLIAM H.; and NORTHUP, ALANA, *The Management of Information Systems*. New York: Columbia University Press, 1981.

KRAFT, A., "XCON: An Expert Configuration System at Digital Equipment Corporation," in *The AI Business: The Commercial Uses of Artificial Intelligence*, ed. P. H. Winston and K. A. Prendergast. Cambridge: MIT Press, 1984.

KULIK, JAMES A., KULIK, CHEN-LIN C., and BANGERT-DROWNS, ROBERT L., "Effectiveness of Computer-Based Education in Elementary Schools," *Computers in Human Behavior*, 1, no.1 (1985), pp. 59–74.

KURTZ, HOWARD, "The Northeast: A Lot of Jobs, but Not Enough Qualified People to Fill Them," *The Washington Post National Weekly Edition*, January 30–February 5, 1989, 6–7.

KUSSEROW, RICHARD P., "The Government Needs Computer Matching to Root Out Waste and Fraud," *Communications of the ACM*, 27, no. 6 (June, 1984), 542–545.

LACHMAN, R.; LACHMAN, J. L.; and BUTTERFIELD, E. C. *Cognitive Psychology and Information Processing: An Introduction*. Hillsdale, N. J.: Erlbaum, 1979.

LA METTRIE, JULIEN OFFRAY DE, *Man a Machine*, tr. Gertrude Carman Bussey. La Salle, Ill.: Open Court, 1912.

LANDY, FRANK J., *Psychology of Work Behavior*, 3rd ed. Homewood, IL: Dorsey, 1985.

LAUDON, KENNETH C., *Dossier Society: Value Choices in the Design of National Information Systems*. New York: Columbia University Press, 1986.

LEACH, BERNARD, and SHUTT, JOHN, "Chips and Crisps: Labor Faces a Crunch," in *The Information Technology Revolution*. ed. Tom Forester. Cambridge: MIT Press, 1985, 480–495.

LEAVITT, H., and WHISLER, T., "Management in the 1980s," *Harvard Business Review*, *36*, no. 6 (November-December, 1958), 41–48.

LEONARD, JENNIFER; STRAUSS, HOWARD JAY; and EDWARDS, JON R., "Vulnerable on All Counts: How Computerized Vote Tabulation Threatens the Integrity of Our Elections," *The CPSR Newsletter*, *6*, no. 4 (Fall, 1988), 12–18.

LEONARD-BARTON, DOROTHY, and SVIOKLA, JOHN J., "Putting Expert Systems to Work," *Harvard Business Review*, *85*, no. 2 (March-April, 1988), 91–98.

LEVY, STEVEN, *Hackers: Heroes of the Computer Revolution*. New York: Dell, 1984.

LEWIS, GEOFF, "When the Chips are Down," *Business Week*, June 27, 1988, 28–29.

LIFTON, ROBERT JAY, and FALK, RICHARD, *Indefensible Weapons: The Political and Psychological Case Against Nuclearism*. New York: Basic Books, 1982.

LIN, HERBERT, "The Development of Software for Ballistic Missile Defense," *Scientific American*, *253*, No. 6 (December, 1985), 46–53.

LOCKHEED, MARLAINE, E., and FRAKT, STEVEN B., "Sex Equity: Increasing Girls' Use of Computers," *The Computing Teacher*, *11*, no. 8 (April, 1984), 16–18.

LOGSDON, TOM, *Computers Today and Tomorrow: The Microcomputer Explosion*. Rockville, MD: Computer Science Press, 1985.

LONDON, JULIUS, and WHITE, GILBERT F., *The Environmental Effects of Nuclear War*. Boulder, CO: Westview, 1984.

LUEHRMANN, ARTHUR, "Pre- and Post-College Computer Education," in *The Computer in the School: Tutor, Tool, Tutee*, ed. Robert Taylor. Columbia University: Teachers College Press, 1980, 141–148.

LUNZER, FRANCESCA Z., "The Little Compact Disk Grows Up," *U.S. News & World Report*, December 26, 1988/January 2, 1989, 114.

LYNN, LEONARD H., "Research and Development in Japan," *Current History*, *87*, no. 528 (April 1988), 165–180.

MCABEE, MICHAEL, "Japan: Land of the Setting Sun?" *Industry Week*, April 29, 1985, 50–53.

MCCORDUCK, PAMELA, *Machines Who Think: A Personal Inquiry into the History and Prospects of Artificial Intelligence*. San Francisco: Freeman, 1979.

MCDONALD, EVELYN C. "The Message Is the Medium," *Government Data Systems*, April, 1988, 6–8.

MCWILLIAMS, GARY, "Airline Control System Dogged by Upgrade Delays," *Datamation*, October 15, 1987, 53–61.

MACK, JOHN E. and SNOW, ROBERTA, "Psychological Effects on Children and Adolescents," in *Psychology and the Prevention of Nuclear War*, ed. Ralph K. White. New York: New York University Press, 1986, 16–33.

MAGRASS, YALE, and UPCHURCH, RICHARD L., "Computer Literacy: People Adapted for Technology," *Computers & Society, 18*, no. 2 (April, 1988), 8–15.

MANTOUX, PAUL, *The Industrial Revolution in the Eighteenth Century: An Outline of the Beginnings of the Modern Factory System in England.* Chicago: University of Chicago Press, 1961.

MARBACH, WILLIAM D., "The Race to Build a Supercomputer," in *The Information Technology Revolution,* ed. Tom Forester. Cambridge: MIT Press, 1985, 60–70.

MARTINEZ, MICHAEL E., and MEAD, NANCY A., *Computer Competence: The First National Assessment.* Princeton: Educational Testing Service, 1988.

MARX, GARY T., "The New Surveillance," *Technology Review,* May/June, 1985, 43–48.

MARX, GARY T., and SHERIZEN, SANFORD, "Monitoring on the Job: How to Protect Privacy as Well as Property," *Technology Review,* November/December, 1986, 63–72.

MASON, CINDY L., "Using Computers in Arms Control Verification," *The CPSR Newsletter, 6*, no. 4 (Fall, 1988), 1–5.

MAYER, RICHARD E., *The Promise of Cognitive Psychology.* San Francisco: Freeman, 1981.

MEINDL, JAMES D., "Chips for Advanced Computing," *Scientific American, 257*, no. 4 (October, 1987), 78–89.

MILLER, ANETTA, et al., "Stress on the Job," *Newsweek,* April 25, 1988, 40–45.

MILLER, KEITH, "Integrating Computer Ethics into the Computer Science Curriculum," *Computer Science Education, 1*, no. 1 (Fall, 1988), 37–52.

MILLER, S. M., "Impacts of Robotics and Flexible Manufacturing Technologies on Manufacturing Costs and Employment," in *The Management of Productivity and Technology in Manufacturing,* ed. P. R. Kleindorfer. New York: Plenum, 1985, 73–110.

MINSKY, MARVIN, ed., *Semantic Information Processing.* Cambridge: MIT Press, 1968.

MIRON, M.; CECIL, J.; BRADICICH, K.; and HALL, GENE, "The Myths and Realities of Competitive Advantage," *Datamation,* October 1, 1988, 71–82

MIURA, IRENE T., and HESS, ROBERT D., "Enrollment Differences in Computer Camps and Summer Classes," *The Computing Teacher, 11*, no. 8 (April, 1984), 22.

MOORE, ROY, and LEVIE, HUGO, "New Technology and the Unions," in *The Information Technology Revolution,* ed. Tom Forester. Cambridge: MIT Press, 1985, 511–527.

MORITANI, MASANORI, *Japanese Technology: Getting the Best for the Least.* Tokyo: Simul Press, 1982.

NEIBAUER, ALAN, "The Computer Literacy Myth," *T. H. E. Journal,* February, 1985, 88–90.

NEWELL, A., "Physical Symbol Systems," in *Perspectives in Cognitive Science,* ed. Donald A. Norman. Hillsdale, NJ: Erhlbaum, 1981, 37–86.

NEWELL, A., and SIMON, H., *Human Problem Solving.* Englewood Cliffs, N. J.: Prentice-Hall, 1972.

NEWMAN, MICHAEL, "Professionals and Expert Systems," *Computers & Society, 18*, no. 3 (July, 1988), 14–27.

NOBLE, DOUGLAS, "Computer Literacy and Ideology," in *The Computer in Education: A Critical Perspective,* ed. Douglas Sloan. Columbia University: Teachers College Press, 1984, 64–76.

NORMAN, ADRIAN R. D., *Computer Insecurity*. New York: Chapman and Hall, 1983.

NORTON, ROBERT E., and BLACK, ROBERT F., "Fitting into a Global Economy," *U.S. News & World Report*, December 26/January 2, 1989, 80–82.

NUSSBAUM, KAREN, "Office High Tech is not Here for Good," *In These Times*, May 24–30, 1983, 12.

Office of Technology Assessment, *Reproductive Health Hazards in The Workplace*, 1985a. Washington, D.C.: U.S. Government Printing Office.

Office of Technology Assessment, *Electronic Surveillance and Civil Liberties*, October, 1985. Washington, D. C.: U.S. Government Printing Office.

Office of Technology Assessment, *Electronic Record Systems and Individual Privacy*, June, 1986. Washington, D. C.: U.S. Government Printing Office.

Office of Technology Assessment, *Intellectual Property Rights in an Age of Electronics and Information*, April, 1986. Washington, D. C.: U.S. Government Printing Office.

Office of Technology Assessment, *The Electronic Supervisor: New Technology, New Tensions*, September, 1987. Washington, D. C.: U.S. Government Printing Office.

OLSON, MARGRETHE H., and PRIMPS, SOPHIA B., "Working at Home With Computers: Work and Nonwork Issues," *Journal of Social Issues*, *40*, no. 3, 1984, 97–112.

ORNSTEIN, SEVERO M., "Computers in Battle: A Human Overview," in *Computers in Battle—Will They Work?* ed. David Bellin and Gary Chapman. New York: Harcourt Brace Jovanovich, 1987, 1–44.

ORNSTEIN, SEVERO M.; SMITH, BRIAN C.; and SUCHMAN, LUCY A., "Strategic Computing," *Bulletin of the Atomic Scientists*, *40*, no. 10 (December, 1984), 11–16.

OZAKI, ROBERT S., "The Japanese Economy Internationalized," *Current History*, *87*, no. 528 (April, 1988), 157–178.

PACEY, ARNOLD, *The Culture of Technology*. Cambridge: MIT Press, 1983.

PAPERT, SEYMOUR, *Mindstorms: Children, Computers, and Powerful Ideas*. New York: Basic Books, 1980a.

PAPERT, SEYMOUR, "Teaching Children Thinking," in *The Computer in the School: Tutor, Tool, Tutee*, ed. Robert P. Taylor. New York: Teachers College Press, 1980b, 161–176.

PARENTI, MICHAEL, *The Sword and the Dollar: Imperialism, Revolution, and the Arms Race*. New York: St. Martin's, 1989.

PARKER, DONN B., *Crime by Computer*. New York: Scribners, 1976.

PARKER, DONN B., *Ethical Conflicts in Computer Science and Technology*. Arlington, VA: AFIPS Press, 1981.

PARKER, DONN B., *Fighting Computer Crime*. New York: Charles Scribner's Sons, 1983.

PARNAS, DAVID LORGE, "Software Aspects of Strategic Defense Systems," *Communications of the ACM*, *28*, no. 12 (December, 1985) 1326–1335.

PEAT, F. DAVID, *Artificial Intelligence: How Machines Think*. New York: Baen Enterprises, 1985.

PELED, ABRAHAM, "The Next Computer Revolution," *Scientific American*, *257*, no. 4 (October, 1987), 56–65.

PEMPEL, T. J., *Japan: The Dilemmas of Success*. New York: Foreign Policy Association, 1986.

PENFIELD, W., and ROBERTS, L., *Speech and Brain Mechanisms*. Princeton: Princeton University Press, 1959.

PINKER, STEVEN; and MEHLER, JACQUES, *Connections and Symbols*. Cambridge: MIT Press, 1988.

POE, ROBERT, "American Automobile Makers Bet on CIM to Defend Against Japanese Inroads," *Datamation*, March 1, 1988, 43–51.

PORTER, MICHAEL E., and MILLAR, VICTOR E., "How Information Gives You Competitive Advantage," *Harvard Business Review*, *85*, no. 4 (July–August, 1985), 149–160.

POWELL, JAMES L., "The Computer as a Presidential Factotum," in *Making Computers Work for Administrators*, ed. Kenneth C. Green and Steven W. Gilbert. San Francisco: Jossey-Bass, 1988, pp. 57–64.

PRESTOWITZ, CLYDE, "Japanese vs. Western Economics," *Technology Review*, May/June, 1988, 27–36.

PRITCHARD, WILLIAM H. JR., and SPICER, DONALD Z., "The Vassar Computer Literacy Program," *EDUCOM Bulletin*, Summer, 1983, 7–10.

"Privacy Invaded—3 Stories," *San Francisco Examiner*, October 7, 1984, A15–A16.

PROVENZO, EUGENE F., JR., *Beyond the Gutenberg Galaxy: Microcomputers and the Emmergence of Post-Typographic Culture*. Columbia University: Teachers College Press, 1986.

PUTNAM, H., "Psychological Predicates," in *Art, Mind and Religion*, eds. W. H. Capitan and D. D. Merill. Pittsburgh: University of Pittsburgh Press, 1967, 37–48.

PYLYSHYN, ZENON W., *Computation and Cognition: Toward a Foundation for Cognitive Science*. Cambridge: MIT Press, 1984.

RADA, JUAN, "A Third World Perspective," in *Microelectronics and Society: A Report to the Club of Rome*, ed. Guenter Friedrichs and Adam Schaff. New York: Pergamon Press, 1982, 203–231.

RADA, JUAN, "Information Technology and the Third World," in *The Information Technology Revolution*, ed. Tom Forester. Cambridge: MIT Press, 1985, 571–589.

RANGE, PETER ROSS, "A 'Triptik' for the Road to Armageddon," *The Washington Post National Weekly Edition*, February 24, 1986, 33.

REIMAN, JEFFREY H., "Privacy, Intimacy, and Personhood," *Philosophy & Public Affairs*, *6*, no. 1 (Fall, 1976), 26–44.

REINECKE, IAN, *Electronic Illusions: A Skeptic's View of Our High-Tech Future*. New York: Penguin, 1984.

REINHOLD, FRAN, "Computing in America: Electronic Learning's 1986 Annual Survey of the States," *Electronic Learning*, October, 1986, 26–69.

REISCHAUER, E., *The Japanese*. Cambridge: Harvard University Press, 1977.

REISS, LEVI, and DOLAN, EDWIN G., *Using Computers: Managing Change*. Cincinnati, OH: South-Western, 1989.

RENNELS, GLENN D., and SHORTLIFFE, EDWARD H., "Advanced Computing for Medicine," *Scientific American*, *257*, no. 4 (October, 1987), 154–163.

RESNICK, L. B., "Task Analysis in Instructional Design: Some Cases From Mathematics," in *Cognition and Instruction*, ed. D. Klahr. Hillsdale, N. J.: Erlbaum, 1976.

ROBERTS, E. and BERLIN, S., "Computers and the Strategic Defense Initiative," in *Computers in Battle—Will They Work?*, ed. David Bellin and Gary Chapman. New York: Harcourt Brace Jovanovich, 1987, 149–170.

ROBERTS, WALTER, R., and ENGLE, HAROLD E., "The Global Information Revolution and the Communist World," *The Washington Quarterly*, Spring, 1986, 141–155.

ROBINS, KEVIN and WEBSTER, FRANK, "Higher Education, High Tech, High Rhetoric," in *Compulsive Technology: Computers and Culture*, ed. Tony Solomonides and Les Levidow. London: Free Association Books, 1985, 36–57.

ROBINSON, A. L., "Impact of Electronics on Employment: Productivity and Displacement Effects," *Science*, 1977, *195*, 1179–1184.

ROGERS, MICHAEL, "The PC Printing Press," *Newsweek*, July 14, 1986, 50–51.

ROGERS, MICHAEL, "Here Comes Hypermedia," *Newsweek*, October 3, 1988, 44–45.

ROSZAK, THEODORE, *The Cult of Information: The Folklore of Computers and the True Art of Thinking*. New York: Pantheon, 1986.

ROTHSCHILD, EMMA, "The Real Reagan Economy," *The New York Review*, June 30, 1988, 46–54.

SAGAN, CARL, *The Dragons of Eden*. New York: Pocket Books, 1977.

SALERNO, LYNN M., *Computer Briefing: Using the Trends for Better Managerial Decisions*. New York: Wiley, 1986.

SALOMAN, ILAN, and SALOMON, MEIRA, "Telecommuting: The Employee's Perspective," *Technological Forecasting and Social Change, 25*, no. 1 (January, 1984), 15–28.

SAWYER, KATHY, "The Mess at the IRS," *The Washington Post National Weekly Edition*, November 11, 1985, 6–7.

SCHANK, ROGER C., "Natural Language, Philosophy and Artificial Intelligence," in *Philosophical Perspectives in Artificial Intelligence*, ed. Martin Ringle. Atlantic Highlands, NJ: Humanities Press, 1979, 196–224.

SCHELL, JONATHAN, *The Fate of the Earth*. New York: Knopf, 1982.

SCHRAGE, MICHAEL, "We're Spending $1 Billion a Year to Gag Our Computers," *The Washington Post National Weekly Edition*, May 6, 1985, 31.

SCHWARTZ, L., "Teaching Writing in the Age of the Word Processor and Personal Computers," in *Run: Computer Education* (2nd ed.), ed. D. O. Harper and J. H. Stewart. Monterey, CA: Brooks/Cole, 1985.

SEARLE, JOHN R., "Minds, Brains, and Programs," in *Mind Design: Philosophy, Psychology, Artificial Intelligence*, ed. John Haugeland. Cambridge: MIT Press, 1981, 282–306.

SEGHERS, FRANCES, and LEWIS, GEOFF, "How Do You Chase a $17 Billion Market? With Everything You've Got," *Business Week*, November 23, 1987, 120–121.

SELIGMAN, JEAN; ABRAMSON, PAMELA; and HAGER, MARY, "Are Computer Screens Safe?" *Newsweek*, June 20, 1988, 53.

SELIGMAN, M. E. P., *Helplessness*. San Francisco: Freeman, 1975.

SHAIKEN, HARLEY, *Work Transformed: Automation & Labor in the Computer Age*. New York: Holt, Rinehart & Winston, 1984.

SHAIKEN, HARLEY, "High Tech Goes Third World," *Technology Review*, January, 1988, 39–47.

SHALLIS, MICHAEL, *The Silicon Idol: The Micro Revolution and Its Social Implications*. New York: Schocken, 1984.

SHAPIRO, JOSEPH P., "Shortchanging the Disabled," *U.S. News & World Report*, July 25, 1988, 50–51.

SHAPIRO, MARGARET, "The Distinct Stock in Trade of the Tokyo Exchange," *The Washington Post National Weekly Edition*, June 13–19, 1988, 20–21.

SHAPIRO, MARGARET, "Empire of the Sun," *The Washington Post National Weekly Edition*, October 31–November 6, 1988, 6–7.

SHATTUCK, JOHN, "Computer Matching is a Serious Threat to Individual Rights," *Communications of the ACM, 27,* no. 6 (June, 1984), 538–541.

SHATTUCK, JOHN, and SPENCE, MURIEL MORISEY, "The Dangers of Information Control," *Technology Review*, April, 1988, 63–73.

SHORTLIFFE, E. F., *Computer-based Medical Consultations: MYCIN*. New York: American Elsevier, 1976.

SIGURDSON, JON, "Forces of Technological Change," in *Technology and International Affairs*, ed. Joseph S. Szyliowicz. Lund, Sweden: Praeger, 1983, 1–30.

SIMON, H. A., and NEWELL, A., "Heuristic Problem Solving: The Next Advance in Operations Research," *Operations Research*, 1958, 6.

SIVARD, RUTH LEGER, *World Military and Social Expenditures 1987–88*, 12th ed. Washington, D. C.: World Priorities, 1987.

SLOAN, DOUGLAS, "Introduction: On Raising Critical Questions about the Computer in Education," in *The Computer in Education: A Critical Perspective*, ed. Douglas Sloan. Columbia University: Teachers College Press, 1984, 1–9.

SMITH, R. JEFFREY, "SDI Comes Down to Earth," *The Washington Post National Weekly Edition*, 1988, April 4–10, 9–10.

SPECTER, MICHAEL, "The End of Easy Access?" *The Washington Post National Weekly Edition*, November 21–27, 1988, 7.

STEFIK, MARK, "Strategic Computing at DARPA: Overview and Assessment," *Communications of the ACM, 28*, no. 7 (July, 1985), 690–704.

STERNBERG, R. J., *Beyond I. Q.: A Triarchic Theory of Human Intelligence*. New York: Cambridge University Press, 1985.

STERNBERG, S., "High-speed Scanning in Human Memory," *Science, 153*, 1966, 652–654.

STILLINGS, NEIL A., et al., *Cognitive Science: An Introduction*. Cambridge: MIT Press, 1987.

STOLL, CLIFFORD, "Stalking the Wily Hacker," *Communications of the ACM, 31*, no. 5 (May, 1988), 484–497.

STONIER, TOM, "The Knowledge Industry," in *Expert Systems: Principles and Case Studies*, ed. Richard Forsyth. New York: Chapman and Hall, 1984, 211–226.

SUPPES, PATRICK, "Computer-based Mathematics Instruction," in *The Computer in the School: Tutor, Tool, Tutee*, ed. Robert Taylor. Columbia University: Teachers College Press, 1980, 248–261.

SZOLOVITS, PETER, "Expert Systems Tools and Techniques: Past, Present and Future," in *AI in the 1980s and Beyond: An MIT Survey*, ed. W. Eric L. Grimson and Ramesh S. Patil. Cambridge: MIT Press, 1987, 43–74.

TATE, PAUL, "Risk! The Third Factor," *Datamation*, April 15, 1988, 58–64.

TAYLOR, FREDERICK W., *The Principles of Scientific Management*. New York: Harper and Row, 1911.

TAYLOR, FREDERICK W., *Scientific Management*. New York: Harper Brothers, 1947.

THOMSON, JUDITH JARVIS, "The Right to Privacy," *Philosophy & Public Affairs*, *4*, no. 4 (Summer, 1975), 295–314.

"The Top 1000 U.S. Companies Ranked by Industry," *Business Week*, April 15, 1988, 270.

TORNATZKY, LOUIS G., "Technological Change and the Structure of Work." Master Lecture Presented at the Annual Meeting of the American Psychological Association, Los Angeles, CA, August 27, 1985.

TOY, STEWART; GROSS, NEIL; and TREECE, JAMES B., "The Americanization of Honda," *Business Week*, April 25, 1988, 90–96.

TRUAX, C. B., and MITCHELL, K. M. "Research on Certain Therapist Interpersonal Skills in Relation to Process and Outcome," in *Handbook of Psychotherapy and Behavior Change: An Empirical Analysis*, ed. A. E. Bergin and S. L. Garfield. New York: Wiley, 1971.

TUCHMAN, BARBARA T., *The Guns of August*. New York: Macmillan, 1962.

TURKLE, SHERRY, *The Second Self: Computers and the Human Spirit*. New York: Simon and Schuster, 1984.

TURNER, JON A., "Computer Mediated Work: The Interplay Between Technology and Structured Jobs," *Communications of the ACM*, *27*, no. 12 (December, 1984), 1210–1217.

TURNER, J. A., "The New Software: Math for Architects, Staging for 'Hamlet,' and Other Graphic Examples," *The Chronicle of Higher Education*, July 2, 1986, p. 4.

TURNER, J. A., "'E-Mail' Technology Has Boomed, but Manners of Its Users Fall Short of Perfection," *The Chronicle of Higher Education*, April 13, 1988, A1–A16.

TURNER, J. A., "Plan for $5-Million Prototype of Electronic Research Library Announced," *The Chronicle of Higher Education*, June 1, 1988, A27.

UNDERWOOD, GEOFFREY and UNDERWOOD, JEAN D. M., "The Computer in Education: A Force for Change?," in *Information Technology and People*, ed. Frank Blackler and David Oborne. Leicester: The British Psychological Society, 1987, 167–190.

VAN DYKE, CAROLYNN, "Taking 'Computer Literacy' Literally," *Communications of the ACM*, *30*, no. 5 (May, 1987), 366–374.

VAN GELDER, LINDSEY, "The Strange Case of the Electronic Lover," *Ms.*, October, 1985, 94–124.

VAN LAWICK-GOODALL, JANE, *In the Shadow of Man*. New York: Houghton Mifflin, 1971.

VOGEL, EZRA, *Japan As Number One*. New York: Harper Colophon Books, 1979.

WALTON, R. E., and VITTORI, W., "New Information Technology: Organizational Problem or Opportunity?" *Office: Technology and People, 1*, (March, 1983), 249–273.

WALTON, R., "Quality of Work Life Activities: A Research Agenda," *Professional Psychology, 11*, no. 5 (November, 1980), 484–493.

WALTZ, DAVID; and FELDMAN, JEROME A., eds, *Connectionist Models and Their Implications: Readings from Cognitive Science.* Norwood, NJ: Ablex, 1988.

WARR, PETER; JACKSON, PAUL; and BANKS, MICHAEL, "Unemployment and Mental Health: Some British Studies," *Journal of Social Issues, 44*, no. 4 (1988), 47–68.

WASSERSTROM, RICHARD A., "Privacy: Some Arguments and Assumptions," in *Philosophical Dimensions of Privacy: An Anthology.* Cambridge: Cambridge University Press, 1984, 317–332.

WEINTRAUB, RICHARD M., "Bombay—Hell in a Very Small Place," *The Washington Post National Weekly Edition*, December 19–25, 1988, 8–9.

WEIZENBAUM, JOSEPH, *Computer Power and Human Reason: From Judgment to Calculation.* San Francisco: Freeman, 1976.

WERNEKE, DIANE, "Women: The Vulnerable Group," in *The Information Technology Revolution*, ed. Tom Forester. Cambridge: MIT Press, 1985, 400–416.

WESSELLS, M. G., *Cognitive Psychology.* New York: Harper & Row, 1982.

WESSELLS, MICHAEL G., "Computer Models and Cognition: History, Impact, and Limits," *Logos, 7*, 1986, 3–15.

WESTIN, ALAN F., *Privacy and Freedom.* New York: Atheneum, 1967.

WHITE, LESLIE, *The Science of Culture.* New York: Farrar, Straus & Giroux, 1949.

WHITE, LYNN, *Medieval Technology and Social Change.* New York: Oxford University Press, 1966.

WILKINSON, BARRY, "The Politics of Technical Change," in *The Information Technology Revolution*, ed. Tom Forester. Cambridge: MIT Press, 1985, 439–453.

WILSON, JOHN W., "Suddenly the Heavyweights Smell Money in Computer Networks," *Business Week*, April 27, 1987, 110–111.

WINNER, LANGDON, *Autonomous Technology: Technics-Out-of-Control as a Theme in Political Thought.* Cambridge: MIT Press, 1977.

WINOGRAD, TERRY, "A Procedural Model of Language Understanding," in *Computer Models of Thought and Language*, ed. Roger C. Schank and Kenneth Mark Colby. San Francisco: W. H. Freeman, 1973, 152–186.

WINOGRAD, TERRY, and FLORES, FERNANDO, *Understanding Computers and Cognition.* Norwood, NJ: Ablex, 1986.

WINOKUR, SCOTT, "Your Financial Records Aren't Your Own," *San Francisco Examiner*, October 8, 1984, B8–B11.

WITT, JOHN, "Sovran to put PRODIGY to work," *Richmond Times-Dispatch*, October 30, 1988, C1–C7.

WOOD, ROBERT CHAPMAN, "The Real Challenge of Japan's Fifth Generation Project," *Technology Review*, January, 1988, 68–73.

WRIGHT, PAUL KENNETH, and BOURNE, DAVID ALAN, *Manufacturing Intelligence*. Reading, MA: Addison-Wesley, 1988.

YU, VICTOR L., et al., "An Evaluation of MYCIN's Advice," *Journal of the American Medical Association, 242*, 1979, 1279–1282.

ZUBOFF, SHOSHANA, *In the Age of the Smart Machine: The Future of Work and Power*. New York: Basic Books, 1988.

ZUREIK, ELIA T., "The Electronic Cottage: Old Wine in New Bottles." Paper presented at a conference on *Technology and Culture: Computers, Values, Creativity*. University of Ottawa, May 8–10, 1985.

Index